HATE

HATE

*The Rising Tide of
Anti-Semitism in France
(and What It Means for Us)*

MARC WEITZMANN

HOUGHTON MIFFLIN HARCOURT
Boston   New York   2019

For information about permission to reproduce selections from this book, write to
trade.permissions@hmhco.com or to Permissions, Houghton Mifflin Harcourt
Publishing Company, 3 Park Avenue, 19th Floor, New York, New York 10016.

hmhco.com

Library of Congress Cataloging-in-Publication Data
Names: Weitzmann, Marc, author.
Title: Hate : the rising tide of anti-Semitism in France
(and what it means for us) / Marc Weitzmann.
Description: Boston ; New York : Houghton Mifflin Harcourt, [2019] |
Identifiers: LCCN 2018042559 (print) | LCCN 2018042805 (ebook) |
ISBN 9780544791343 (ebook) | ISBN 9780544649644 (hardback)
Subjects: LCSH: Antisemitism—France—History—21st century. |
Muslims—France—Social conditions—21st century. |
Jews—France—Social conditions—21st century. | Muslims—
Cultural assimilation—France. | Judaism—Relations—Islam. |
Islam—Relations—Judaism. | Social integration—France. | France—
Ethnic relations. | BISAC: HISTORY / Europe / France. | SOCIAL SCIENCE /
Violence in Society. | SOCIAL SCIENCE / Jewish Studies.
Classification: LCC DS146.F8 (ebook) | LCC DS146.F8 W45 2019 (print) |
DDC 305.892/4044—dc23
LC record available at https://lccn.loc.gov/2018042559

Book design by Kelly Dubeau Smydra

Printed in the United States of America
DOC 10 9 8 7 6 5 4 3 2 1

For Philip Roth
R.I.P.

Contents

Preface

The trap that led to the abduction, torture, and murder of Ilan Halimi, in January 2006, had been set on the Boulevard Voltaire, in Paris, months earlier by a twenty-seven-year-old first offender named Youssouf Fofana.

Fofana was the fifth child of Ivory Coast immigrants living in the southwest Paris suburb of Bagneux, in one of the derelict projects there that the French call *cités*. He had gathered around him a bunch of ethnically diverse kids aged sixteen to twenty-six, faithful members of a group he had christened the "Gang of Barbarians."

Under Fofana's leadership, the gang had set itself the task of making money by going after the one community that controlled everything everywhere. Jews were kings. Everybody knew they swallowed the money of the state, while he, being black, was a slave to that same state and therefore to them as well.

Fofana's first plan consisted of sending anonymous threat letters or Molotov cocktails sent to public figures such as the president of Doctors Without Borders, Rony Brauman, the then director of the French cultural channel Arte, Jérôme Clément, a lawyer by the name of Joseph Cohen-Saban, and others who were (or appeared to be) Jewish. As this came to nothing, Fofana concocted another idea, which consisted of randomly abducting Jews. But that plan failed, too, largely, it seems, because of the fury of the gang members themselves. In one of the rare nearly successful attempts, the abducted man, Mickaël Douïeb, fifty, was found by police, handcuffed and swimming in his own blood after the gang beat him to cries of "kike" and "dirty Jew" before running away.

Finally, in January 2006, they started to pace the Boulevard Voltaire looking for "Jewish stores" and potential victims there. The group's methods, meanwhile, had somewhat gained in sophistication, as Fofana had encountered his improbable muse. She was a seventeen-year-old called Emma the Bait, a.k.a. Yalda. Her real name was Sorour Arbabzadeh, and she remains by far the most arresting character of this grim story. Although obviously smart, she still was in the tenth grade. She had been raised in Iran, where her mother, a nurse by trade, had been in an arranged marriage with a violent man diagnosed with paranoid schizophrenia, who beat Sorour throughout much her childhood. After he died, in 1999, the family had ended up in France, with political refugee status; Sorour was ten. When she was fourteen, three teenagers—from her own suburb, it seems—raped her. (A complaint filed by her mother against the boys was soon withdrawn, possibly under pressure from the neighborhood.) The battalion of juvenile court judges, trained caregivers, and social workers who'd followed the girl since then had been unable to prevent her from making multiple suicide attempts.

Plan number four, as elaborated by Fofana, was this: A girl, carefully selected by him for her sex appeal, would flirt with one of those loaded Jewish guys; she would get a date with him; and, at the end of the evening, she would ask to be brought back home to Bagneux, where the rest of the gang would be waiting. When a signal was given, the youngest members of the gang would set a car on fire as a diversion for any cops patrolling around while the rest would jump on the guy and lock him up in the trunk of a car. Then they would send their ransom demand.

Fofana had confided his idea to Tiffen, a semi-homeless twenty-year-old woman born in Brittany to a Catholic family. Tiffen had converted to Islam at fifteen. She had responded by suggesting to Fofana several possible targets for kidnappings in the *cité,* among them some of her own friends. But, either because none were Jewish or because Tiffen thought she lacked the necessary confidence to play the vamp part in the abduction plan, none had been acted upon. Then Tiffen came up with Sorour, a high school girlfriend, whom she introduced to the gang. Sorour's sex appeal was not lost on Fofana. "I can work wonders with you," he is reported to have told Sorour when they met.

According to what Sorour Arbabzadeh later confessed, she accepted Fofana's proposal to be used as a honey trap as "a favor to him," and with the promise of a payment of three to five thousand euros once the ransom was paid. She denied having become involved sexually with Fofana or any of the other gang members.

On January 16, 2006, Sorour entered a cell phone store on the Boulevard Voltaire, where she chatted up Ilan Halimi, a twenty-two-year-old clerk. They set a date for a drink four days later at 10 p.m. *He's nice,* she confided to Tiffen afterwards, *he's cute.* The twentieth was a Friday, and, as he did every week, Halimi spent the Shabbat dinner at his mother Ruth's house, along with his sisters — but without his Chinese, non-Jewish, girlfriend. Then he went to meet his new acquaintance for a drink at the Paris Orléans, a café she'd chosen because it was close to the south beltway of the capital, leading to Bagneux.

Twenty-four days later, Halimi was found in the southern suburb, walking on the tracks of the regional train line, naked, handcuffed, and in a state of deep exhaustion. He had three knife wounds and was covered with third-degree burns on two-thirds of his body. He was taken to the emergency room but died a few hours later.

• • •

Sorour Arbabzadeh had had no trouble getting Halimi to drive her to Bagneux, or giving the proper signal—searching in her purse for her keys—right after they'd arrived and gotten out of the car. In her testimony, she said that she'd heard Halimi crying out for two whole minutes as he resisted the gang members, who had lifted him up from the ground and, carrying him by his arms and legs, were trying to lock him up in a car trunk. Students on an adjacent street also saw him struggling from afar, but, because of the high pitch of his voice, they took him for a girl and thought—or preferred to believe—that the whole thing was a joke.

After the car took off, Sorour was in tears. She found comfort in the kind words of one of the gang members who had stayed behind with her. Maurice was a computer engineer by trade, from Martinique, in the French West Indies, who had converted to Islam. *Don't worry,* he told her. *This is not your fault. Besides, it's all over.*

In fact, the event called for a celebration. Around midnight that same evening, after Halimi was taken care of, Fofana invited Maurice, Sorour, and her then boyfriend, Sami—who was trying to establish himself as a fashion model, and whom she'd recently met on the Internet—to have dinner in Paris. They stopped in Montparnasse, at a French steakhouse chain restaurant called Hippopotamus, where she had an ice cream. When dessert was over, Fofana also offered Sorour and her boyfriend a 109-euro three-star hotel room nearby for the night.

In the morning, as she discovered a few days later, Sorour was pregnant. She spent the three following weeks—the three weeks during which Ilan Halimi was wrapped in tape from head to toe, with only a hole left for him to breathe ("He looked like a mummy," one of his jailers told the police afterwards), fed through a straw, and untied only when toilets or showers became absolutely necessary, lying, the rest of the time, day and night, first on the cold ground of an unheated, empty apartment of the Bagneux *cité,* then in the building's boiler room, in the cellar below, where the ground was even colder and where his situation worsened significantly, because now he could only piss in a bottle and defecate in a plastic bag, which infuriated his jailer, who had to hold the bag for him each time and felt humiliated and beat him for it more than once as a result—three weeks during which he was burned with cigarette butts because Fofana was frustrated that, despite his daily phone threats and pressures, "the Jews" did not seem to be willing to pay the 450,000 euros he demanded for his hostage's release—three weeks during which Ruth Halimi and her two daughters were harassed on the phone and on the Internet, and the police were at a loss, and every newspaper in the country wondered who the Gang of Barbarians were and what all this really meant, since anti-Semitism was too dull a fantasy to even contemplate—three weeks at the end of which, finally, Ilan Halimi was cleaned up, first with cheap soap and water and then with acid, because his jailers, inspired by the details they'd gleaned from TV shows, were convinced that acid would erase any traces of their DNA, then beaten again, handcuffed again, and, naked, simply covered with sheets, put in a trunk again, and driven into the woods, only to be stabbed and practically burned alive—three weeks that Sorour, for her part, spent wrestling with one question and one question only, as her obsessive text messages to Tiffen during the period indicate: Should she break up with Sami, have an abortion, and call Maurice, with whom she had fallen in love, or should she stay with Sami and have his baby?

The trial of the Gang of Barbarians opened three years later, in April 2009. No fewer than twenty-nine people stood in the dock. Twenty-two were charged with kidnapping, torture, barbaric acts, and murder, six for having knowledge of these crimes and not having denounced them. Among the latter was the concierge of the building, Gilles Serrurier, thirty-six years old and of Christian background, who broke down in tears in the courtroom. Not only had he given Fofana's gang the key to the apartment where Ilan Halimi had been held, but, when it turned out that the place was going under construction and couldn't be used anymore, it was he who had opened the building's boiler room for them. Without him, as the state prosecutor remarked, the crime couldn't have possibly been carried out. He spoke of his fear of the gang, of the pattern of kidnappings in the *cité,* and of his alleged ignorance of the conditions of Ilan Halimi's detention.

It soon emerged that the number of defendants—twenty-nine—was, in fact, a low one. If one added the friends, boyfriends, girlfriends, and sometimes parents of the accused, the total number of people who had known what was going on was closer to fifty. Given that the case had been widely covered in the French press during those fatal three weeks of Ilan Halimi's detention, just one anonymous phone call to the police would've been enough to stop everything.

Jérôme Ribeiro's parents were a case in point. Ribeiro, also Christian-born, was an unemployed container packer who had served as one of Ilan Halimi's jailers. At some point during his detention, the prisoner's health had begun to deteriorate, and Ribeiro had started to panic. He had confided in his girlfriend, Leila, and the two had gone to see his parents. "The guy, he's not gonna make it." Ribeiro's father, Alcino, however, had advised him to keep silent and asked Leila to do the same.

One of the things they feared, besides police, was the power of the community they thought they had targeted and defied: things were bad enough as they were—no need to get public in addition. That fear ran so deep among the gang members that after Ilan Halimi's death, one of Fofana's "lieutenants" went into hiding—not from the police but, as he later admitted, from the Mossad, which, he said, had no doubt sent its commandos from Israel to Bagneux to take revenge on each member of the Gang of Barbarians. As everyone knew, Jews had special powers and no mercy. (In Jérôme Ribeiro's room, police also found anti-Semitic leaflets and Nazi-oriented posters.)

Fofana's personality added an even more sinister twist to the story. In February 2006, a few weeks after Halimi's death, as the police were arresting most of the gang members, he had managed to escape to the Ivory Coast. From there he continued to make threatening phone calls to the victim's family. He was interviewed there by French TV reporters and, on French national television, appeared with a proud smile on his face and a girlfriend at his side. "Let's just say that if the guillotine were still around, one might suggest it for me," he answered, with a studied, movie-like ambiguity, when the reporter asked him whether or not he'd been the one to kill Halimi. His greatest wish now, he confessed on the show, was to become a warlord in some African rebellion. Once caught by the Ivory Coast police, extradited, and put in jail in France, he attempted, through his lawyer, to find a publisher for his memoirs.

Fofana was a narcissistic media addict. His Islamist stand during the trial and since sounds like a retroactive justification on his part. He is said to have become a devout radical Muslim only in jail, and there is no doubt that he also was influenced by his first lawyer, Isabelle Coutant-Peyre. A former associate of the Nazi Klaus Barbie's lawyer, Jacques Vergès, Coutant-Peyre had grown up in a Catholic French bourgeois family before converting to Islam in 2001 in order to marry the international terrorist Carlos, the Jackal, who was incarcerated in France and for whom she served as lawyer. Born in Venezuela as Ilich Ramírez Sánchez—a name given to him by his father as a reference to Lenin—Carlos had been recruited by the KGB in 1968 and sent to training with the Popular Front for the Liberation of Palestine in Amman in the early seventies. The PFLP was a dissident Palestinian group, controlled by Syrian-Russian intelligence. Traveling with leftist German terror groups infiltrated by East German secret services, Carlos had traveled across the Middle East to accomplish several missions before finding refuge in Damascus in the mid-eighties—and before being arrested in Sudan in 1991, when the Cold War ended and the Syrians judged him useless.

Sent to France, he had been sentenced to life for the bombing of the Saint-Germain drugstore in 1975, and it was during his trial that Coutant-Peyre met him and they fell in love. Prior to this, Coutant-Peyre had been counsel to Roger Garaudy, a French intellectual and former Communist turned Holocaust denier. Some years later, she admitted to having been hired by Iran.

France's current situation with terror cannot be fully understood without this Cold War background—and without the over-ideologized intellectual atmosphere pervading the country during the second half of the twentieth century, a period during which the Communist Party affected virtually every aspect of the cultural life with a force unmatched in the West. After the Cold War ended, as we will see, some former leftists and Communists in search of a new anti-capitalist stand turned their attention toward the worst reactionary tendencies of Islam, and met along the way former extreme right-wing militants who shared their disappointment. But this ideological aspect of things falls short of explaining the journey of individuals such as Fofana.

Prior to the crime, Fofana does not appear to have attended any mosque on a regular basis, nor to have befriended would-be jihadists or even surfed propagandistic websites. And yet, as all his accomplices testify, his obsessive anti-Jewish hatred was, from the start, utterly genuine. His parents and his brother, who appeared in court, seemed as flabbergasted by it as anyone else and offered no explanation. The more passive anti-Semitism of the rest of the gang was no less evident—to begin with, the crazy amount of ransom money they asked for. The sum was based on the assumption of everyone in the gang that "the Jews" would pay, because Jews stick together, and if the family didn't have that kind of money, as was the case, the community would provide. The fear of "the Mossad" was another example of how the gang members were under the spell of a narrative in which "the Jews" were both a fantastical threat and a legitimate target. It is important to understand that this narrative predated any Islamist propaganda that Isabelle Coutant-Peyre may or may not have provided her client with during the trial. In other words, at the time they abducted, tortured, and killed Ilan Halimi, none of the gang members were "Islamist militants"; in fact, as the case of Jérôme Ribeiro indicates, not all of them were even Muslims. Yet, during the hearings, the link between these messy, semi-conscious anti-Jewish biases and possible future ideologically trained organized terror groups was hard to miss. (Isabelle Coutant-Peyre's presence, for one, indicated that such a link was indeed possible.) "Is the worst yet to come?" asked the leftist website Rue89 in an op-ed piece, concluding, "We've been lucky so far that thugs and future killers of the suburbs haven't yet dared to use their weapons," an allusion to the number of Kalashnikovs known to be held in the *cités*. In the next decade, however, they would. But the connection between a spontaneous anti-Semitic impulse and more ideologically trained terror acts targeting everybody would remain an enigma, one that would plague French attempts to combat terror to this day.

In the 2000s, by and large, incredulity and embarrassment prevailed. Part of the media thrill with the Ilan Halimi murder found its source in a fascination with the prospect of a new rising tide of anti-Semitism in France. Yet editorialists and authorities alike exerted a fantastic amount of energy denying that this enticing possible storyline was in fact true. Police investigators had insisted from day one on the thoroughly villainous nature of the crime — "villainous" as opposed to ideological. The official statement the investigating magistrate gave, against all evidence, in the days following Ilan Halimi's death went even further: "There isn't a single element," he said, "allowing us to attach this murder to an anti-Semitic purpose or an anti-Semitic act." The collective view that came to prevail was that if the notion that Jews have money is clearly a racist cliché, the mere fact that the Gang of Barbarians acted according to that cliché did not make them anti-Semites. Rather, they simply were illiterate and ignorant. It was as a consequence of that ignorance that they let clichés dominate their lives. The minister of interior at the time, the future president Nicolas Sarkozy, commenting on the case at the National Assembly, summed up the prevailing attitude when he defined the gang's mindset as "anti-Semitism by amalgam"—an expression whose absurdity illustrated, above all, the confusion the French faced in the wake of the situation.

Part of the general embarrassment came from the sudden confrontation with the strange, unknown world from which the gang seemed to spring: a half-medieval, half-twenty-first-century world, quite hard to define, that had nothing to do with the old, familiar working-class universe to which the country was used to assigning the people from the *cités*. Hence the piece the leftist senator Esther Benbassa (herself Jewish) published in *Le Monde* arguing that to emphasize anti-Semitism in this case would have the effect of encouraging tribalism. During the trial, two defense lawyers for Fofana's accomplices—Gilles Antonowicz and Françoise Cotta—came up with an article of their own expressing the same idea: "Only people with political motivations," they wrote, "would try to sell the opinion that anti-Semitism is eating away at French society. Such a plague, as we all know, is, fortunately enough, almost nonexistent in the country."[1]

It was, of course, a perfectly legitimate argument: How statistically significant, after all, is one crime—especially when this crime involves so improbable a series of pathological characters? The warnings that anti-Jewish violence was rising in the *cités* were consequently widely dismissed as exaggerated, if not politically oriented. A few years after the case, Antonowicz dedicated a whole book to the Halimi murder story, in order, he wrote, "to fight the belief that in 2006 a young Frenchman has been killed by a bunch of savages for being Jewish."[2]

The present book began as a series of five articles that I wrote for the U.S. online magazine *Tablet* between May and August 2014, five years after the trial, on a series of violent anti-Jewish incidents in France. As a French writer, my choosing a New York–based, English-language medium was based on my absolute conviction that there would not be any chance to interest a French outlet in such an issue. At least not in the way and at the length I felt the subject should be covered. Something was on the rise. After the murder of Jewish children in Toulouse in March 2012, anti-Jewish brutalities had multiplied. In January 2014, the first anti-Jewish slogans to resonate in Paris since World War II had been heard, during a right-wing demonstration. On December 31 of that same year, one week before the *Charlie Hebdo* massacre, the number of anti-Jewish incidents across the country had reached eight hundred, more than two per day, for a Jewish population of 500,000. Yet only Jews perceived any of this, and besides, the nature of what they perceived wasn't entirely clear.

Then in early 2015 came the killings at *Charlie Hebdo* magazine and the attack on the Hyper Cacher kosher market, in the suburb of Vincennes, two days later. November of the same year saw the synchronized attacks on the café terraces and in the Bataclan theater that claimed 130 victims and wounded more than four hundred; on July 14 of the following year, on the national holiday, occurred the Nice attack, which killed eighty-four people. Several other, more minor killings and attempted attacks took place in between. (The most notable among them were the beheading of a small entrepreneur, Hervé Cornara, by his Islamist employee in June 2015; the attack on the Thalys train the following August, during which a massacre was avoided thanks to three U.S. soldiers on vacation who were present on the train; and the grim throat-slitting of Father Jacques Hamel during mass in his own church near Rouen on July 26, 2016.) By the end of 2016, the terror death toll in France had risen to 239 over those two years, with several hundred more left permanently injured. Although this number was small compared with the 25,621 victims of terror worldwide that same year, two-thirds of them in the Middle East and North Africa,[3] it still was a significant figure for a European country.

But what did it signify?

Months had passed since I signed the contract for a book based on my 2014 reporting for *Tablet,* and from the Jewish viewpoint I had adopted in writing them, the terror wave now under way both clarified and confused the matter. If the attacks confirmed, to a point, the intuitive fears that had first triggered the writing, they also raised a damning issue, one that is now at the heart of what follows: What was the connection between, on the one hand, a series of random, spontaneous brutalities perpetrated by regular individuals against one group only—the Jews—and, on the other, planned terror attacks led by determined individuals aiming at the French population indiscriminately?

To assume that there was no connection at all—that the dramatic rise of anti-Semitic incidents in France in the months preceding the first terror attack was a simple coincidence—did not track; yet to claim, as most of the Jewish community leaders did, that every perpetrator of an anti-Semitic attack was an Islamist militant was absurd and simply did not jibe with the facts.

The torturers and killers of Ilan Halimi in 2006 were no Islamists. Kobili Traoré—the young Frenchman of Malian background who, in April 2017, sneaked into the apartment of sixty-five-year-old Sarah Halimi (no relation to the first victim) and, while quoting verses of the Koran, beat her savagely before throwing her over her balcony was no Islamist. She died from the fall, and police said that her face was unrecognizable as a result of the beating. One year later, in March 2018, Yacine Mihoub stabbed his neighbor, the Shoah survivor Mireille Knoll, age eighty-five, eleven times, then tried to burn her body. His accomplice later testified that, before the crime, Mihoub had complained about "the richness of the Jews" and shouted *"Allahu akbar"* during the murder. (Mihoub's mother was later indicted for trying to hide the knife he had used.) Yet nothing in the file suggests that Mihoub or his mother were Islamists. Clearly, without these random expressions of anti-Jewish hate, the terror wave France has experienced since 2015 would not have occurred on such a scale. Yet the link between the two—and with the extremist right-wingers who shouted anti-Semitic slogans in January 2014—was by no way obvious.

France sent more jihadists to Syria than any other Western country; less quantifiable was the atmosphere of violence pervading the country since the rise of the National Front during the early 2000s. Paralleling the anti-Semitic brutalities in the *cités,* a populist reactionary wave was in the air, and, with the influx of people fleeing the Syrian war, this populist wave rode on the back of a refugee crisis of unprecedented scale. It was from this corner, the populist far right, that the first anti-Semitic slogans had indeed been heard during a demonstration in January 2014.

Despite its anti-Muslim stand, this populist wave shared many things with the Islamists: reactionary views on the role of women, a frank hostility to gay rights, and, if one was to believe the slogans, an ambivalence, at best, toward the Jews. In the last months of 2016, with a Socialist Party virtually killed by the anti-charismatic President François Hollande, and with Emmanuel Macron still in the wings, everybody assumed that a reactionary, pro-Russian candidate —possibly Marine Le Pen, more probably the right-wing François Fillon—would succeed in the coming presidential elections, set for the following April. The country was beginning to look like a laboratory for the worst tendencies of the new century.

Then, between November 2016 and April 2017, things changed again, radically and unexpectedly. Instead of the reactionary candidate the French were supposed to elect, it was the unforeseen Emmanuel Macron who won, some six months after the no less unforeseen victory of Donald Trump in the United States. It looked at first as if the two countries had switched places. Seen from Paris, however, Trump was even less a surprise than his chief strategist, Steve Bannon, was. The disorganized, bookish mind, the narcissistic sense of his own intellectual grandeur, the nihilistic verbosity, the nationalism mixed with the claim of "authenticity": What could be less American than that? What could be more French? Indeed, from a French viewpoint, the familiarity each time Bannon spoke on CNN was unmistakable.

By his own admission, Bannon's first intellectual mentor *was* French. "We are at the end of the Enlightenment," he is reported to have said to a French official in Washington, D.C., in 2016. "Have you read Charles Maurras?"[4] Charles Maurras! To an American ear, such a reference could only be lost, but for the French, it was only too obvious. Between 1898 and the late 1930s, Maurras had been one of the most successful journalists in Paris.

Like Bannon, he was blessed with an innate talent for intellectual marketing. Maurras was the first in Europe to rephrase the intellectual quarrels against the cosmopolitan "elite" of the Enlightenment tradition into something new, by focusing it on nationalistic and social issues. He had made his journal, *L'Action Française,* an instant success by mixing high-culture charges against modernity with the low, popular anger against international finance then personified by Jewish bankers. Maurras stood for a society of castes, for the Catholic Church, and for restoring the king, and *L'Action Française* was three things in one: a royalist political movement, a journal, and a nationalistic philosophical system allegedly based on the rational principles inherited from the positivist school. Of course, it was also anti–American.

It was under its influence that the name Rothschild became, in France, a code word for the rage against the combined forces of the U.S.-imported capitalist system backed by the foreign "kikes" who were said to control it. Maurras was, in other words, the very first "populist" in the sense Europeans give to that term.

Embattled in a royalist and anti-Semitic fight, he prefigured in many ways the Vichy regime, which collaborated with the Nazis during the Occupation years and which Maurras supported. Maurras was anticapitalist.

Anti-Semitism was the cornerstone of his thought and of his action. In 1898, the year he created *L'Action Française,* the journal's avowed first purpose was to fight against the rehabilitation of Alfred Dreyfus, a captain of the French army and of Jewish origins, who four years earlier, in 1894, had been accused of spying for the Germans and sentenced to life imprisonment in the penal colony of Guyana. Dreyfus's public military degradation that year had given way to anti-Semitic cries such as "Down with the Jew!" In 1896, new elements surfaced as a lieutenant colonel named Georges Picquart discovered a document proving that another officer, Ferdinand Esterhazy, was the real traitor, and not Dreyfus. The army, however, tried to cover up the discovery. Dreyfus's condemnation had been so public a case that to admit a mistake would have been humiliating, and besides, that a Jew had figured as the guilty party had come as a blessing. It had helped prove, by contrast, the strength, the sense of honor, and the honesty of the "authentic" French soldiers. In the minds of the generals, then, the matter was settled. Then, four years later, in January 1898, as Dreyfus rotted in a Guyana jail, the case erupted again in Paris.

The reason for this new development was a piece written by the novelist Émile Zola in *L'Aurore,* in which he defended Dreyfus — an article that, under the title "J'Accuse . . . !," would crown its author the first of that French species known as the *"intellectuel engagé"* — the committed intellectual. One month later, with the help of two nationalist friends, both in response to Zola and in order to launch a new form of nationalism, Maurras founded his own journal, *L'Action Française.*

The French Revolution, according to Maurras, had been plotted all along by Jews and Freemasons, and he saw proof of that in the very Declaration of the Rights of Man and of the Citizen that ended slavery and emancipated the Jews. Since then, not only was the country losing its "authentic, eternal values," but the decadent and individualist cosmopolitanism resulting from the republic was spreading in all Europe.

According to that view, Dreyfus's innocence was, for Maurras, beside the point. What mattered was national honor and the French army. If Dreyfus had been a real patriot and a real soldier, he would have accepted his fate, guilty or not. That was what knightly honor commanded. But democracy, with its emphasis on individualism, favored feminine morality based on words rather than actions. Speeches, personal rights, won over masculine values such as heroism and self-sacrifice. Dreyfus clung to those petit bourgeois rights, because, as for any stateless, rootless Jew, these rights and the law were the only guarantors of his citizenship—and there, for Maurras, lay his real treason. Thus, in a Kafkaesque twist, it was by trying to prove his innocence and clinging to the law that Dreyfus proved he was guilty. His personal interest was more important for him than the honor of the French army. Therefore, he should stay in jail, *regardless of the facts*. Disdain for the truth, which is now everywhere, finds here one of its deepest roots.

The key notion sustaining Maurras's reasoning was the opposition he drew between two different visions of France. He called them, on the one hand, "the legal country"—that is to say, the fictions and lies of an international political culture of merchants, based, since the Revolution, on the Declaration of the Rights of Man—and, on the other, "the real country," which was to be found, in his eyes, in regional, local traditions, in the existence of "a people" of peasants and an opposition to merchants—a people whose identity expressed itself in a natural love for the national soil, the Church, and the memory of the kings. Having no state, and therefore no national soil of their own, the Jews were bound to support the first, which explained why they cared about nothing and could never be trusted (in addition to having crucified the Lord).[5] In this opposition, we may recognize what is today known as "identity politics."

In our age of fake news, one can only be struck by Maurras's disdain for facts and words as a journalist, while he emphasized the importance of "eternal" nationalist and religious values, pretty much as Bannon does—and with him all the figures of the "anti-globalist" current, from the nationalists in Russia to the Wahhabite theologians. One should note also the strange organic link between fake news and anti-Jewishness. Anti-Semitism was, of course, widespread even before Maurras came on the Parisian scene. Indeed, the atmosphere of hate was so toxic during the so-called Belle Époque in Paris that, in 1893, Theodor Herzl, the future "inventor" of political Zionism, who was then freelancing in the French capital as a correspondent for the German press, could write the following to the novelist Arthur Schnitzler: "There will be a revolution here this year. If I don't escape in good time, I'll probably be shot as a German spy, as a bourgeois, as a Jew, or as a financier."[6] He wasn't wrong. The hammer dropped one year later—only not on him, but on Dreyfus.

Maurras used that atmosphere to launch *L'Action Française*. But in doing so, he also contributed to the process of framing this hate into a coherent, pseudo-rational narrative, by which it spread even more. By 1901, Maurras was so successful in doing so that, by witnessing this particular Parisian *air du temps* he had helped to create, two agents of the tsarist secret police at the Russian embassy in Paris, Pyotr Rachkovsky and Mathieu Golovinski, came up with the idea of forging a hoax that would accuse the Jews of plotting to control the world. Their initial goal with this project was not so much to hurt the Jews as to spread rumors and a general feeling of paranoia, in order to undermine the political liberalism of Western Europe, which was seen in Russia as a potential threat to the order of things. Given Maurras's narrative and success, using the Jews simply sounded easier.[7] Yet *The Protocols of the Elders of Zion*, which they ended up publishing first in Paris, turned into the most successful fake news of all time, spreading across Europe and into America. Forty years later, it would be distributed en masse to the soldiers of the Wehrmacht to help convince them of the righteousness of what they were doing. After the war, it also spread across the Arab world, with the help of former Nazis sheltered by Nasser in Egypt, where the book is still a bestseller to this day.

So what is it in France that makes the country such an inspiration for anti-liberal tendencies of all kinds? Could it be that something in the Maurras heritage, while helping Bannon to form what passes for his theories, also contributed to the blindness with which France put up with the new wave of anti-Semitism in the suburbs from the early 2000s on? Is it a coincidence that Putin's chamber philosopher, Alexander Dugin, came to France as a young man, in the early nineties, to search for intellectual mentors — before he came up with his own theories in which, among many other things, he pleads for a Russian-Muslim alliance against the West? Is it really too far-fetched to see in Wahhabism and Salafism — the Muslim ideologies pleading for a return to an "authentic Islam" divorced from globalism and modernity — a kind of Muslim translation of Maurras's profession of faith for "the real" against the fake global cosmopolitanism?

Thanks to the Enlightenment and to the Declaration of the Rights of Man, as imperfect as the text may appear today, France was the first country to emancipate the Jews and to abolish slavery, in 1791. Shortly after that, however, it distinguished itself again, this time by inventing political terror and the guillotine. Could it be that the country has been at war with its inner demons ever since, and that the noise of this war attracts demons from abroad? Is it what contributes to making France a sort of laboratory for the global fury we see today?

This book, needless to say, does not pretend to answer these questions the way a history book would. Yet it is with them in mind that it has been written. They constitute the backdrop against which the dangerous fate of the Jews of France is being played out today. In fact, the fury started with them.

HATE

ONE
The Return of the Repressed

O n April 15, 2015, in the paved courtyard of the majestic Hô-
tel des Invalides, the French state paid the last tribute to my
great-uncle Jean-Louis Crémieux-Brilhac, *conseiller d'État*
and war hero of the Resistance, who had just died. The
warm light of a Parisian late-morning sun poured in on the
crowd—two hundred people, perhaps, among them three sitting
government ministers, various leaders of the Jewish community, and
members of my great-uncle's family, enclosed within the ancient
freestone walls.

The hotel is the official secular temple of France. Military personalities deemed worthy of the country's gratitude have been honored
in this courtyard since the emperor Napoleon made the first-ever
presentations of the Légion d'Honneur in it in 1804. The building was built two centuries earlier by King Louis XIV as a hospital dedicated to the disabled soldiers of the brand-new French Empire. As the first of the French meritocratic decorations, the Légion
d'Honneur took the place of the Order of Saint Louis, which until then had been the kingdom's highest honor, and the exclusive

privilege of nobility. Napoleon's remains are now buried in the hospital's crypt.

The slow beat of the drums ushered in a Republican Guard officer in full regalia, who slowly walked toward my great-uncle's coffin, resting on a trestle in the middle of the courtyard, and set down on it a folded French flag. The military orchestra played "Farewell to Arms," Chopin's Funeral March, and "La Marseillaise," and three rifle shots resounded under the empty blue sky. The short silhouette of President Hollande, cramped in a suit, his tie knot askew, crossed the courtyard to reach the white lectern set under a white tent a few feet away from the coffin. The speech he gave was brief, not particularly memorable, and the ceremony ended, the politicians left the scene. My family gathered together for the journey to the Montparnasse cemetery, where Jean-Louis Crémieux was to be buried, and an hour or so later, with the funeral convoy leading the way, we began to proceed, passing by Sartre and Beauvoir's grave, beneath the deep, shiny green of the leafy trees and the warm sun, up to the vault of the Crémieux family.

That there are two Crémieux vaults — one within the Jewish quarter, and Jean-Louis's located a few feet outside of it — was a slightly sensitive matter. The presence of Rav Haïm Korsia, head of the Consistory, the religious institution of the Jews of France set up by Napoleon in 1808, had been requested by Jean-Louis's niece Laurence, but was counterbalanced by the demand by Laurence's uncompromisingly ultra-secular sister Martine that he not make a speech, let alone say a prayer. As a result, the rabbi was reduced to a mere shadow, if someone who spent his time exchanging gossip with Pierre Nora, Jean-Louis's publisher and a member of the Académie Française, can be called that.

My great-uncle, who, after retiring, became a historian of the Gaullist Resistance movement during World War II, belonged to the most French branch of our family. He was a Jew from Provence, a community whose settlement in the country can be traced back to the Roman Empire — at a time when Jewish merchants followed the Roman legions as far as Marseille.

Jewish soldiers, some of whom had fought Rome in the two great, doomed Jewish uprisings of the first and second centuries before joining the legions, were posted in southern France, and as far north and east as Cologne. In the Middle Ages, the Jewish community of Provence grew wealthy, and the region became an important spiritual center. This was where Isaac the Blind, born in 1160 in the small village of Posquières (now Vauvert), one hour south of Avignon, wrote the first commentaries on the *Sefer Yesira* (*The Book of Creation*) and created some of the most basic notions of what would later become the kabbalistic tradition, such as the *En-Sof* (the infinite presence of the hidden God) and the *Sefirot* (the ten spheres of the creation linking the perfect hidden divine language to imperfect human words).

Things being what they are, the Jews of Provence were periodically assaulted and even massacred by Crusaders on their way to the Holy Land and back, or by the population who held them responsible for the Plague. But a defining moment for their ancient community took place in the fourteenth century, when the popes, having deserted Rome and settled in Avignon, enacted special laws to protect them. "In exchange," as it were, Jews were to wear a special yellow hat and pay extra taxes, and they were forced to attend special sermons in churches calling for conversions. Yet after a decree to expel the Jews from the kingdom of France was issued in 1394, it is thanks to the popes that Provence remained the only region, along with Alsace, in the North, where a Jewish presence was tolerated. Known from then on as *les Juifs du pape* ("the pope's Jews"), they were existentially nurtured, so to speak, one century later by the experience of the Marranos, Jews converted by force to Christianity, who were said to Judaize in secret — undoubtedly the first community ever, in the West, to experience the modern feeling of a split conscience and of a double belonging. The Marranos expelled from

Spain passed through Provence on their way to exile in Amsterdam or in the Ottoman Empire, and in some cases decided to stay.

Because of that specific story and despite their number—only two thousand people as of the sixteenth century—these *Juifs du pape* ended up giving birth to a very specific regional form of secular Jewishness in France, one that over time became nearly devoid of any particular religious content and was to have an important influence on that specific form of secularism the French call *laïcité*, which in 1905 was enshrined in France's Law on the Separation of Church and State.

With the rise of the Enlightenment in the eighteenth century, the fate of the Jews improved throughout Western Europe, but nowhere better than in Germany and France. Under the French philosophers' influence—Montesquieu's in particular—Louis XVI authorized the Jews to farm the land and abolished the extra taxes they had to pay. Yet they still were subjected to daily controls and forbidden to travel freely. Then, in 1791, in the wake of the Declaration of the Rights of Man, which had been issued two years earlier and would so repel Maurras one century later, the representatives of the French National Assembly voted to abolish slavery and emancipate the Jews, thus recognizing them as French citizens.

This was no little matter. Despite the small number of Jews in France at the time—forty thousand people in a total population of 23 million—the National Assembly took up the question of whether they could be citizens no fewer than thirty-two times in two years. According to Professor David Nirenberg, from whom I borrow these numbers, "in the Christian polities of Europe, the right to decide the fate of the Jews . . . was a defining prerogative of the sovereign. In claiming to determine the status of the Jews, the Assembly was therefore asserting its sovereign power."[1] The hothouse debates over the Jews involved questions that would seem shocking today: "I always believed that [Jews] were men," argued Abbé Henri Grégoire, one of the main advocates of the emancipation, which implied that the humanity of the Jews was not at all obvious. "I had always thought that one could re-create those people," he added, "bring them to virtue and leave them in good will."[2] (Under the same premises, Abbé Grégoire was also a strong abolitionist.) Jews were thought to be at the limit between humanity and non-humanity, between reason on the one hand and madness and superstition on the other. For the proponent of the Enlightenment tradition, the question of the limits of reason went hand in hand with the issue of universalism. To be human—to be "a man"—was to be gifted with the powers of reasoning. Women were excluded from the right to vote on the ground that they weren't human. Secular Voltaire, for one, thought that Jews, having written the Bible—this self-contradictory catalog of superstitions—weren't, either. By implication, the notion that Jews were crazy and therefore not fully human went together with the idea that Jewish men were not "real men." Dating from the Middle Ages, a popular tradition had it that Jewish men suffered from the same curse as women: they menstruated. If, on the other hand, Jews were indeed gifted with reason, as Abbé Grégoire advocated, then they were at least potentially full members of the human race—"real men"—and consequently deserved to be citizens. Such reasoning would provide the basis for the concept of "assimilation," intrinsically linked with the notion of progress, according to which all men are equal, providing they receive the right education in reason and civilization.

Although they did have an impact on the lives of actual Jews in the country, these debates over the *regeneration* of the Jews and their emancipation were, above all, as David Nirenberg puts it, "a subset and a surrogate for the much larger debate over how to achieve the conversion of tens of millions of French subjects, peasants and princes, peddlers and priests, into citizens."[3] Once passed, the law on the emancipation of the Jews would influence all of Europe and help spread Moses Mendelssohn's Haskalah, the Jewish Enlightenment, in nearby Prussia and, from there, led to the freeing of European

Jewry from the miserable ghettos in which they had been confined for centuries, and to the creation of the secular Jewish world from which sprang the Jewish life of the nineteenth and twentieth centuries in Europe as we remember it. This issue of Jewish manhood and the regeneration of the Jews was furthermore destined to have tremendous repercussions in the modern narratives of anti-Semitism, but also in the way Jews conceived themselves.[4]

But in the context of the French political implementation of the Enlightenment tradition in the eighteenth century, another development is worth noting in this issue of the link between Jews and reason. Either because of France's tradition of centralized power or its Cartesian tendencies, or both, the French are inclined to believe that rationality is by nature the source of human behavior and that, conversely, only one type of human behavior — the more rational — will impose itself naturally on people, providing they're being talked into reason and receive the right education — that, in other words, progress is the natural direction of human affairs. Following this mindset, by the mid-eighteenth century, the current known as the Enlightenment had gained in France a political importance unmatched anywhere else in the West. Even though they disagreed among themselves, French philosophers all concurred that, if correctly applied, the principles of the Enlightenment would solve most political problems, while science would improve human life. At the end of the century, the French Revolution was seen as the ideological translation of these optimistic principles, and for a short while — before the souvenir of the guillotine slowly sank in — France embodied for everyone the best that the Western world could offer. That was when, seven years after the emancipation of the Jews, in 1798, the future emperor Napoleon Bonaparte, then only first consul, launched his expedition in Egypt in what was to become the first cultural confrontation between the Islamic world and the West. To emphasize his point, Napoleon brought with him a delegation of scientists and a delegation of rabbis from Provence.

Of course, there had been encounters between the Muslim world and Western travelers before. But Napoleon's histrionics collided with the Mediterranean anachronism in a spectacular way. In the Ottoman Empire, typography had appeared in the fifteenth century but was confined, mostly, to the Jewish, Greek, and Armenian communities. The printing press was either forbidden or subject to strict control. Ottoman and Egyptian civil servants were flabbergasted by the number of books Napoleon brought with him. As Christopher de Bellaigue argues in *The Islamic Enlightenment,* the Sublime Porte was confronted with "the most self-consciously modern society on earth — and its new dynamo, Napoleon. His military brilliance [was] offset by a vast ego and the attention span of an adolescent. Napoleon was not only a general: he was also inspired by the intellectual vigour of the Enlightenment and the transformative potential of the French Revolution. Recently elected to the Institut de France ... he was an accomplished mathematician and a keen debater on matters ranging from habitable planets to the interpretation of dreams. He also bought enthusiastically, and with characteristic self-interest, into France's post-revolutionary imperialist doctrine, which would — in the words of his future ally Talleyrand — 'set everything in order ... in the interest of the human species.'"[5]

Along with the exhibition of scientific experiences and the philosophical discussions on political freedom and individual rights, which both fascinated and worried the Egyptian imams, Napoleon and the rabbis of Provence also revealed to them a new, developing form of Judaism.

None of this went without opposition. In Cairo, the head of the *diwan,* Sheikh Abdullah al-Sharqawi, was quick to denounce the French occupiers as "materialist, libertine philosophers who deny the Resurrection and the afterlife and ... the prophets."[6] During the same period, in Europe, the ultra-conservative Catholic philosopher Joseph de Maistre, a future source for Maurras, was among the first to attack the Declaration of the Rights of Man as the source of all troubles. "This mad pronouncement, 'Man is born free,' is the opposite of truth," he wrote, and the main beneficiaries of this lie were the scientists, the philosophers, the Freemasons, the democrats and the Jews.[7] Surely they had plotted a secret "conspiracy" to overthrow the ancient divine order and its aristocracy in France, and now, spreading liberalism, they threatened to do the same with the entire continent and beyond. The improbability that such a small community could have accomplished an event of such magnitude as the Revolution was precisely, for de Maistre, the proof that this was so, for the strength necessary to achieve such a goal as to defy God's eternal order had nothing to do with numbers. It proved that Jews and Freemasons were nothing less than *the Army of Satan* and that he marched behind them.

Meanwhile, another Egyptian luminary, Abd al-Rahman al-Jabarti, who was one of the first to fully realize the significance of the wave of modernity breaking on Islam and would soon turn to the nascent current of Wahhabism in reaction, remarked, amazed, that France was "a country without religion but which obeys the judgment of reason."[8] For someone like Jabarti, who believed that reason comes *from* religion, this was a contradiction in terms. And while his statement was more than exaggerated at the time — despite the Enlightenment, France was deeply Catholic and would remain so until at least the end of the 1950s — it certainly is an apt description of what the Jews of Provence ended up being.

By the end of the nineteenth century, you couldn't be more a part of the spirit of the French Republic than these *Juifs du pape*. Often left-leaning, they were widely seen, by their fellow Jews and by others, as the most successful specimens of the unique French-Jewish symbiosis that dominated the end of the nineteenth century. Yet, aside from this symbiosis, and countering it, an anti-modern, anti-Enlightenment current had grown among the best intellectual circles in the country. De Maistre was widely read by Balzac, and above all by Charles Baudelaire, the greatest poet of the era, who borrowed from him much of his dark irony and sharp style. As early as the 1830s, France entered an age of Restoration, marked by a will to restore the kings and the aristocracy (a current from which Maurras would later derive). But because nobody can undo history, the result of those efforts was marked by decades of malaise and restlessness. Now that "real" aristocracy was gone, ambitious people — immortalized by Balzac's Rastignac — bought or invented for themselves particles such as "de," giving themselves fake names and fake origins to enter the Parisian salons in which virtually nobody was what he or she pretended to be. While "legitimacy" became the catchword, everyone saw himself as a fraud. That the Industrial Revolution and its corollary, the rise of a corrupt urban life, were decadent and ugly was a commonplace of the times. (De Maistre thought they were produced by God's wrath as a punishment for the Revolution.) "Real" culture, "real" France, belonged to an idealized past of a pure, romantic world where honor, true love, and knighthood once reigned. With time, this mindset evolved into a toxic atmosphere of intrigue and caste obsession, and the Jews, needless to say — as symbols of new money, of urban life, and of the entrepreneurial spirit — became the appalling embodiment of this untraceable purity of blue blood.

So while law enshrined the French-Jewish symbiosis, in actual practice, the effect was less obvious. Finally, this symbiosis fell into crisis with the Dreyfus affair, described above, before being destroyed beyond repair in 1940 by the war and, above all, by widespread French collaboration with Nazi Germany.

My great-uncle Jean-Louis Crémieux grew up as a perfect representative of the species. Although his grandfather was a rabbi, he owed his early intellectual training not to the Talmud Torah but to his uncle Benjamin Crémieux, a star literary critic of the Parisian

early twentieth century, a friend of Proust's who introduced Piran-
dello to the French reading audience and died in Buchenwald in
1944, as both a Jew and a member of the Resistance.

At twenty, in 1937, Jean-Louis was the youngest member of the
French Comité de Vigilance des Intellectuels Antifascistes (Vigilance Committee of Antifascist Intellectuals). He also entered the
prestigious military academy of Saint-Cyr, the French West Point.
At the beginning of the war, he was appointed as an officer cadet
on the western side of the Maginot Line, the defensive fortifications
that were supposed to protect France forever but instead crumbled
almost immediately in front of the German army. Captured by the
Wehrmacht in 1940, he managed to hide his Jewishness and was sent
to a prison camp in Pomerania, from which he escaped after several
months. Underground, penniless, on foot, and a Jew, he implausi-
bly managed to cross Germany, walking until he reached the USSR,
where the Russians, then Germany's allies, jailed him in the Lub-
yanka prison. They most certainly would have sent him back to the
Nazis if not for Hitler's decision to violate the German-Soviet pact
and invade Russia—an event that probably saved my great-uncle's
life. Instead, he was given permission and the means to embark for
London, where he worked directly with Charles de Gaulle as the
chief of the propaganda committee for the French Resistance.

But Resistance fighters in London were not exactly Jew-friendly
at the time. Products of the anti-parliamentary atmosphere of the
1930s, they owed their intellectual training to Charles Maurras's
L'Action Française, probably the best-written and most stimulating
newspaper in the country, which had framed the best minds of two
generations of intellectuals. In the beginning of the war, then, most
of the Resistance fighters tended to see Jewish influence on the
decadent republic as the main cause of French defeat—in much the
same way that the Nazis blamed Germany's defeat in World War I
on weak, greedy, traitorous Jews.

As a Jew and a former officer of the Maginot Line, Crémieux

had seemed a walking example of France's wartime humiliation. Small and seemingly frail, he certainly looked more like an intellectual than a warrior—a perfect illustration of what anti-Semites in those days referred to as the "effeminate Jew." But Jean-Louis was a mensch. He had more than enough strength to bear suspicions while helping to form the small group of Jewish Resistance fighters who were to play a key role in repositioning the Gaullists' vision. By the end of the war, in good part thanks to this Jewish nucleus, the Gaullist resistance had turned from a nationalist, reactionary semi-military formation into the first right-wing party in twentieth-century France to unambiguously embrace democracy.

The most prominent figure in that group was not my great-uncle, however, but Pierre Mendès-France, who later, in the mid-fifties, served as de Gaulle's minister of finance and then prime minister and with whom Crémieux worked closely. Both Crémieux and Mendès-France were pragmatic, moderate left-wingers. With the Resistance now in power, on the shoulders of de Gaulle, the French could claim a seat among the winners. Yet, through the Vichy regime, which had been the official government for four years, the country had aligned itself with the losing, murderous side—and the Jewish presence reminded everyone of that embarrassing fact. Then there was the difficult question of how efficient the Resistance had really been, whether or not it had represented anything more than a symbolic force, and, if not, what it meant in terms of political legitimacy. How *real,* in other words, was French power?

In her novel *Les Mandarins,* written and set during the period, Simone de Beauvoir has that bleak mindset of self-doubt summarized, tellingly, by the sole Jewish character of the book, a man named Scriassine, based on Arthur Koestler: "The poor French. They don't know whether they won or lost the war. To succeed with the future, you first need to look at the present head-on. And I've got the feeling that people here do not realize what the situation is at all . . . They seem to believe they'll be able to go on living the way they used to live before the war."[9] These questions would plague the country's policy for decades to come.

But it was Mendès-France who, in the mid-fifties, publicly unearthed the issue. He understood that because of the past—because of the economic situation resulting from it—and because of a new environment dominated by two superpowers, France had lost the legitimacy as well as the means (which are often the same thing) to sustain an empire. He was properly vindicated as a result. After de Gaulle seized power in a bloodless coup of sorts in 1958, Mendès-France and my great-uncle Jean-Louis left the government, in part because they opposed de Gaulle's stubborn support for keeping colonization going. That same year, 1958, Mendès-France, now a simple *député* fighting for the independence of Algeria, found himself the subject of an anti-Semitic campaign. Its most outspoken voice was Jean-Marie Le Pen, at the time the youngest parliamentary representative, who, after starting out in politics as an anarchist, had volunteered to fight in Indochina for the fading French Empire and now aligned himself with the settlers in Algeria. "You are aware that your character is the focus of a certain amount of patriotic and almost physical repulsion," Le Pen said during the debates at the National Assembly. Mendès-France, meanwhile, received far more explicit letters, by the dozen, from simple citizens accusing him of being "a traitor" and "a dirty Jew." He never recovered a prominent position in a French government. My great-uncle Jean-Louis, who specialized in higher education and science, had been one of Mendès-France's closest collaborators and remained a "Mendèsist" all his life. He disappeared from the scene.

No Kaddish was said before we were invited to march one by one past the open grave and, as a last salute to Jean-Louis, to either toss in a rose or, according to Jewish custom, put a stone on its side, which I chose.

Among the various speeches delivered there, the most vivid for me, in part because the questions it raised seemed to me to be left unanswered, was by Jean-Louis's son Michel, who undertook the complex task of explaining why, in his opinion, even though Jean-Louis refused religion, and even though trying to make him cross the threshold of even the most liberal synagogue on Yom Kippur was a herculean task, Jean-Louis had nevertheless insisted on defining himself as a Jew throughout his life.

"To be Jewish, for Jean-Louis," said Michel, setting the tone,[10] "was to be the heir of the Jewish Enlightenment. In the twenties, the Crémieuxes saw themselves as Jewish the way others defined themselves as Auvergnats or Bretons. They gathered on Sundays in Paris to eat cakes and argue with the rocky accent of the Cathar region or the singing one of Provence. They were Socialists . . . , put all their hopes in justice and fraternity. As for anti-Semitism, they were convinced it was a pre–World War I antiquity and that it would soon be swept out completely. When labeled as a Jew by the anti-Semites, Jean-Louis fought not only to defend himself, his family, or his tribe, but to defend the republican principles to which he was viscerally attached."

Then Michel added: "You think: 'Who are you to speak this way? You yourself married someone from Auvergne, your cousin has married a Protestant, your nephew someone from Poitou. We are no longer Jews . . .' Well, hear me well: I'm not speaking to you about race, or blood, and even less religion. I'm speaking to you about the most precious thing Jean-Louis passes on to you today, about what he was the most attached to and that you receive today as his heritage." But then, what heritage was that?

Michel's speech reminded me of my own words at my father's funeral, nine years earlier, in 2005. As a Communist, my dad was even less of a Jew than Jean-Louis ever was. He'd gone through the war first in hiding with his brother, then, when they were of age, in the Resistance. But being Jewish wasn't something he ever mentioned, not even when I hammered him with questions. Without the family presence of his Zionist brother, I probably would not have guessed that we were Jews at all.

I mustn't have been more than nine when, because I had asked my parents about our family's background, they managed their uneasiness by pretending that our name was German. In fact, as I would learn much later, it was Polish-Ukrainian. My great-grandfather Mordka—Max—Weitzmann had left his shtetl, set in a part of Ukraine ruled by Poland, in the 1880s with the intention of immigrating to the United States by way of Greece and then Egypt. But because the boat he took in Cairo was quarantined in Marseille due to a typhus epidemic, and as he had no money for a second ticket, he simply stayed in France. Later he reached Paris, and in Paris he reached the Pletzl—today's Le Marais quarter—where everybody spoke Yiddish and where, after some time as a cap manufacturer, he managed to open a small hat store.

But "German": that was what my parents said that day. At nine, the word led me to a short but intense period of fascination with the Wehrmacht soldiers in the American war movies we watched on TV on Sunday nights, and to choose German instead of English in my first year of high school. (Why the German professor, a small, dark, agitated man full of passion, who never missed an opportunity to teach us that Hitler had *also* done good things, such as inventing the Volkswagen, held me in such contempt all year long remained unfathomable.)

A stage actor, my father worked for the state, as a civil servant in a theater company that was appointed to various cities across the country. In the sixties and seventies we lived far from the capital, and far from any distinctly Jewish environment, in towns like Reims and Besançon, where we led a very regular middle-class life—except, that is, for my father's slightly erratic behavior.

Something was off with him, but what? What accounted for the pathological distractions that, when away on tour, sometimes made him send us blank postcards with no words at all on them; that, when in town and encountering my mother by chance in the street, made him salute her with a sweet, absent smile as if she were a perfect stranger? Once, just back from a trip, he even passed her by after she'd come to the train station to welcome him, taking the arm of another woman instead, someone he had never seen before, and it wasn't until my mother called out his name—"Serge!"—that he turned, realized what he had done, and laughed, which was his default mode when embarrassed. Also there were the worries—the anxiety about being late, which meant that, when going to Paris to visit the rest of the family, with the train station a five-minute walk away, we left the house at eight for the ten o'clock train. He worried about being late on his taxes, and being late on his union subscription—in short, of being caught unprepared for whatever anyone might require of him. He worried about displeasing authority, any kind of authority, even the lowest employee at the social security office could set off a burst of anxiety in him, not to mention the theater directors he auditioned for, and in front of whom he stammered and mumbled, which was the reason he worked for the state in the first place—so he would not have to pass audition. He had, in his own eyes, no justification for living, and the very idea of competing with anyone and fighting for his own interest trapped him in a series of unbearable contradictions. Needless to say, when I reached fifteen, this mix of placidity and deep-rooted fear began to drive me mad.

Of course, he had been a hidden child during the first years of the Occupation. But his own father, my grandfather Henri, had also contributed to his unsettled state of mind. Born in 1901, growing up in the nationalistic atmosphere of World War I, Henri bore in his youth all the inner conflicts an ambitious son of Jewish immigrants might try to contain in post-Dreyfus France. Eager to belong, and to distance himself from his own father, Max, who barely spoke French—and who was in an arranged marriage with Henri's mother, Caroline, who betrayed daily signs of frustration and unhappiness—Henri joined the army out of patriotism and, once there, found no other way to manifest himself than to climb the barracks roof and plant there a red flag in the name of the international revolution. This was two years after the Bolshevik coup in Moscow. The clash between a rising Communist ideology and the Action Française movement—between rebellion and identity, as we would say today—was turning into France's main political issue. The incident led to my grandfather's confinement for some weeks in the psychiatric ward of the military compound. From there he began to write frantic love letters to my future grandmother, Nelly, a young Jewish girl of delicate constitution whom he'd met a few weeks earlier in some Socialist circle but whom he suddenly decided, from that military loony bin, that he *had* to marry. After he was released from the army and did marry her, however, conjugal life turned out not to suit him that much after all.

What gave him his restless nature? Was it because, in those years, to be both a nice, steady Jewish boy and an ambitious, energetic Parisian was somehow a contradiction in terms? In the best circles of the City of Light, with the miasma of the Dreyfus affair still hanging in the air, it wasn't rare to see Jews being called out to duels by "real Frenchmen" in order to prove their manhood, an ordeal that could end with the death of the Jewish contestant. "In France, Jews are kindly treated, especially in death," Theodor Herzl had remarked sarcastically twenty years earlier, in the correspondence quoted above. "When their splendid lives, for which they are so envied, are happily over, Judenmenschen are no longer discriminated against, but are buried alongside Christenmenschen, in the same cemeteries. Moreover, when a Jew, by his inborn cunning, goes as far as to sacrifice his life in a fine gesture of chivalry, his noble act is greeted with murmurs of approval . . . No Jew, without being modest, could truly ask for more." Herzl spoke from direct experience. He had attended the funeral of a French Jewish officer, Captain Armand Mayer, called to such a duel by the notoriously anti-Semitic

Marquis de Morès. Mayer, having trouble with his right arm, could not lift the heavy Colichemarde sword he'd been given and was almost immediately killed by his opponent.[11]

Marcel Proust defended his own life in this way twice—once in the context of the Dreyfus affair—and during my grandfather's youth, the young literary critic Léon Blum, future leader of the left-wing coalition the Popular Front, had to fight duels as well. Forty years later, in the 1960s, my brother and I still played with the sword cane—a long, thin blade, surmounted with a copper pommel and hidden in a wooden sheath, that we had found in a closet with a top hat—with which, according to his own account, Henri had fought no fewer than three times.

The crisis of manhood, this other name for modernity, is the backdrop against which these duels were fought. As Hemingway, D. H. Lawrence, and others would soon show, such a crisis affected every Western country as a consequence of the Industrial Revolution and of the advancements of technology. The mass graves of the Great War had just shown what the new age meant for the old ideal of chivalry. Yet, perhaps because of the vestiges of the French aristocratic order and the guilty nostalgia for it, perhaps as a result of the humiliation of defeat in the Franco-Prussian War of 1870— even perhaps as a result of the French emphasis on good manners and the famous French *galanterie* or because of all of that—this crisis had been anticipated in France and could be felt with a special intensity in Paris's upper and intellectual classes. Jews were especially targeted because, as we've just seen, more than being viewed simply as traitors and cosmopolites, their manhood was considered questionable at best. While Jewish women were supposedly gifted with a savage sexuality (*"la belle juive"* had been a French stereotype since Balzac), Jewish men, if they weren't imagined menstruating anymore, were considered to be secret sodomites. There was a strong link at that time, in the French and European mind, between "unmanned" homosexuals, decadence of manners, and the "international foreign interests," which, according to Marshal Philippe Pétain in 1940, would threaten the country. Words like *homosexuality, cosmopolitanism,* and *Judaism* had practically become synonyms to designate the democratic poison of the republic undermining France's strength and honor. Already in 1894, in addition to treason, one of the charges against Dreyfus had been his alleged "acquaintance with sodomites."[12] Some thirty years later, in 1933, the journalist star Léon Daudet, in attacking Léon Blum, whose parents were observant Jews from Alsace and who had just been elected parliament member at the National Assembly, wrote that Blum was a "hybrid ethnic and hermaphrodite" freak. Charles Maurras, for his part, called Blum "a perfect homosexual," while other journalists in *L'Action Française* referred to Blum as either "a girl from the ghetto more suited to hold deliquescent purposes in perfumed salons," "a nervous woman," "a female homosexual whose eyes shine with lubric desire," "a delirious prostitute crying out for male power," "a presidential fag," "a perfumed female camel," and "a Palestinian mare." Blum—who was heterosexual and wrote a book preaching free love between men and women—was also considered to possess a special "serpentine charm" expressing "the hypocrisy of his race and the duplicity of his character." *L'Humanité,* the paper of the Communist Party, called him *"la grande coquette"* (the great coquette).[13]

In other words, to put it bluntly, under the notion that Jewish males were unmanly and lacked virile virtues lay the secret, obsessive fear of a threatening Jewish seduction whose corrosive effect would result in turning every "real French" man into a homosexual. It was in this context that, after his marriage, my grandfather Henri, who had turned into a young financial journalist and a lover of theater and literature, went out every night, befriending politicians and writers and, by his own account, accumulating as many mistresses as he could, probably as much by taste as yet another sign of his belonging to the real Paris crowd. Then, eighteen months after my uncle was born, Henri's frail wife, Nelly, gave birth to my father and, a few weeks later, died of blood poisoning in the hospital. Feeling perhaps some retrospective guilt at having been so distant and careless, or simply out of rage and because, for someone so eager to belong to the Parisian standard, "failure" was not an option and he needed someone to blame, my grandfather picked on his newborn son. He gave him up to Nelly's brother, and, even after he took him back, a year later, he never ceased to believe, and to have *him* believe, that my father owed his life to his mother's death. This was my father's education: caught between, at home, the guilt of being born and, at school, the guilt of being born Jewish—as underlined by the Action Française demonstrators who, on account of the number of Jewish students in the Janson-de-Sailly high school he and his brother attended, gathered regularly before the school gates, yelling out, "Jews! France doesn't belong to you!"—*Juif! La France n'est pas à toi!*—or, more clearly, "Death to the Jews."

There was far worse to come. In 1936, Léon Blum's election at the head of the left-wing Popular Front coalition set off an outburst of anti-Semitic fury in France. At the vanguard stood *L'Action Française,* which announced, "It is because he is Jewish that we must see, conceive, hear, fight, and put down the Blum." Blum, wrote another newspaper, "is everything that repels our blood and gives us gooseflesh. He is evil, he is death." At the National Assembly, congressmen openly referred to Blum as "a repugnant member of the Jewish scum." These labels were also assigned to the Jewish minister of the interior, Marx Dormoy, and the Jewish minister of education, Jean Zay. Death threats were made against Zay, who also received anonymous letters at home. Read one of them: "Each of your kin is followed and watched and will be shot with the greatest calm."

These were not simply words. In 1937, an Action Française militant by the name of Jean Filliol, who one year prior had tried to stab Blum with a sword on the Boulevard Saint-Germain, used the same weapon against a Jewish banker and, this time, killed him. No charges were pressed. After the war broke out, on a summer night in 1941, Marx Dormoy, no longer minister, had his head cut off by the bomb that a young French actress put under his bed before leaving the room where they had just made love. As for Jean Zay, in 1944, a group of French extreme-right militants entered his prison cell, took him to the woods, and shot him. By then, though, my father, along with the rest of the family, had long been in hiding.[14]

In the eulogy I gave for my father, I drew, more or less convincingly, a link between his Communist convictions—which had led him to forget any sense of personal interest—his strange personality, and the history of the Jews in France. His traits, I had argued, were manifestations of the decaying of the Franco-Jewish symbiosis that had reached its peak during the last decades of the nineteenth century, before being attacked and finally destroyed. That model of Jewishness, of which, in my mind, my father was the pathological version and Jean-Louis, his elder by ten years, the healthy one, could no longer exist. Not surprisingly, Jean-Louis had come to me afterwards to mark, as gently as he could, his disagreement.

Jean-Louis had joined the Resistance not as a Jew but as a Frenchman. France, for him—*the real France*—was with de Gaulle in London rather than in Vichy. In his view, France had therefore won the war, not lost it. He could not admit that the Vichy years had broken the mold in which men like him were made.

As a Jew, furthermore, he could also not envision that the arrival of the Sephardic community in the sixties, in the wake of the Arab countries' independences—whose first measure, once freed from the grip of French and English colonial occupation, had been to expel the Jews en masse—had entirely reshaped the way French Jews saw their bond to France. Nor did he see how, for the younger generations of Jews—aware of the Vichy past and born into a world where the state of Israel was easily reached with a low-cost five-hour flight—the old ambivalences with which one envisioned his Jewishness as French, or the sorts of contradictions with which one defined his Frenchness as a Jew, could not have seemed more radically distant.

My conversation with Jean-Louis continued a few weeks later, in his apartment on the Boulevard Saint-Germain, near the Seine, where he, my cousin Laurence, and I went to have dinner. Jean-Louis, the embodiment of successful secular assimilation, spent a good part of the evening displaying pictures of the Crémieux branch of the family, such as his rabbi grandfather and his cousins, doing so while explaining the brutal circumstances in which several of them had been assassinated by the Nazis with the help of the French police.

The backdrop against which these family discussions took place gave them a dramatic relevance, at least in my eyes. Since the fall of 2000, anti-Semitic brutalities had been occurring in poor suburbs, inhabited largely by North African Muslim immigrants and their offspring since the mid-1980s. These suburbs had been built during the first decade of the twentieth century for the French working class, and, during the over-ideologized French atmosphere of the Cold War, most of them had fallen under the control of the Communist Party. Communists ran the urban neighborhoods in the north, south, and east of Paris—a territory nicknamed for that reason "the Red Belt"—and, between the 1950s and the '70s, had developed there a vast program of agitprop subsidized through the cultural departments of their municipal administrations. Given my parents' staunch left-wing politics, it was inevitable that they would end up spending their retirement years in one of these places. In the mid-eighties, pretty much at the same time as the last remnants of the French working class were leaving the place and the lower part of the migrant population was moving in, they bought their apartment in the town of Bobigny, in the rough district of Seine-Saint-Denis.

Some months prior to our dinner with Jean-Louis, in February 2005, in the midst of the beginning of the rise of anti-Jewish brutalities, someone had sprayed a swastika on the old wooden wagon that stands at the entrance of the memorial of the transit camp of Drancy. Ten minutes away from Bobigny, Drancy is now a suburb like any others, but it was from there that, during World War II, seventy thousand French Jews arrested by the French police were herded before being sent to death camps, my grandfather Henri among them. The swastika was five feet tall, and drawn upside down. There had been an attempt to set the wagon on fire, and a leaflet found on-site was signed "Bin Laden." My eighty-year-old father was in shock.

His father had been confined in Drancy after his arrest at the end of 1943. Although it was managed by the prefecture and the French police, the administrator of the camp at the time was none other than Aloïs Brunner—one of the most notorious war criminals of the Nazi regime. A few months before this, Brünner had supervised the extermination of the Jews of Greece, and in the summer of '44, after the liberation of Paris, which forced him to leave Drancy, he would be successfully appointed to the same task in Hungary. (Brunner, who survived the war, found refuge first in Egypt, then in Syria, where he became an adviser on security issues for Hafez al-Assad, the father of the current slaughterer, Bashar, and helped set up the Syrian secret services with the help of the Soviets. He died in the 2000s, in unknown circumstances.) Brunner was a fanatic anti-Semite and, in Drancy, had established a set of brutal internal rules for the Jewish detainees that ranged from a prohibition against smoking and confinement to barracks to a virtual famine and beatings. Tonsure was mandatory. My grandfather was submitted to it all, escaping deportation by a hair, thanks to an administrative imbroglio inside the camp. He was still there in June, when Paris was liberated.

What I'm piecing together here comes, of course, from my own research—not from Henri's or my father's confidences, since neither of them ever spoke about it. This is to say that, in February

2005, the lunch my brother and I attended at our parents' the Sunday following the swastika incident was the first time I ever heard my father mention the war years voluntarily. That day, he also informed us of the grand plan he had concocted against what he saw as "the return of fascism." To remain passive when something like this occurred so close to home was unbearable. He had found in his archives an old play he'd written twenty-five years earlier, a collage adapted from revolutionary French poets of the prewar era, and with it, he would do the only thing he thought he knew: he would set up a new theater company. Confident in the ideological bond that tied him with Bobigny's Communist municipal team, he would call City Hall's cultural service, apply for a public subsidy, and use the money to hire a handful of young, average citizens of Bobigny —Muslim immigrants, Africans, Pakistanis, Hindus, and French— to whom he would teach who Brecht was and the basics of revolutionary theater and then, with the limping, round silhouette of my eighty-year-old father in the vanguard, they would tour the whole Seine-Saint-Denis department, defying fascism and the resurgent violence. The stroke that eventually killed him struck some months later, at the very hour he was to call City Hall to discuss the municipal subsidies he needed.

To say that my parents weren't religious would be an understatement. Neither am I—nor, for that matter, is anyone in the family. So to end my eulogy for my father with the Kaddish prayer was not exactly a rational decision on my part. The prayer is in Aramaic, and I'd learned it phonetically a few days earlier, without even trying to understand what it meant. But in the tradition, the Kaddish is to be said by the firstborn, a practice that in the Yiddish-speaking world led to the use of the word "Kaddish" as a nickname for the eldest son, which I am. So from this connection between an enigmatic prayer for the dead and the filial bond, I sort of figured that reciting it would stand as a good summary, perhaps even a kind of homage, to the mutual incomprehension of son and father that had been the basis of our relationship for as long as I could remember.

Also, I thought, in a way that was not necessarily more coherent than my father's, that it stood as an assertion of a more assured form of Jewishness in a time of rising tension. The past five years, I had been discovering, with growing incredulity, that on certain issues people saw me first and foremost as a Jew. At the newspaper where I worked, my perspective was questioned because of my last name. When the subject of anti-Jewish brutalities in the suburbs came up, colleagues speculated that — if these incidents were even real — the Mossad itself was probably behind them. To object to that bizarre hypothesis was to out myself as a "communitarian" and an identity politics nut. All this — both the context and my answer to it — stood in the background of these discussions with Jean-Louis after I had said the Kaddish for my father and we began to see each other.

But now, at Jean-Louis's funeral in the Montparnasse cemetery, I wasn't so sure. Did my saying the Kaddish make more sense than the stone I had just put on Jean-Louis's grave? Had I been trying to please my indecipherable father — who probably would have thought I was mad — or to distance myself from him even further? Was it more meaningful than the religious circumcision I had undergone at the age of thirty? Of course, our Communist parents had not had us circumcised. At thirty, when I was in analysis, it had suddenly seemed of the greatest importance to remedy that. I was as atheistic then as I am now, however, so to be lying half-naked on the operating table while the surgeon removed my foreskin and the rabbi stood at my side with a Torah in his hands, making me repeat the Psalms, felt like complete lunacy. As did the bar mitzvah that followed some weeks later, during which I stood at the altar reciting the *parsha* with a nonstop and rather painful erection hidden in my pants because of the blood rushing into my penis, a consequence of the operation. (The erection, which it was out of the question to relieve, lasted a full month, the time it took the stitches to heal.)

Why we do what we do, sometimes, remains as mysterious as the meaning of the Kaddish itself. In front of Jean-Louis's grave on that sunny spring morning in April 2015, all I could say was that if I had to do it again, I would. But why—I couldn't tell. Given the turn of events in the country, it seemed that my whole attitude toward my Jewishness and toward France—what Jean-Louis's son, my cousin Michel, had called our "heritage" a few minutes ago—could be seen as much as an affirmative act against the rising tide of national madness on the subject of the Jews as my own personal contribution to it.

As Jean-Louis's burial was ending and the crowd was beginning to disperse, and I left the tomb and started walking the alley with my cousin Laurence, we remembered Jean-Louis's vast apartment, which was soberly decorated with furniture practically unchanged since the early fifties, where she and I had had dinner with him and where he had shown us the pictures of his ancestors and ours.

And only then did it dawn on me that this place, Jean-Louis's apartment, was situated at the very corner of the Boulevard Saint-Germain and the Boulevard Henri IV, which meant that, before he died, Jean-Louis had certainly seen and heard the anti-Semitic chants shouted by thousands of participants in the demonstrations of January 2014, one year earlier, as they had crossed the Seine on the Pont de Sully. I wasn't in France at the time. I had followed the demonstrations online without giving much thought to the route they'd taken, so the connection with Jean-Louis hadn't even crossed my mind. But now it did. Set up against the Socialist government, the demonstration had been called by right-wing and Catholic organizations, and they had christened it the Day of Wrath, from the Book of Revelation.

As we approached the gates of the cemetery, I began to imagine what my great-uncle might have thought, in the months before his death, having fought for his country and served it at the highest levels, listening to the howls from the river of people below:

JUIF! LA FRANCE N'EST PAS À TOI!

These were the very same words, the very same chants, that my father had heard at the gates of the Lycée Janson-de-Sailly such a long time ago. *Jew, France is not yours!*

STATISTICS OF HATE

There are roughly a half million Jews in France, and they account for less than 1 percent of the country's population. In the weeks and months following the Day of Wrath march, however, the number of anti-Jewish acts, which had begun to rise in the suburbs in the early 2000s and constituted the backdrop of my dialogue with Jean-Louis, reached an unprecedented point.

By the end of that year, Jews had been the targets of 49 percent of reported hate crimes in the country.[15] Yet, in themselves, these numbers are somewhat misleading. They miss the extremely violent and otherwise bizarrely motiveless nature of the incidents that year.

To give only a few examples:

Two weeks after the Day of Wrath, in February 2014, in Villeurbanne, a Lyon suburb: Armed with a hammer and a crowbar, a man charged his female neighbor and her child in their garden while yelling, "Dirty Jew, go back to your country." The woman was hit on the shoulder but, along with her child, she managed to get inside her house, escaping the aggressor. (She still bore bruises and had difficulty walking when I met with her for this book more than a year after the incident.)

That same month in Thiais, near Paris: As he smoked a cigarette outside the family pavilion, a young man was assaulted by two men who stole his cell phone and beat him with cries of "Dirty Jew, we don't like Jews here. This is no Israel, this is Palestine!" The victim was hospitalized for forty-two days.

May, Créteil, a suburb near Paris: On his way home, a man was accosted by men in their twenties, yelling, "You bitch, you Jews, you're all the same!" They beat him up and broke his arm.

June, Nice: A young woman and her mother were attacked by an unknown passerby who slapped the younger one in the face while yelling, "Dirty fucking Jew, dirty French, we're gonna blow everything up! Synagogues will blow up, you bitches!"

A few days later in Pantin, near Paris: Five female students were saved from an attack by a bus driver who closed the door of his bus while cries of "Dirty Jewesses, fucking race with your shitty religion!" could be heard through the doors.

One week after that, in Grenoble: A man pushing his son's wheelchair was assaulted by three men who exclaimed, "You Yehudi, you Jew!"

Also in Grenoble, around the same time, a woman was attacked by a neighbor who grabbed her, shook her, and spat in her face while yelling, "You Jew, you have money, you're gonna burn in hell, we're gonna take all your money, I'm gonna burn you! You're gonna see what I do to you and your child!" She managed to escape, locking herself inside her home.

Et cetera. The list could go on and on, and further examples will be given later. The point here is that none of the recorded eight hundred brutalities and aggressions that year were terror-related. None, it seems, were perpetrated by Islamist militants, or politically motivated. Mostly they were carried out spontaneously, in an overwhelming number of cases by individuals of Muslim background leading inconspicuous lives — if sometimes delinquent ones — who were apparently overcome by a free-floating, anti-Jewish rage.

In the last of those incidents that year, on December 1 in the suburb of Créteil, a newlywed couple residing in the husband's Jewish parents' house were attacked at home by three young men looking for "the Jews' money," who totally ransacked the place and were unable to find anything of value, so one of them raped the woman instead. That story was the only one that year to make it on the front pages in the national press and on TV, and a debate, raised by then prime minister Manuel Valls, ensued on anti-Semitism in the suburbs for the first time. It lasted until Christmas. Then the new year started, and on January 7 came news of the massacre at the magazine *Charlie Hebdo,* which killed twelve and wounded nine, followed two days later by the attack at the Hyper Cacher market, in Vincennes, which killed four. Five weeks later, on February 15, Omar Abdel Hamid El-Hussein, who had attacked the Krudttønden, a cultural center and café, in Copenhagen, in the middle of the afternoon the day before, with the intention of killing the Swedish cartoonist Lars Vilks, who was starring at an event there and whom he missed —shooting a participant instead—made a point of shooting a Kalashnikov in front of the city's Great Synagogue the following night, killing a guard before being shot by police. It was beginning to look as if there was some sort of connection between the spontaneous anti-Jewish violence and these terror attacks, which were obviously more planned and aimed at a wider crowd, but of which nature? And how to comprehend it without succumbing to the temptation of this capital sin known as generalization? And what about the right-wing Day of Wrath demonstration my great-uncle may have heard through his windows one year earlier? How did it figure into all this?

In April, when we buried him, I found myself wrestling with those questions, and I would continue to do so while writing this book—or rather, as it sometimes seemed, as the terrorists wrote it for me while I ran behind them, painfully trying to take notes.

And as I ran, and as I took notes, it became clear that in order to make sense of the complexity, I first had to distrust many of the words that are usually associated with the subject. Words such as "Muslims," to begin with. And "immigrants." And of course words like "Islamophobia." And "racism," "fascism," and even "Jews." That ubiquitous vocabulary of international TV and social media, as if these words meant the same thing for everyone everywhere—a plastic grammar of commonplaces that wards off the fear and explains nothing.

For what could be more different from a Muslim financial engineer from Pakistan living in New York, for instance, than the offspring French Muslim from Algerian parents living in a French *cité*? French Jews, whose demographic today is overwhelmingly Sephardic: have they anything in common with their American counterparts? The very word "immigration," which for an American is still connected to hopes of renewal and a new start: what does that word even mean for the rural immigrant from the Djurdjura Mountains, in Algeria, who settled in post-imperial France in the fifties or sixties? What does it mean for his children?

Terror is the black mirror of globalization. To write about it would be to write about a global phenomenon from a particular viewpoint, and, conversely, to discern, in the particulars of a situation, reflections of the global issue.

So before I deliver my French story of terrorist violence and anti-Semitism, a lesson on language: as I've tried to give at least some notions of the particularities of the French Jews, let us now see what the word "Muslim" means, and what the word "immigrant" means, *in the French context.*

"MIGRANTS," "MUSLIMS"

As a young writer in the 1980s, I witnessed the birth of the immigrant Muslim culture in the suburbs of Paris. I worked then at an alternative weekly newspaper called *Sans Frontière—Without a Border*

—which bore no connection with the medical NGO of the same name. *Sans Frontière*'s team was composed of Marxist militants and political refugees from the Maghreb (northwest Africa), and it was the first media outlet to take an interest in, and cover, immigrant youth. The paper helped initiate and structure the civil rights movement, which fought police violence and racism throughout the country. In 1983, it played a crucial part in the national March for Equality—nicknamed the Marche des Beurs (*beurs* being derived from a slang word for "Arab")—that constituted the apex of that movement. I can testify that at that time, very few of these youths, if any, defined themselves first and foremost as Muslims. Born in France for the most part, or having arrived in the country at a very early age, they were engaged in a struggle about equal rights, jobs, and access to consumerism and other "privileges" of the middle class.

What had sparked the March for Equality was a series of random hate murders against kids of Maghrebian origin that had taken place that year in various suburbs across the country. The youngest victim, Toufik Ouanès, ten years old, had been shot in July in a Parisian suburb by a neighbor, a bus driver, whose sole motive, he said, was that he was "exasperated by the noise in the street." The driver was sentenced to just two years for manslaughter. Social riots that same summer in a Lyon suburb had ended in bloodshed, with the nineteen-year-old leader of the protest, a Franco-Algerian by the name of Toumi Djaïdja, wounded by a bullet fired by a cop. Then in September, in the city of Dreux, near Paris, the National Front had won its first municipal elections, causing a political tremor. That was when two veterans of the fights for migrants, Christian Delorme and Jean Costil, inspired by Martin Luther King and Gandhi, came up with the idea of a march across the country. Delorme was a Catholic priest, and Costil a Protestant pastor. As for the team from *Sans Frontière* who soon joined, they mostly fought for human rights. With Toumi Djaïdja at its head, the march took off in October in Marseille and grew daily as it went from one city to the next. It arrived at Place de la République, in Paris, in mid-December— a flood of 100,000 people. By then the initial demands, as devised by Delorme and Costil—an end to racism, and papers for undocumented migrants—had evolved into something much larger.

For the first time in its history, France was confronted with the results of decades of immigration policy, and with the heritage of its lost empire. This result took the form of a population the country realized it knew nothing about. The timing, however, could not have been worse.

President François Mitterrand had come to power two years earlier as the candidate of "the United Left." In addition to members of the Socialist Party, his government included three Communists. Overseas, Reagan and Thatcher were implementing neoliberalism, Khomeini had ushered in political Islam, China was implementing liberal reforms, and the Red Army was invading Afghanistan. But while the world was already heading toward the next century, France, where unemployment was on the rise, was turning its attention toward nineteenth-century Socialist ideologies. It was a crisis of identity as much as a crisis in economy. Mitterrand's electorate was composed mostly of the children of a working class that had risen into the middle class during the previous three decades of a prosperity backed by a strong state policy—and whose success was due, in good part, to the migrants whose children were now asking for their slice of the cake. This former working class was essentially white, and its narrative, on which Mitterrand had based his political campaign, was similarly monochrome and enclosed into the national borders. It found its roots in mythological episodes of French history, such as the storming of the Bastille, the Paris Commune —during which, in the winter of 1870–71, the proletariat of Paris had taken hold of the capital—and the 1936 Popular Front. Faithful to the Enlightenment tradition as the French understand it, it was also a story of constant, linear progress, in which the decolonization chapter played, at the time (this would change later on), only a distant part—a part in which, furthermore, the French left congratulated itself for having helped the Algerian people against French imperialism. As for the realities of immigration in this tale, they were limited to fighting the racism lonely migrant workers suffered at the hands of the police or the administration. Nobody had thought of their children as citizens, let alone of the specific contradictions at play in their families.

Several factors complicated the matter. One was President Mitterrand himself who, as minister of the interior during the Algerian War of Independence, twenty years prior, had supported the setting up of special military courts to cover war crimes and torture, and personally ordered the execution of forty-five Algerians activists by guillotine. Algeria was where most of the immigrants were coming from, and the nationalist nerve there was irritated at the prospect of seeing the offspring of Algerian citizens declaring their allegiance to a former empire led by such a man. In Algiers, the good relations Mitterrand had established with President Chadli Bendjedid—both were "Socialists"—had to be kept as discreet as possible.

To add to the complexity, however, many prominent figures in Mitterrand's government had entered into politics on the other side of the anticolonial struggle. In the sixties, a significant number of them had helped provide money and guns to the Algerian revolutionaries. This meant that they were friendly with the Algerians weary of Mitterrand, and that they also maintained good relations with the secret police operatives who, under the cover of a network of "cultural associations" and *"amicales,"* had controlled the social and religious lives of the immigrants on French territory since the fall of the French Empire.

This discreet handling of migrants was part of a deal set up with the first official immigration plan of the French administration in the early sixties—when, with de Gaulle, the right was in power. From its outset, that first plan was conceived as the domestic chapter of a global new diplomacy with France's now independent former colonies, a diplomacy that would come to be known as France's "Arab policy." The main goal of this policy, in addition to access to gas and oil resources and cheap manpower, was to reassert France's prestige after the loss of its colonies. The maintaining of friendly relationships between French politicians of all parties and USSR-backed oligarchs in the Maghreb was good business all around. Cash from the oligarchs, sent via diplomatic pouches, financed French election campaigns during the sixties and seventies and allowed the political class of France to keep entertaining the delusion that they still ruled an empire. On the domestic side, the former colonies provided a malleable workforce that progressively replaced the French proletariat, a large portion of which was now enjoying the benefits of a middle-class life.

Yet that workforce had to be watched closely: on this, both sides of the Mediterranean agreed. The French feared what had happened during the Algerian War of Independence, when hostile networks had sprung up on French soil among the migrant workers, and as for autocratic Algerian and Moroccan counterparts, they felt concern with the possible rise of discontent among a population exposed to liberal Western ideas about individual rights, freedom of speech, and democracy. Having virtually no social or cultural existence in France, the migrants were reduced to passing shadows, nonexistent entities whose stay was nonetheless scrutinized by two pairs of eyes: the French *and* Maghrebian secret police. This status of invisibility, however, had a longer history.

The first workers from the Maghreb had come to France in the early 1920s, during the empire. A vast majority were men, from rural mountain areas and small villages in Algeria where diplomas were scarce and traditions plentiful. Some had lost their lands to French settlers. They worked in the French armament industries and later in construction, with the intention of returning home later on — which explains only partly why they were not seen as citizens. The dominant view of their arrival in "the metropole," as one called the French homeland, was best summarized in a famous speech de Gaulle made in 1959, four years into the War of Independence in Algeria: "We are, above all, a European people of the white race, of Greek and Latin culture and the Christian religion. The Muslims, have you seen them with their turbans and their *jellabas*? You can see clearly that they are not French."[16] That de Gaulle in this speech spoke of the Harkis—the Algerian Muslims fighting with the French army against the Algerian freedom fighters—is, of course, highly significant. It means that, in de Gaulle's mind, even the Algerians on the French side could not be seen as French. Consequently, the Harkis' fate, after the War of Independence was over, was a tragedy—a tragedy that constitutes one of the most shameful episodes of France's post-imperial policy. Thousands were simply left behind by the French in Algeria, to be slaughtered, along with their families, by the new regime. As for the Harki soldiers of the French army who did manage to come to France, they were parked in the same camps that had been used by the Vichy regime in the forties for the Jews and the Spanish refugees fleeing fascism, and were discriminated against all their lives. (The last of those camps did not close until the end of the seventies.)

This French view of "the Muslim" as a ghost had been framed in Algeria ever since the dawn of the colonial area. What motivated it was a vision much more complex and paradoxical than a simple apartheid, and it is crucial to understand it because it still largely determines France's mindset toward Islam to this day.

Soon after its conquest, in 1830, the Algerian territory had been given the administrative status of a French department. This meant that in theory, its population was French by law. And yet a special status imposed in 1865, called *le statut personnel musulman*—the Muslim personal status—deprived Muslims of any political rights. Although French, they could not vote. Worse still, if they wanted to benefit from the political rights attached to their French citizenship, they had to apply for naturalization, despite being French. And even if they became naturalized, which was rare, their new status could not be passed on to their children, who had to go through the whole process again. In effect, this Kafkaesque labyrinth resulted in what the writer Kamel Daoud demonstrates so chillingly in his novel *The Meursault Investigation:* during colonial times, Muslim citizens simply did not exist.[17]

Whether deprived of rights, as the Algerians were, or simply undocumented, like the Tunisians and Moroccans who illegally migrated to the metropole from French protectorates, during the imperial age, these first immigrants were invisible to the French population. It was that situation that was reproduced in different forms, as we've seen, through the 1960s and '70s, thanks to the network of the secret police of the Maghrebian regime and under the supervision of the French government. Because they were poor and had no real plan to settle in France, immigrants from the Maghreb in those years slept in shantytowns, in cheap hotel rooms, and, above all, in awful hostels for workers run by the French administration and managed by public servants, most of whom had been employed in the colonial administration before independence. There, migrants were subjected to humiliating treatments, to frequent controls from French police, and to the constant surveillance of snitches working for the Algerian and Moroccan secret services.

Until at least the early eighties, this political control exerted by foreign powers on French territory was performed for the most part under the guise of "cultural associations" set up in every city, with the official purpose of connecting the migrants with their countries of origin. But another means of control was the mosques, whose imams were de facto appointed by Morocco and by Algeria, in collaboration with the French. In the nineties, this arrangement would come to play a crucial role in the Islamist propaganda denouncing the traditional, moderate imams as the product of a "neocolonial" policy.

As corruption and an economic crisis deepened in the Maghreb countries in the 1970s, however, a significant percentage of the migrants decided to settle in the former metropole for good, and this situation of heavily regulated invisibility began to change. France contributed to this decision by closing its borders to further legal immigration while, on the other hand, passing a law called *regroupement familial* (family reunification) that allowed, for the first time, those migrants already living in the country to be joined by their wives and children and to become French. But given the colonial past and the current French collaboration with the Arab regimes, this law, which should have improved the situation of the migrants, only created new ambiguities.

In their hearts and minds, out of nostalgia as much as pride, and also out of rampant hostility toward the former empire, migrant fathers did not easily acknowledge their decision to settle in France. They still saw themselves as someday returning home. Yet parents seldom discussed this ambivalence with their children, who'd come to France as babies or were born there as French citizens. And to complicate matters, the French also felt the need to avoid hurting the nationalistic pride of the Maghreb autocracies, which could not easily admit that a rising fraction of their population had left. As a result of all this, the *regroupement familial* largely remained an administrative measure and was never accompanied with an active policy, which would have helped the new population to integrate. Basically, they were left to themselves.

All this is important because it means that in France, the word "migrant," when applied to the populations of the former empire, has a very different meaning than it may have, for instance, in the United States. A "migrant worker" in France is not somebody who crossed the sea to start a new life. He came *with* his past, connected to his place of origin by every means possible, while making a living in a country haunted by the loss of its colonial glory. It is this common bitterness that should be kept in mind in order to correctly assess the frame through which immigration was perceived in France *on both sides,* that is to say by native-born French as well as by migrants. Among migrant families, this bitterness often took the form of conflicting duties and obligations, passed on to children by fathers who were mutely trapped in their wounded honor. And there was no knowledge, either, of what France required from these children—if, indeed, it required anything at all. Migrant youth were therefore abandoned by both sides, in a cultural no-man's-land. It was in order to free themselves from this history, to clarify it, to leave the no-man's-land and become fully French, that they rebelled at the end of the seventies, shaking up not only French conservative blindness, but their parents' traditional values and the "cultural associations" linking their families to the autocratic regimes ruling their countries of origin.

Such are the facts. Yet, as the essayist Yuval Noah Harari has it, humans think in stories rather than in facts. In order to understand how the demands of these migrant youth were received, and what followed, it is first necessary to explore the narrative with which France conceived of these facts during and after the colonial era. What was the French imperial tale that justified the discrimination of Muslims, in a country that, at the same time, paradoxically glorified "the Orient" as a solution to the contradictions of modernity?

IMPERIALIST EMBARRASSMENT

Neither the ordeal of the Jews today in France, nor the religious trap in which the Muslim youth of the country fell at the end of the eighties, can be fully grasped without first exploring what can only be called a French imperialist *embarrassment.*

Upon conquering Algeria, in 1830, France was confronted with a deep crisis of self-doubt. With the rise of industrial capitalism, the turmoil of the patriotic wars of the Revolution and of the

Napoleonic conquests through which the country had thought to spread universal ideas of freedom and equality seemed to have ended in bitterness and mediocrity. Napoleon's self-assurance during the expedition of Egypt, thirty years earlier, was long gone. "The age of chivalry is gone. That of sophisters, economists, and calculators has succeeded; and the glory of Europe is extinguished forever."[18] These lines from Edmund Burke, contemplating the French Revolution from London in 1790, now seemed prophetic. Many in France were beginning to think like him—or like Joseph de Maistre, who, writing from St. Petersburg, had scoffed at the Declaration of the Rights of Man and the universalism that underpinned it: "Man? I met Italians; I met Englishmen; I met Germans and I even met Frenchmen. As for Man, I do not know what that is."[19] The worth of the Enlightenment that the country had promoted for so long was called into question. An inner war was raging, and France, confronted with its own modernity, seemed caught between two periods and two visions of itself.

In Paris, royalty had been restored. But King Charles X hesitated between a post-revolutionary heritage of liberalism and an impossible return to the past. The Parisian salons were haunted by the ghosts of the Terror and the Revolution and by fantasies of blue blood. Everyone was obsessed with purity of lineage. It was the time of the Rastignacs and Rubemprés immortalized by Balzac's novels—the ambitious nouveaux riches who dreamt of restoring a "pure" aristocracy while exchanging favors in bedchambers and adding nobiliary particles to their names in order to erase their own plebeian "impurity." The culture of the salons was a mockery of the Ancien Régime's court culture: a culture of corruption played out in the name of ideals, a culture that Baudelaire would soon call *satanisme badin*—lighthearted Satanism.

Because their emancipation in 1791 had been seen as the first consequence of the passing of the Declaration of the Rights of Man —the abolition of slavery being the other—Jews, as we've seen, were considered one of the main symbols of this age of miscegenation, of new money and of the new urban life. Furthermore, the emancipation had spread in Europe, encouraging Jews to come out of the ghettos. A secular Jewish world would come to populate European cities and embody liberalism, to the dismay of European royals. Charles X's abdication and exile after the riots of 1830 only made things more confused.

It is in this context that Algeria was conquered, and that, in order to find hope again and regenerate the notion of universalism, liberal philosophers and politicians began to call for the building of a new French Empire, to succeed Napoleon's. One of the founding fathers of liberalism, Tocqueville, pretty much set the tone in 1841, eleven years after the French army set foot in Algeria, and six before the territory was annexed by France: "I do not think that France could seriously think of leaving Algeria. The desertion it would thus create would appear to the eyes of the world as the sure announcement of its decadence . . . Should France step back in front of such an action . . . it would seem as if it bent to its own powerlessness."[20]

The second reason invoked by Tocqueville for colonizing Algeria was to bring the Enlightenment to the "ignorant races" inhabiting Africa. During most of the colonial era, it was this argument that was invoked by the progressive camp, not the reactionary one, in favor of colonization. Victor Hugo, the author of *Les Misérables,* favored colonization in the name of the Declaration of the Rights of Man.

Conversely, news of the conquest was received with exasperation by the reactionary camp. For those nostalgic for blue blood, empire meant the management of a new, barbaric population and, above all, the reawakening of dangerous ideas such as universalism. It could only put at risk the restoration of the Ancien Régime that was now under way, and serve the partisans of the new global era. As a scandalized Baron Jean-Jacques Baude, representative of the Loire department, phrased it at the National Assembly, "It is to the benefit of the Jews that we conquer Algiers!" In other words: to the benefit of miscegenation and global money.

By the same token, the worst massacres perpetrated by the French during the conquest were the deeds of high-ranking officers who despised the Enlightenment and did not believe in the colonization they were fighting for, like the war criminal General Thomas-Robert Bugeaud, for instance, who famously gave his soldiers the order to either burn the Arabs' crops every year or exterminate them all. Jacques Leroy de Saint-Arnaud, one of Bugeaud's officers, smoked out the caves in which Muslim civilians found refuge and killed by suffocation thousands of men, women, and children. Yet neither of those men favored the colonizing of Algeria, "a costly possession of which our nation should be glad to get rid of," as Bugeaud put it at a hearing at the National Assembly.

In many quarters of the colonial administration, during the following years, these rifts and contradictions led to a curious mindset. Napoleon's campaign in Egypt had had the effect of splitting the Muslim world in two. While a minority of religious dignitaries had fallen in love with the ideals of Enlightenment and were trying to translate them into Muslim terms — and were often marginalized in their own countries for doing so — a majority of imams were generally opposed to Western Enlightenment, and, as paradoxical as it may seem, this Muslim influence began to be seen favorably in reactionary and utopian French circles as a solution to the crisis of the modern age.

Several civil servants of the rising colonial administration thus began to take genuine interest in Muslim traditions, in what sounds like a prefiguration of what we would today call multiculturalism. But it is important to frame this word in its historical context. For these French, multiculturalism was cosmopolitanism in reverse: in other words, an identity politics. By and large, it was the anti-modern elements of the Muslim traditions that these high-ranking civil servants found so appealing. Many, for instance, used Islamic law to

marry young, Arab girls, often under age, only to repudiate them after a few months in accordance with the Muslim practice, and with
the blessing of local imams. Probably the most fascinating character
in this crowd is the man who in 1860 would become Napoleon III's
"special adviser for oriental affairs"—i.e., the affairs of the Ottoman
Empire and Muslim relations—and whose thinking would inspire
the discriminative law on Muslim personal status.

THE "MUSLIM PROPHET" OF THE FRENCH EMPIRE

Thomas-Ismayl Urbain[21] was born in 1812 in Cayenne, the son of a
woman whose mother was an emancipated slave. He was of white
complexion but was one-eighth black, an octoroon, which is probably why his father, Urbain Brue, never recognized him. At eighteen,
like so many of Balzac's characters, he changed his name. Taking his
father's first name, he made it his own family name, then left Marseille, where he had spent his childhood, for the Paris of the Restoration to establish himself as a writer.

In the salons, obsessed with the blue blood fantasy, racism was
the rule. "He stinks, the Negro, open the window!" is the sentence
attributed to one of the great stars of the day, Mademoiselle Mars,
after a visit in her living room by Alexandre Dumas, who was one-
quarter black. Dumas's huge ego, arrogance, and talent, however, allowed him to pass beyond prejudices and become one of the most
popular writers of his time, which was much more than Urbain
could say for himself. Marginalized, deprived of any introduction
to enter the salons, and afflicted with what he called the "double
shame" of being part black and the grandson of a slave, Urbain had
little chance to make it. He soon joined the legendary Parisian *bohème,* this "floating, decomposed, and confused mass of third-rate
writers and journalists," as Karl Marx put it, where aspiring men of
letters, utopian thinkers, professional revolutionaries, and snitches

interacted. From there he joined the crypto–Christian Scientist and Socialist sect that was the rage in the vanguard of the days, the Saint-Simonians. The Saint-Simonians, from among whom most of the French pre-Marxist Socialists originated, preached a "rational faith," that is to say, a mix of mystical love for humanity and utopian totalitarian social organization whose ambition was to solve the crisis of modernity opened by the overthrow of the Ancien Régime and the Industrial Revolution, by reconciling technology and science with religion. When Urbain joined them, the leader of the movement was a Barthélémy Prosper-Enfantin, whom everyone called Père Enfantin, half an intellectual star and half a guru, who had set himself the task of uniting the materialist West and what he saw as the more spiritual "Orient" through a spiritual and physical wedding between himself and some woman he hoped to find in Egypt. The following extract of one of his speeches, typical of his pseudo-prophetic style, also conveys the French disarray of the days: "Thrones are shaken, families are torn apart, kings and love are no more. A new religion, a new politics, a new moral: here is what I bring to you. And only I could bring them to you because you have loved me and because I love you."[22]

Urbain soon fell under his spell. ("I love you, Father, like a child," he wrote, underlining the word "Father" three times, as he would do in all his letters to Enfantin until the guru's death.) Enfantin himself seems to have been quite taken with Urbain's intensity, and especially with his blackness. Another of the Saint-Simonians, Gustave d'Eichthal, the son of a Jewish banker who had converted to Catholicism, was so struck by what he called "the dramatic power of Urbain the Black" that the two men began a homosexual relationship that lasted all their lives. This point matters because Urbain himself was ashamed of his slave ancestry. The homoerotic emphasis on his blackness, even though he was of white complexion, seems to have helped him to get in touch with the narcissistic drive that would soon lead him to define himself as "a black Muslim prophet, representative of the Muslim races elected and proclaimed by God,"[23] and consequently start a career in the French colonial administration.

His conversion to Islam occurred in 1833, during a trip of the Saint-Simonians in Egypt, on the trail of Napoleon's expedition there thirty years earlier, but with the goal of finding for Père Enfantin "the Messie woman" he would marry according to his mystic vision. (It seems that Enfantin was instead spotted ravaging all the brothels of Upper Egypt before he was expelled from the country.) Urbain fell in love with Muslim culture, learned Arabic, got circumcised in Egypt — which says something of his determination, given that anesthesia was likely unavailable — and took the name Ismayl. "Thank you, Prophet!" Père Enfantin wrote from Paris as soon as he heard the news. "You are the first of my children to have joined the Orient."[24]

Three years later, in 1837, back in Paris, Thomas-Ismayl, who, by then, had had all the time to measure the distance between his literary dreams and reality, accepted a job as a translator in Algeria, where he started to work with General Bugeaud — the war criminal. This was when he began to speak of the Arab Muslims as "my People." "To me," he later wrote in his memoirs, "this was the continuation of my mission in the Orient . . . I would work at unifying the Muslim society of North Africa with the French civilization." The letter he wrote to Enfantin after settling in Algiers in the spring of 1837, however, gives perhaps a more accurate idea of his deranged messianism at the time: "I hope to be one day the representative of the Muslim races elected and proclaimed by God. One day, if God would make my work fecund, and my people [the Muslims] would like to follow me, I will bring you to them to be known and loved by them."[25]

Three months after this letter, his first act as a self-proclaimed Muslim prophet to bring together the Muslims from Algeria and the French was a diatribe he wrote in the national press against the Jews.

• • •

Indeed, Algerian Jews, discriminated against under Ottoman rule, tended to welcome the French arrival in the territory. The colonial administration, for its part, relied on Jewish merchants for its daily needs in food and equipment. This was precisely what displeased Urbain. At the time of his arrival, a couple of financial scandals involving French officers and one Jewish grocer had hit the news in Algeria, giving him an opening for his ire: "Generals and civil servants have given up the honor and dignity of France to these degraded pariahs [the Jews]," he wrote in *Les Débats,* a newspaper of the day. "Such an attitude," he added, "can only distance the Arabs from us, and make them say, with some disgust, that French and Jews are one."[26]

It is crucial to note that, despite how it appears, Urbain's burst of anti-Semitism here is *not* a consequence of his conversion to Islam. It is a product of the kind of Frenchman he was.

As we've seen, for the reactionary camps, Jews symbolized the degraded modern age, and, as a result, many a French civil servant thought exactly as Urbain did. "The Algerian Jew is a base and contemptible being for whom everything is summarized in money," wrote, for instance, someone named de la Pinsonnière, in an official report on Algeria in 1833.[27] Bugeaud, under whose orders Urbain worked, saw the Jews of Algeria as "a people despised [by the Muslims] and very worthy of it, for they have reached the ultimate height of abjection, deceit and greed." So if there's any causality at all between Urbain's anti-Semitism here and his conversion to Islam, it is this: *Because* Jews were seen as the embodiment of modernity, Urbain was, like many of his contemporaries in France at the time, an anti-Semite. It was this uneasiness with modernity that had eased his way toward the Muslim world in the first place. Whether or not Muslims in Algeria actually despised Jews the way he claimed they did is not the subject here. What matters is that Urbain, like Bugeaud, perceived them to do so: "Muslims hold the Jews in contempt," he wrote, a perception that was already natural for him. And it is this perception that led him to look for an alliance with the Muslims on these grounds, in order to save the West from its nihilistic materialism.

In this context, it is also worth mentioning Urbain's views on slavery and on his own blackness. His intimate friend and lover d'Eichthal was obsessed with the slave trade. Drawing from Urbain's example — or, rather, from his fantasy of Urbain's example — he had written a whole "scientific" theory according to which "the black race," as he wrote, was in essence feminine, whereas "the white race" was masculine. He dreamed of a mystical union between the two that would "restore domesticity," in the sense that the "black would perform the domestic function" as a woman in the interest of the white. Urbain, like most of the Saint-Simonians, had had anti-slavery convictions in his youth. It seems that Urbain accepted d'Eichthal's theory as a middle position between his past anti-slavery stand and the situation he had found in Algeria, where he had adopted a much more cautious attitude on the question of slavery in general as he witnessed, with no apparent repulsion, the slave trade that went on to the benefit of the upper classes of Muslim society.

Since its abolition during the Revolution, slavery in France had been a subject of hothouse debates. Napoleon had reestablished it in Haiti, and in the French West Indies of Guadeloupe and Martinique, it still constituted a de facto reality sustaining the sugar industry. Finally, in 1848, under pressure from the abolitionist militant Victor Shoelcher, the National Assembly voted to abolish slavery once and for all everywhere in the empire. Everywhere, that is, except the Maghreb, where the colonial administration was keen to maintain good relations with the imams and the Muslim upper classes. Thus, in 1848, Algeria counted 18,329 slaves, and three thousand were sold each year. By 1880, two thousand slaves a year still entered the country, while the number of slaves in Morocco reached 100,000. (In Egypt, the number reached 515,000.)[28]

Urbain was of course no stranger to this French administration's mindset. He saw his blackness, however discreet, as an obstacle to his social climbing in France, which may have been one of the reasons he converted to Islam in the first place. But now, as a Muslim from the colonial administration with contacts in the world of the ulema (doctors of Islamic law), he certainly was not ready to risk this position over a conflict on slavery.

Another field, somewhat related, in which his being a Muslim helped him to overcome "the shame" of his origin was marriage. "A rich marriage was unworkable for me because of the original stain of my birth and my modest resources," he wrote in his memoirs. And a poor wife was no solution, either: "If she were as educated as I am, she would suffer from my mediocre means," whereas, if she had an inferior education, she would "make my life painful." Therefore, "in such uncertainty, I resolved to take a Muslim wife." Which he did, in the person of Djeyhmouna Bent Messaoud Ez Zebeiri, twelve years old. The marriage was performed by an imam in 1840, with the blessing of the girl's father.

Urbain's correspondence shows that he assumed at first that he would repudiate her after a few months, as so many French civil servants did at the time. In the end, he remained married to Djeyhmouna, who eventually gave him a daughter but whom he treated all his life as some sort of inferior being. As he wrote to d'Eichthal, his true lifelong confidant, "I was not strong enough for an equal marriage."

THE FRENCH MUSLIM PROPHET AND ITS HERITAGE

I have expanded a bit on Thomas-Ismayl Urbain because his trajectory gives a sense of the paradoxes and complexities with which colonial France approached Muslim traditions and cultures. Probably the climax of those contradictions occurred in the 1860s, when Urbain became Napoleon III's special adviser for oriental affairs and, as one of the leaders of the "Arabophile" lobby, drew the outlines of France's "Muslim personal status" law, which would have the unintended consequence of creating a quasi-apartheid system depriving Muslims of any rights.

Urbain was as much against the French settlers, whose sole policy consisted in stealing as much land as they could from the Arabs, as he was against an integration policy that he feared would risk destroying the Muslim customs and spirituality that, in his view, saved Algeria—and ultimately could save France as well—from Western nihilism and decadence. It is not too much to say that the theory he landed on anticipates by more than a century what we would today call "identity politics." The name he found for it was *l'associationisme* —a barbarism even in French, but, in short, it meant that the only harmonious way for France to manage its empire while avoiding a corrupted universalism was to favor the rise of two separate societies that would live side by side under the same administration, but without mixing. "Nobody," he wrote, in order to rationalize his notion, "can say my political law, my social organization, my lifestyle represent for humanity the final expression of progress. Progress cannot have the same form for the Arab and for the French, for the Muslim, and for the Christian." Urbain's speculations found a political echo in Napoleon III, who had come to the throne in 1852 after a coup d'état and was desperately looking for an imperial destiny worthy of his uncle's glory.

They had a lot in common. Both were eccentrics and somewhat losers, both had nostalgia for France's glory days, and both had spent their youth among the Parisian *bohème,* fomenting great designs and eager to make history. When, after a trip to Syria in 1860, Napoleon III realized that fifteen million Arabs lived under Ottoman rule, he began to imagine that he could free this population from the Turks and become their leader. France could turn into a powerful *"royaume arabe"*—an Arab kingdom—over which he would benevolently rule, thus finding a role worthy of the Bonaparte name. Algeria turned into a kind of test for that grand project, and acquired a critical importance. That was when he called Urbain to his side.

For Urbain, as well as for the conservative imams he was in touch with, the problem in allowing Muslims to become citizens and benefit from expanded civil rights was that they would have had to submit to the Civil Code instituted by Napoleon I in 1808, which defined the rules of citizenry in France. In practical terms, to obey the Civil Code meant giving up traditions such as polygamy, repudiation, and slavery that benefited the Muslim upper classes. A Muslim personal status, on the other hand, would allow those traditions to live on, although at a price that would mostly affect the lower classes of Muslims. Thus the Muslim status was instituted.

In the end, the Arab Kingdom never saw the light of day — Napoleon III's reign ended ten years later, with the Franco-Prussian War of 1870 and the Paris Commune, and was succeeded by the Third Republic. Meanwhile, in Algeria, French colonial settlers used the status law in order to marginalize the Muslims even more and monopolize land. But in terms of civil rights, the consequences of the personal status had been obvious from the start.

This discriminatory system against the lower classes of the Muslim population in Algeria in the name of Islam shaped French imperialism until the crumbling of the empire. It was the basis for the quasi invisibility the migrants suffered when they began to travel to the metropole. As late as 1947, when de Gaulle passed a law to reform the Muslim status and give Muslims a say in local elections, Muslim women were denied the right to vote, in order to appease the Muslim clerics. Everywhere else on French territory, women had had the vote since the end of World War II.

To make things perfectly clear: I am not suggesting that an interest in Islam necessarily leads to identity politics and apartheid, nor that Urbain and his like were wrong to point out the dilemmas of the modern crisis. The search for transcendental meaning is, in a sense, part of that crisis itself and probably can't be avoided any more than modernity can. But, at least since Napoleon's expedition in Egypt, the same crisis also affected the Muslim world. And while some of the religious dignitaries there fought to develop an "Islamic Enlightenment" based on a dialogue with the West, a majority simply took shelter in a conservative view, and people like Urbain, eager to escape the West and full of the enthusiasm of the convert, were naturally inclined to turn to them.

Let us take a look at how this vision of Islam spread across Europe long after Urbain's death and in a completely different context. Let us turn our attention to "Judaism and Islam as Opposites," an article that the Nazi propagandist Johann von Leers published in 1942 in *Die Judenfrage,* an anti-Semitic propaganda journal of the Nazi regime. Von Leers explained in it what was, in his view, the superiority of Islam as far as "the Jewish question" was concerned: In the Muslim world, he wrote, "Jews are despised in the filthy lanes of the mellah [where] they lived under a special law which . . . kept them in a state of oppression and anxiety. If the rest of the world had adopted a similar policy, we would not have a Jewish question."[29] Isn't this almost word for word the conception French civil servants like Urbain had of the way Muslims *despised Jews*? Like Urbain, von Leers saw the Muslim world as an escape from the curses of modernity, but he took this view to its extreme. And, in his case, the word "escape" is to be taken literally: in the mid-1950s, on the run after the Nazi defeat, he ultimately found refuge in Cairo, where Gamal Abdel Nasser, the Egyptian Socialist leader, put him in charge of anti-Jewish activities (and where he was joined later by Aloïs Brunner, the commander of the Drancy camp during my grandfather's incarceration, on his way to Syria). Like Urbain, von Leers also converted to Islam, taking the name Omar Amin, and it was under this name that von Leers helped expel the Jews from Egypt in 1956 before being appointed head of the Institute for the Study of Zionism, in Cairo, where he began recycling the Nazi anti-Semitic propaganda from World War II into an "anti-Zionist" narrative aimed at the Arab masses. One of his accomplishments was the translation into Arabic of *The Protocols of the Elders of Zion*. The translator was French, a former collaborator of the Vichy regime.

This is, of course, an extreme example. But more to the point, perhaps, is the case of one of the greatest French writers of the twentieth century, Jean Genet. Sartre admired Genet, who—despite avowed homosexual fantasies involving murderers and Nazis —labeled himself a left-winger. Genet wrote extensively in the seventies to claim his support for the Black Panthers, in the United States, as well as for the Palestinians. In 1983—the very year of France's Marche des Beurs—he undertook the writing of what would become his last book, *Un Captif Amoureux* (*Prisoner of Love*) in which he recounts his visits to Palestinian training camps in south Lebanon in the early seventies.

In the book,[30] Genet, like Urbain before him, sees the Muslims as having a more "authentic" identity than the average bourgeois Westerner may ever hope to attain. What modernity calls individual freedom is, for Genet, merely the bourgeois illusion that, by obeying reason and social convention, one frees oneself from history, from identity, and from secret impulses. Only the criminal, the sociopath —and the Nazi—manage to escape this race into the void, because crime is so individual an act that the extreme violence required to accomplish it has the effect of an inner electric shock, so to speak, that destroys conventions and connects the individual to his own inner being. Such sociopaths are the real thing. They can lie, but they are never fake.

By the same token, writes Genet, "there was no tradition of the fake in the [Palestinian] fedayeen." Watching them dance Bedouin dances, for instance, makes him realize that the fedayeen identity and culture have been preserved "from corruption thanks to the dryness of the desert sand that kept them for two or three thousand years." In one of the most telling passages, he describes a failed attempt by the PLO to build a fake military base to which they can invite the international press for propaganda purposes; once on-site, however, journalists are quick "to note the details proving that this base is phony," writes Genet. He concludes that Palestinians are unable to master modern technologies of communication: they can't lie consciously, as Western journalists do.

It is important to understand that Genet does not say that Palestinians do not lie. What he says is that, lacking a culture of the fake —being no hypocrites—they are indifferent to what is true and what isn't in what they say. For what matters to them, according to Genet, is what is "authentic"—what transcends, in other words, the brevity of modern time. Remarkably, then, Genet, describing the Palestinians, finds here, almost naturally, Maurras's logic on the Dreyfus affair. For Maurras, as we may remember, facts must pale, so to speak, in front of the telluric call for the authentic values of the national honor.

For Genet, religion is a way to express this "authenticity," even though the fedayeen he describes in the book are said to be Marxists. He thus suggests that Marxism, for them, is only a superficial tool that they borrowed from the West in order to "learn the causes and setbacks of the Industrial Revolution," almost a ruse, while their real "sources wait in the desert."

"My wife will never be a nurse"—that is to say, a woman trained according to Western criteria—Genet has a Marxist fedayeen saying at some point in the book. "I want her to be a virgin. I want a real woman, a real marriage. My wife will be a virgin and a Muslim." The virginity of the potential wife here is another sign of an "authenticity" that Western women are deprived of.

In direct line with Urbain's mystic search for an escape from the West, this emphasis on authenticity on Genet's part leads far enough. It allows him to praise suicide attacks, for instance, as expressions of the "authentic" self freed from any "bourgeois" attachment. He goes as far as to compare the kamikaze to the transsexual, as two expressions of the same disdain for the subjective, illusory self. The suicide bomber, he writes, is like the young boy "who after long days of worries and perplexity decides to change sex. As he finally reaches his decision, a joy invades him, a joy nearing, perhaps, dementia. It is the equivalent of death expected, yet feared, and isn't it comparable to suicide? Thus the Palestinians, the Shiites . . . saw themselves blowing up in thousands of pieces of laughter . . . Joy of the transsexual, joy of the Requiem, joy of the kamikaze . . . joy of the hero." (That *Prisoner of Love* was publicly praised by official representatives of the PLO in Paris and elsewhere despite such lines is mystifying.)

To what extent was this narrative of Islam as an alternative to the Western crisis to be found in France, and in French governmental circles, in the early eighties, when the migrant youth marched for their rights? Roland Dumas, Mitterrand's minister of foreign affairs, for one, was intimate friends with Genet and also his personal lawyer, and would act as his executor after Genet's death in 1986, the very year *Prisoner in Love* was released. (In 2015, the same Dumas would blame Prime Minister Manuel Valls's defense of secularism on his being "under Jewish influence," because Valls's wife at the time was Jewish.)

More tellingly, perhaps, two years after the march, in 1985, the minister of education, Jean-Pierre Chevènement, commissioned a French Islamic scholar by the name of Jacques Berque to write the first government report on what France should do about its migrant youth. Born in 1910 in Algiers, the son of a colonial administrator, Berque was a translator of the Koran and a militant supporter of the Palestinian cause. He also was the president of an organization called Amitiés Franco-Irakiennes (Franco-Iraqi Friendship Society), set up that same year to promote cultural and commercial ties between Paris and Saddam Hussein, to whom Paris sold weapons.[31] A close friend of Berque's, Chevènement, who also was a member of that group, was, and is to this day, a Socialist. Berque—who died in 1995—also defined himself as a Socialist, as did Saddam Hussein. The secretary-general of Amitiés Franco-Irakiennes, Gilles Munier, however, was a former correspondent in Algiers for *La Nation Européenne*—*The European Nation*—a newsletter printed by the neofascist movement Jeune Europe during the sixties. Jeune Europe had been created by an aging Belgian militant called Jean-François Thiriart, the former head of Les Amis du Grand Reich (Friends of the Greater German Reich), the main collaborationist organization in Belgium during World War II. In a seemingly contradictory move, Munier had written a series of pieces for Thiriart's publication supporting, as Genet did, both the Palestinian fedayeen and the Black Panthers. In 2014, in an interview for an extremist Catholic French radio station called Radio Courtoisie, Munier compared today's jihadists to the anti-Nazi resisters.

As disconcerting as all this may be at first, at least to anyone used to drawing clear distinctions between "the right" and "the left," it begins to make sense once we place it in the context of an existential war of French modernity with itself—an inner struggle against the very universalism of the Enlightenment tradition that France helped to define. As we've seen earlier, this war found echoes in the Arab world far beyond religion, and with the same results. The full name of the Baath Party, of which Saddam Hussein was a member, for instance, was the Arab Socialist Resurrection Party. Although a Greek Orthodox Christian, its founder, in 1947, Michel Aflaq, saw Islam as "the soul of the body of Arabism." The goal of the Baath Party was a fight for "resurrecting the authentic Arab, untainted by imperialist influences."[32] When Aflaq died, in 1989, Saddam Hussein, who gave the eulogy, claimed that Aflaq had converted to Islam in the last years of his life, a statement later confirmed by his son. In 1941, in any case, this quest for authenticity had led him to support Rashid al-Gaylani, an Iraqi politician who, after seizing power in Baghdad through a coup in 1941, threw the English out of the country and opened the door to the Nazis. It won't come as a surprise to learn that Aflaq had been a philosophy student at the Sorbonne during the 1920s, a time when, by his own admission, his political views were framed through the readings of Lenin, the French anarchist Proudhon, and, unavoidably, Charles Maurras.

What I'm trying to point out here is a narrative arc, one that — from Urbain's utopian quest and nostalgia for blue blood to Maurras's "real country" to the romanticism of a pure Arab "Socialism" — defines modernity as its chief enemy: a narrative for which France served as a source. I think this narrative is key to understanding the curious link between both the far-right and extreme-left French networks and Islamist ones in France from the nineties on, and, stranger still, the fact that some of the most prominent leading figures of the global populist wave, such as Steve Bannon and Alexander Dugin, turn to France for reference and inspiration.

Predictably, in 1985, Berque's report solution for integrating the migrant youth fell along those lines. France, he wrote, was to refuse "Anglo-Saxon cosmopolitanism," as well as its own Jacobin tradition of assimilation — the two Western political forms of universalism — in favor of what he called a new "generous emotion" directed toward "the potential contribution to our cultural identity" that the youth of the suburbs could bring. This contribution, in Berque's mind, was of course Islam.

Again, the point here is not to discuss the merits or faults of Islam — nor, for that matter, of any religion or culture. It is to point out a narrative. In France in the mid-eighties, this narrative framed the government's answer to the migrant youth civil rights issue into a cultural and religious discussion. The will to integrate was answered with the notion that, in order to become better integrated, the youth should return to a religion they hardly knew and to traditions that, for the most part, they fought about at home with their parents.

WHAT WE TALK ABOUT WHEN WE TALK ABOUT "MUSLIMS" IN FRANCE

What should give hope is the realization that, despite such a heavy context—despite, also, the flux of violent news and what the extreme right loves to believe—by and large, in France, integration worked. The fight of the migrant youth in the early eighties helped change the French cultural and political landscape beyond recognition. Today movie stars, singers, doctors, teachers, policemen, journalists, and TV hosts of Maghrebian and other African origins are embedded in the French cultural scene in a way that would have been unimaginable thirty-five years ago.

Yet the progressive, if difficult, assimilation of that generation coincided with France's fall into economic crisis, which was marked by mass unemployment. As a result, while a majority of these migrant children assimilated, a minority of them did not. Instead they fell into poverty. It is this minority that wound up being stuck, with children of their own, in the *cités,* the poor suburbs, along with the degraded remnants of the French white working class. Needless to say, that fraction of the youth was particularly receptive to this narrative that sent them back to a religious background most didn't possess. Then, in the nineties, a new wave of immigrants joined them in those suburbs, along with satellite TVs, new technologies, discount plane tickets, and, yes, Islamist networks set up either by the Muslim Brotherhood or, more decisively, by Algerian Salafis with close ties, as we'll see, to the bloody civil war then raging in Algeria, only two hours away by plane. Before examining the influence of these networks, let us first try to quantify this minority of outcasts.

French custom forbids the categorizing of citizens according to cultural, religious, or ethnic differences, even for the purpose of sociological study. For decades, no data was available on the Muslim population of France, allowing every paranoid fantasy to thrive. Yet in 2016, a French liberal think tank, the Institut Montaigne, published a survey supervised by a political adviser and former consultant of the Chirac government, Hakim El Karoui, now a consultant for President Macron. According to this study,[33] the first of its kind, between three and four million Muslims live in France (5.5 percent of French nationals over age fifteen), of which 46 percent define themselves as entirely secular and integrated. Although the Institut Montaigne does not specify their origins, there is reason to think that this percentage is the result of the civil rights movement of the late seventies and early eighties.

The survey also showed the existence of two other groups, consisting of 26 and 28 percent of the French Muslim population. Members of the first claim that religious law is as important for them as the laws of the Republic, and, as for the second group, said to be the youngest and the more dynamic, its members asserts that, for them, Sharia law matters more than democracy. There is hardly a doubt that the troubles France is encountering today primarily have to do with this last subset, whose members do not recognize democracy or the rule of law as primary.

There is an ambiguity in the study — as in French reality — as to whether the label "French Muslims" refers only to Muslims who are French by right, and therefore vote, or to the whole population of the Muslim faith living on French soil, regardless of nationality. An additional difficulty lies in the fact that, given the history between France and Algerians, Algerians can be both by law. Lastly, the survey of course can't take into account the fluctuating number of undocumented migrants who come and go, so the total number of Muslims present on French soil is probably higher than what the report indicates. Given this complexity and the volatile nature of some of the interviewees, one can safely assume that the number of Muslims who place Sharia in front of democracy is closer to 30 percent than 28. In March 2018, a second study, by two French sociologists, Anne Muxel and Olivier Galland,[34] focusing more specifically on teenagers, found that 32 percent of Muslim adolescents consider religion "an absolute"—versus 6 percent of non-Muslim French. In any case, this means that between 940,000 and 1.12 million Muslims in France can be thought of as "secessionists." While by no means an insignificant figure, this still points to a minority.

The trouble, however, begins when one realizes that from the extreme right to the Muslims themselves, almost everyone in the country focuses on this minority as if it were representative of the whole. To give an example: When Radia Legouad and Latifa Ibn Ziaten, the mothers of the two French soldiers of Muslim faith killed in a terror attack in Montauban in 2012, came to testify during the trial of the killer's brother, in October 2017, to deliver powerful speeches on behalf of their patriotic Muslim sons, they came alone. No Muslim dignitary had found it necessary to accompany and support them. Left-wingers, so eager to launch petitions and write op-ed pieces against Islamophobia, were nowhere to be seen, either. The contrast with the empathetic attention given to the killers by the press, Muslim dignitaries, and anti-Islamophobic activists couldn't have been more striking. Somehow these assimilated Muslims, who had found their way in French society, are not seen as the "real" ones, and as a result, the dysfunctional minority of outcasts gets to shape the narrative of the majority. The crucial question is why? The answer, in my view, lies in the anti-modern narrative—both French and Salafi—according to which "authentic" Muslims are the ones who do not fit.

As the civil rights movement began to die down, and disillusionment grew, that fraction of the youth sent back to the *cités* and to Islam gave in to their anger. The first riots began in 1992, in the *banlieue* of Vaulx-en-Velin, near Lyon, after a young man, aged eighteen, was shot by policemen as he was charging them with a stolen BMW.

During the three nights of riots that ensued, commercial centers were looted, cars were burned by the dozens, and, for the first time in France, gunshots were fired against a police station.

Around the same time, through an organization called Jeunes Musulmans de France—Young Muslims of France, or JMF—the Muslim Brotherhood, under the guidance of charismatic leader Tariq Ramadan, began to spread its propaganda. Salafi killers from the Algerian civil war, on the other hand, were settling down in France with the avowed purpose of setting up underground cells to support their fight.

THE BEGINNING OF THE ANTI-JEWISH VIOLENCE

Ten years later, in the fall of 2000, the peace process in the Middle East collapsed. In France, the coverage of the riots in Jerusalem and Hebron was huge. French journalists sent their reports from West Jerusalem or the West Bank, where they worked for the most part with Palestinian translators, and, in general, spoke a bit of Arabic and not a word of Hebrew. The daily *Libération* published a "human interest" piece on a female suicide bomber. Op-ed pieces analyzed Israel's existence as "a cancer." In the trendy cultural magazine I then worked for, journalists spoke of the young Arab stone throwers in Jerusalem as the "new rockers"—as in *rock 'n' roll*—of the twenty-first century.

The peak of that coverage occurred in October 2000, when the national public channel France 2 aired on its evening news a spectacular document: the filmed death of a nine-year-old Palestinian child soon to be known worldwide as Muhammad al-Durrah, killed in an exchange of fire between Israeli soldiers and Arab gunfighters, while his father was wounded. Although not present on the scene at the time, and with no way to check on the circumstances of the incident, the French journalist presented the sequence as the cold-blooded murder of a Palestinian child by a Jewish army. The power of images showing a child and his father looking for shelter behind a small, useless wall before getting shot carried the day. A few weeks later, while in the West Bank, two Israeli reservists ended up in Ramallah by mistake and were lynched by a mob in retaliation for "the murder," and in France, the synagogue of a suburb near Paris called Trappes was burned down in what appears in retrospect to have been the first serious anti-Jewish incident in the country. Things spiraled downward from there.

That winter, the director of the Service de Protection de la Communauté Juive (SPCJ), Ron Azogui, started getting calls for protection. "Not just around Paris," he told me, "but in cities like Lyons and Marseille, where Jews were feeling threatened. Stones were thrown against synagogues, and buildings were vandalized and attacked. We listed 111 anti-Semitic aggressions that fall and winter, against only nine for the whole year in 1999."

As winter was followed by spring, and spring by summer and fall, and a next year, and another after that, anti-Jewish incidents kept rising. On the wall of a Jewish building in Marseille that was attacked and burned down, one could read the words BIN LADEN WILL WIN — DEATH TO THE JEWS! The media reported the incident cautiously, avoiding any mention of the second part of the sentence in order, as the journalist later put it, "not to inflame passions." Such caution soon became the rule, the unpleasant details appearing only in police records, and in the copies of those records kept by the SPCJ. There were incidents now reported in public schools, too. A growing number of Jewish parents, religious as well as secular, started to pull their children out of the public school system and put them into Jewish private schools — not for religious reasons, but out of fear for their safety.

By 2003, the problem of anti-Semitic harassment and violence against Jewish children in French public schools had turned serious enough for a general inspector at the Ministry of Education named

Jean-Pierre Obin to be assigned to compile a specific report on the subject:

"The situation had degraded so much in a couple of years that for the first time in France since the war, schools, in some suburbs, had become Judenrein," Obin told me in a 2015 interview, recollecting the period. "My team and I met with professors who had no problem admitting what was happening. But they thought there was nothing they could do to prevent it. Jewish kids who were outnumbered when harassed at school were in no position to fight back, so why not go elsewhere, where they'd be better off? This from left-wing secular professors, teachers who not only fought discrimination on a daily basis but also made a point of standing firm against any form of communitarianism. People who hated the very notion of private school to begin with! But suddenly, Jewish kids under threat were pushed out of the public system toward religious establishments, and this was no problem for them anymore. Sociological dynamic, they called it, a natural evolution of things. We were shocked."[35]

Teachers who did react to what was going on in their schools found themselves confronted with another problem. A history teacher at the Lycée Voltaire, in Paris, Hélène Roudier de Lara, faced several anti-Jewish incidents in those years, including walls tagged with swastikas, blunt refusals to study the Holocaust in class, and physical aggressions against Jewish students. Although she duly reported each and every one of these incidents to her superior, they never made it to the statistics at the Education Department. "One year," she says, "I had to deal with at least ten such incidents. That same year, though, the Ministry of Education reported that not one anti-Semitic incident had been noticed in *any school in France at all*."[36]

Roudier de Lara had a friend at the minister's cabinet, and she called her to investigate the discrepancy between these official numbers and what she could see on the ground. The answer, she was told, was technical. "The ministry simply didn't have any specific entry for anti-Semitism. It wasn't supposed to exist. So swastikas were labeled as 'depredations,' and anti-Semite aggressions as 'racist' or just plain 'aggression.'"[37] Didier Leschi, the former prefect of the Seine-Saint-Denis department during the 2000s, confirms: "From the reports coming back to us during the whole decade, it was clear that we had a problem with anti-Jewishness in the suburbs. But no one knew what to do, so the particulars of the incidents disappeared once they joined the stats charts. French administration simply wasn't ready to cope with words as heavily charged as 'anti-Semitism.'"[38]

It had taken a half century for France to officially recognize the full extent of the Vichy regime's responsibility in the persecution of the Jews during the Occupation years. Virtually undiscussed during the fifties and sixties, when both the Gaullist and Communist narratives prevailed, stating that the whole country had resisted the Nazis, the subject had come into focus during the seventies, thanks largely to the work of American historians, Robert Paxton in particular. Then, during most of the eighties and nineties, the painful process continued through the release of Claude Lanzmann's *Shoah* and through several trials of remaining Nazis and former high-ranking French collaborators like Klaus Barbie and Maurice Papon. The silence of the previous decade contrasted with what was becoming an obsession with France's past. In truth, contrary to other European countries prone to pogroms, such as Poland and Hungary, most of the French population during the war had helped the Jews, hiding them and protecting them from the persecution (my own family was saved that way), a fact that explains why two-thirds of the Jews in France survived the war—and a fact that should have made the country proud.

Instead, first silence and then shame prevailed on that subject. Why? The problem was that, in contrast with other European countries, in France the betrayal had come from above. It was the elite

of the country of reason, the bearers of reason themselves — the intellectuals, the politicians and the military — who had first collaborated with the Nazis. It was among them, too, as we've seen, that
the anti-modern mindset was born, planting the roots of fascism
throughout Europe in reaction to the best of what Paris had given
to the world at the end of the eighteenth century — the Declaration of the Rights of Man, the abolition of slavery, the emancipation
of the Jews. The French capital, in other words, was a battlefield for
and against modernity. What New York represented for the jihadists prior to 9/11, Paris symbolized in 1940. Where else could Hum-
phrey Bogart and Ingrid Bergman have witnessed the Nazi invasion
of Europe in Michael Curtiz's *Casablanca*? Its fall in a mere three
weeks that summer symbolized for the world the strength and ruth-
lessness of the Nazis. And Hitler understood it. Paris was the only
one of the conquered cities that he took the pain to visit — char-
tering a special plane to see the Eiffel Tower and Napoleon's tomb
in the Invalides. In *The Zone of Interest,* the novelist Martin Amis reminds us that the conquest of that city filled the Führer with the
feeling that he could now do anything he pleased. And what he did
was invade the USSR and implement the final solution.

I think the memory of this past grandeur and the sense of a special responsibility in what happened helps explain the obsession of
the French for the collaboration after the years of silence on the
subject waned. The fate of the Jews reminded the French of the
country's elite disgrace. Finally, in 1993, between the trials of Klaus
Barbie and Maurice Papon, it was revealed that François Mitterrand
himself, a Socialist president, had maintained a very close, lifelong
friendship with one of France's most notorious collaborators, René
Bousquet, who personally engineered the largest mass arrest of Jews
in France during World War II. Bousquet was said to have partly financed Mitterrand's campaign in 1981. His subsequent murder, by
an unstable Frenchman shortly after the revelation erupted, only

added to the general discomfort with what was clearly a combustible subject. To come to terms with yet another wave of anti-Semitism seemed unbearable.

And Jean-Marie Le Pen's breakthrough in the first round of the 2002 presidential elections—less than a year after the attacks on New York and D.C.—added to the heavy atmosphere. While the left was in disarray, President Jacques Chirac, running for a second term, confronted Le Pen in the second round by presenting himself as the sole democratic alternative to fascism. But his subsequent victory, with an improbable 80 percent of the ballots—a result close to those enjoyed by the populist dictators Chirac was so fond of—only revealed the depth of France's political crisis. Everybody was scared. Raising controversial opinions about immigration or Islam in such a context was out of the question, since they might reinforce the strength of the far right.

In 2004, a second report commissioned by the prime minister, to the writer Jean-Christophe Rufin, focusing on anti-Semitism at large, concluded that anti-Jewish violence in the suburbs was on the rise. This violence, it concluded alarmingly, had to be addressed as seriously and as quickly as possible by French authorities in order to reinforce the country's domestic security in the years to come. Nothing was done.

The next year was the year of the swastika in Drancy. It was the year my father, appearing one Sunday more calm and confident than he ever had been since being forced into early retirement from acting twenty years earlier, announced his grand project to me and my brother.

In the wake of his announcement, I felt divided—happy that my father had found an activity at all; fearful that his request for subsidies might not be approved by the mayor's team; and fearful of what would happen if it did, imagining my limping father as he walked Bobigny's wild streets. The following Monday he was noticeably anxious about having to call City Hall that day to discuss his project. A few minutes before the appointed time for the call, he had a massive stroke.

I do not mean to suggest that he was a collateral victim of the swastika: he had been a heavy smoker for decades, he had phlebitis, he was overweight, and he never exercised. He was a perfect candidate for a stroke; any occasion of tension could have done it. And yet, it was this one and no other. And in which other country, at which other period, would his last weeks of existence have sent him back to his youth of permanent fear?

The Drancy memorial was vandalized again several times in the following years as the violence grew. The perpetrators were never caught. This was France; it could've been anyone.

TWO
The Year of the Quenelle

ew, France is not yours. The march during which the very anti-Semitic slogan my father had heard as a child in the thirties was chanted in the streets of Paris for the first time in *my* lifetime occurred on January 26, 2014, one year before the terror wave began.

As explained above, this demonstration inaugurated a dramatic rise in the number of anti-Jewish random aggressions, emanating mostly from Muslim individuals, that had started fourteen years prior all over the country. And yet the event was in no way related to those incidents. Nor were the thirty to forty thousand "rebels" who gathered in the wet, icy fog of that drained, gray early afternoon. Two years ahead, in fact, and, language notwithstanding, they could have been Trump supporters.

The main difference lay in the unlikely French shambles with which they were trying to define who and what they were: a junk catalog of nationalist folklore where regressive placards held by six-year-old children standing on their fathers' shoulders and claiming I WANT A DADDY AND A MOM!—a remnant of the anti-gay-marriage demonstrations of the previous year—mixed with French flags of every size; with drawings of Marianne, the symbol of the French Republic, wearing a Phrygian cap, with a blouse added to cover her breasts; with bloody sacred hearts surmounted with the cross of the ultra-royalist Chouans, who in 1791 opposed the Revolution; with blue flags printed with white lilies, the flower of the kings and of French nobility; with diverse signs inspired by the swastika, the ornament of modern crusaders at war against Islam in France and against international Jewry.

The woman who called the march was Béatrice Bourges, a Catholic militant who, two years prior, as discussions at the National Assembly over the legalization of gay marriage were unfurling, had claimed to have had a divine intuition that gender theories and same-sex marriage would "destroy Western civilization." She had then put together a political movement called Le Printemps Français, the French Spring, which joined together several ultra-conservative and extreme-right homophobic groups. Although the law had ultimately been passed, the French Spring had proved able to mobilize several thousand demonstrators on its behalf, proving, if need be, that there was indeed a place in France for such sentiment when it focused on a subject as divisive as gay marriage seemed to be.

Another thing the French Spring had demonstrated, however, was its curious appeal to forces far distant from its normal political boundaries. Groups of young Muslims who usually did not march with conservative Catholics, let alone extreme-right militants, and who in 2012, according to every poll in the country, had voted overwhelmingly for François Hollande's Socialist Party, were shocked enough by the prospect of gay marriage that they were now marching against the left. Although Muslims and neofascist groups did hate each other, they united side by side under the rain that day, performing a ritualistic gesture, for which they regularly stopped the procession to take selfies that they posted to Facebook. Somewhere in that mess, the cry resonated: *Juif! La France n'est pas à toi!*

Part Nazi salute, part *fuck you* gesture, the motion in question involved crossing one hand to the opposite arm or shoulder as if performing a *Sieg Heil!* and was called *la quenelle*. It had been introduced onstage the previous fall by a forty-eight-year-old half-French, half-Cameroonian stand-up comedian called Dieudonné M'Bala M'Bala, whose theater, La Main d'Or, near Bastille, had turned, in a few years, into the epicenter of anti-Jewish hate in Paris. The walls of the bar adjoining the stage had been decorated for years with posters of Hamas, with praises to Mahmoud Ahmadinejad, who during his presidency had partly financed Dieudonné's small Anti-Zionist Party, and with leaflets emanating from extreme-right student unions close to Jean-Marie Le Pen, the former leader of the National Front, who also was Dieudonné's daughter's godfather. After the show, fans of "Dieudo," gathering around beers and sandwiches — a lower-middle-class public that far outnumbered the immigrant children of the *cités* who had been his first fans — were sometimes granted a friendly appearance by the star at their table.

Dieudonné had begun his career in the nineties as a left-wing anti-racist satirist. His anti-Semitic remarks onstage began to increase in early 2000, as the first tensions around the subject were beginning to be felt in the country, but it was the marketing stroke of genius of *la quenelle* that brought him to quasi-star status nationwide. By 2014 his shows included scatological insults hurled against prominent Jewish intellectuals such as the philosopher Alain Finkielkraut, celebrations of deniers of the death camps, like Robert Faurisson, who appeared as a guest star onstage, and phone conversations with the convicted terrorist Carlos from his jail cell. Dieudonné also relied on his website, Dieudosphere.com, to spread his message with even more clarity through "comic" videos in which he commented on the news. In 2013, a classified note focusing on "the Dieudonné

phenomenon" and sent to President Hollande had explicitly compared the tremendous audience of the comedian's videos on You-
Tube and Facebook with the poor ratings for any TV interview
given by Hollande himself.

The president's lack of charisma was notorious. He was at his
lowest in the polls, with barely 20 percent approval ratings after
only eighteen months in power—the worst showing by any French
president since the birth of the Fifth Republic. Hollande's prime
minister, Manuel Valls, had launched a war against Dieudonné, publicly denouncing his anti-Semitism and trying to legally ban his
shows, the only result of which had been to reinforce the anti-gov-
ernment sentiment and in the defense of freedom of speech.

"I pissed on the Wailing Wall" . . . "The Holo-cost us an arm"
. . . The more outrageous Dieudo's "jokes" were, the more he was
loved by his public—young, urban, partly white petit bourgeois and
partly from immigrant working-class backgrounds—but the jokes
were nothing compared with the invention of la quenelle. Sold to his
public as an emblem of rebellion against "the system," la quenelle was
used both as a sign of recognition between "rebels" and as a cryptic
signal denouncing anything allegedly connected with Jews, Israel,
and America—that is to say, the masters of the world. Dieudonné's website rewarded the most imaginative stagings of this gesture,
which were infinitely reproduced on social media, with a special
award called the Quenelle d'Or (the Golden Quenelle). That winter
of 2013–14, prizewinners included the football star Nicolas Anelka
and Dieudonné's extreme-right militant lawyers in Brussels, Henri
Laquay and Sébastien Courtoy, friends of Jean-Marie Le Pen's and
counsel, in 2009, for the Belgian Islamic Center in its defamation
trial for having compared Israeli foreign minister David Levy to
Hitler on its website.

The success of la quenelle during the fall of 2013—a success
boosted by the multiple attacks and trials against Dieudonné from
Jewish associations and by the prime minister's attempts to silence

him—had sent his popularity through the roof. Now, in January, at his request, his fans were filling the Day of Wrath march. They were the ones chanting "Jew, France is not yours."

For everything there is a hate, and a time for every hate. It was the Ecclesiastes of counter-knowledge, this Day of Wrath, the new gospel preached through social media, against unemployment, against liberalism, and against the state; against excessive taxes, against welfare; against the hardship reserved for French peasantry; against family planning and against gay marriage and gender theories; against corrupt politicians, against capitalist America's European lackeys and the "media elites"—in short, against anything that could be interpreted as a sign of our chaotic era, except, of course, themselves.

THE SPREADING OF A HATEFUL JUBILATION

In the weeks and months following the Day of Wrath demonstration, as the number of anti-Jewish incidents rose across the country, the *quenelle* gesture seemed ubiquitous. Anonymous people started to infiltrate the live audiences of TV shows to do it; TV technicians invaded news sets to perform it behind the journalists during the eight o'clock news. In numerous cases, the set chosen for a selfie *quenelle* was a Jewish location or a place connected with World War II. Two youths, for instance, performed it in the ruins of Oradour-sur-Glane, the small village in the north of the country where, during the war, more than six hundred men, women, and children were massacred by an SS squadron. Some made the trip to Berlin to have their picture taken performing the gesture at the Holocaust Memorial. In Toulouse, a man planted himself in front of the Ozar Hatorah Jewish school, targeted two years prior by a terror attack in which three children had been killed. Meanwhile, other incidents were reported. In Antwerp, Belgium, a doctor refused to visit a ninety-year-old Jewish woman who had broken her rib. "Send her to Gaza for a while," he is reported to have said on the phone to the woman's son. "She won't hurt any longer." On the Brussels–Paris line, a train was stopped in the middle of nowhere, its alarm plugged, and a voice, never identified on the loudspeakers, announced that all Jews should get off and change to the train for Auschwitz.[1]

On May 4, at the request of a young Belgian parliament member named Laurent Louis, Dieudonné and his fans gathered in Brussels for a *quenelle* demonstration. Authorities who had forbidden it, due to its obvious anti-Semitic character, sent the police to disperse the gathering with water cannons. Two weeks later, on May 20, the Jewish Museum in that very town was attacked by a man armed with an AK-47, who killed four people. After the alleged perpetrator was arrested near Marseille the next day and identified as a French national by the name of Mehdi Nemmouche, Dieudonné's lawyers and friends Laquay and Courtoy offered him legal assistance.

The following summer, "anti-Zionist" demonstrations against the war in Gaza degenerated into riots against at least two synagogues in Paris and the suburb of Sarcelles. In Paris that September — among the many anti-Jewish aggressions of the period already listed above — a seventy-four-year-old man walking to the synagogue, a yarmulke on his head, was hit by a stranger, who went on beating him after he'd fallen on the asphalt, yelling, "I'm gonna kill you, son of a bitch!" The same month, in the Paris suburb of Épinay-sur-Seine, a teenager coming out of school had her hair pulled and her head shoved against the wall by a girlfriend who'd just learned she was half-Jewish.

A CONTEMPORARY NATIONAL SOCIALIST

Dieudonné M'Bala M'Bala was born in 1966, the son of a Cameroonian accountant father and a white sociologist mother, a Buddhist, from Bretagne. His first name, Dieudonné, as it turns out, was the second name of Louis the XIV, under whose reign the slave trade became an industry in France, and the infamous Black Code was written to govern its practices. While this detail may seem irrelevant, it might actually be of importance for someone as obsessed as Dieudonné with "roots," identity issues, and the notion that Jews were the main operators of the slave *negocio*. What a thing, after all, to be a black man and bear the name of the person who made the slave trade one of the main resources of your own country. All the more so, perhaps, when your white mother comes from Bretagne, from which most of the ships sailing toward Africa and the Caribbean in the seventeenth century embarked, which could only make you live with the rampant suspicion, however ungrounded, that at least some of your own ancestors may well have had slave traders themselves.

In any case, after Dieudonné's parents divorced, his mother raised him in a middle-class suburb near Paris, where, as a teen, he attended Catholic school and learned judo, piano, and jazz saxophone. He got his degree in computer science, then started out onstage in the early nineties along with a childhood friend—a Sephardic Jew named Élie Semoun. After six years of success, the duo split and Dieudonné launched his solo career as a sort of black second-rate Lenny Bruce—left-leaning, mocking racism, satirizing "all religions" so much that, at the time, people compared his humor to that of the caustic *Charlie Hebdo,* a parallel that would often be used later by his defenders.

Dieudonné's own account of his split with his Jewish friend in 1996 centers, not surprisingly, on a financial dispute. That same year was the year of his "awakening" to the duplicity of the Jews after an encounter with representatives of Louis Farrakhan's Nation of Islam, who for a while envisioned opening a bureau in Paris. (The project never materialized.) As an additional motivator in his political journey, Dieudonné also mentions his failed attempts to finance a historical motion picture on slavery, because of the Jews who, he claims, control the movie industry as they once controlled the slave trade.

But Dieudonné's career as the messiah of anti-Jewish hate probably would never have taken off without a prophet, the person in the wings gifted with the brains to articulate in a coherent narrative the disordered visions of the chosen. It was through an appearance on a live entertainment program called *You Can't Please Everybody,* in December 2003, that Dieudonné met his. That evening, Dieudonné performed a number disguised as an Orthodox Jew, sarcastically advising his audience to "convert like [him] and join the axis of Good, the Zionist-American axis that offers so many opportunities to its followers." He concluded his sketch shouting *"Isra-heil!"* and making the Nazi salute. It was a prime-time show, aired on France 2, the context was the Iraq War, and everybody laughed.

A few days later, a tall, well-built man in his early forties named Alain Soral got in touch with the comedian. Soral, who presented himself as a sociologist, was, in fact, an ex-journalist, a failed actor, and the author of several books on subjects as various as fashion, seducing women, and what he called the "feminization" of Western societies — in his view, a synonym for decadence. He was also a former member of the Communist Party, a member of the National Front, a ghostwriter for Marine Le Pen's speeches, a kickboxing practitioner, and, surprisingly or perhaps unsurprisingly, given his anti-gay vehemence, a closeted homosexual.

According to Dieudonné's own account of that first meeting, Soral started by criticizing him for the poor quality of his act: he had been too clownish, too much of an amateur on such a serious issue as the Jews — in short, he needed help. Soral could provide it, along with political clout.

Today Soral describes himself as a "National Socialist," and having met him once, on the set of a TV show in 2010, where I was presenting one of my books, I can only testify to the strict accuracy of this self-assigned label. In 2016, on his website, Égalité et Réconciliation, or E&R, Soral posted a picture of himself handcuffed and wearing a T-shirt labeled GOY, to better illustrate his daily martyrdom in defending France against international Jewry. He had been condemned that same year to a conditional sentence of six months and a 70,000-euro fine for having commented on his Facebook page on a picture of Nazi hunters Serge and Beate Klarsfeld receiving Germany's highest medal of honor in Berlin. The comment said, "Here's what happens when you don't finish the job." One year later, in 2017, the French sociologist Antoine Bevort published a one-year study analyzing the success of political websites in France. E&R came in at number one, with an average of eight million visitors a month. The day we met on that TV show, in 2010, he was presenting a new book of his own, *Comprendre l'Empire*—*Understanding Empire*—which attributes everything going wrong in the world to the Jews (with the help of the USA). By 2014, this modern rewriting of *The Protocols of the Elders of Zion* had sold 100,000 copies, mostly through Amazon, where he ranked at the top position in the political essays category.

He showed up in the TV dressing room "protected" by five or six bodyguards his size, and the tension rose immediately. The palpable atmosphere of collective male violence, the insults disguised as "jokes" that he exchanged with his men, turned out to be directed not against me, as I thought it could've been, but against the sole female guest on the show, who was pregnant and had to be moved to a separate dressing room to avoid a physical incident.

As for the talk show on which we met, it was one of the main cultural programs on France 2 at the time, and that Soral was invited at all was in itself a problem. The host, a Frédéric Taddeï, who has a reputation in France for being the most well-read TV host in the country, was also said by his own team to be quite obsessed with the Jewish Question. Tariq Ramadan was one of his regular guests, and he had invited Dieudonné on his show no fewer than three times. In the fall of 2018, after sixteen years at France 2, he would begin a new talk show on RT network—the international Russian news channel backed by the Kremlin, which in 2005 financed an Axis for Peace conference hosting, among others, Dieudonné.[2]

That day in 2010, it was Soral, and as I made a point during the show to expose him for what I thought he was, I appeared, in the eyes of Taddeï, and probably not just his, as another paranoid, clumsy Jew unable to accept freedom of speech or to keep up with an intellectual debate.

STAVROGIN AT THE FRENCH COURT

Born in 1960, the son of a Franco-Swiss father from the Savoie mountains who beat him for most of his childhood and ended up in jail for fraud, Alain Soral ran away from home at seventeen and ended up in Paris in the early eighties, drifting between temporary jobs and trendy nightclubs. He borrowed money from friends, crashed on other friends' couches. He practiced intensive kickboxing and intensive street pickup, and later wrote a whole book to draw "sociological conclusions" from the seven hundred women he had allegedly picked up on the street and "penetrated." "What glory can one get from girls when one knows that they have been physically, psychologically and sociologically programmed for that?" he wrote.[3] In 2016, however, Soral was convicted for harassment after sending offensive text messages to the African model Binti, who had refused to be "penetrated" by the esteemed sociologist. To give a taste of the messages, as published by the weekly *Marianne:* "White men take black women for whores, which they are most of the time." "Finally, you'll be stuck with fags and Jews. Fags as friends to hear your cry that your fate is to be a Jew's whore."[4]

Other than that, Soral entertained a Genet-like taste for male meanness, for bulimic disorganized reading and endless philosophical-political discussions. Then as now, he spent most of his time with men—the only creatures worth talking to. He tried his luck as a painter, as an actor, as a filmmaker, as a writer, as a fashion critic.

The pattern will sound familiar to any reader of Dostoyevsky's novels; there's not much to add except perhaps a note on the context and the specific emphasis put on culture in France in the early eighties, when Sofral was trying to establish himself as a cultural figure. The Socialists had just come to power and Jack Lang, as minister of culture, was making Paris a feast. Everyone with a bit of ambition, it seemed, could enter the party provided he found the right people to court, learned to master the right social codes and the right behavior. Then, in due time, it was assumed, this would lead him or her to the right public subsidies provided by the state. Public subsidies in culture aren't necessarily bad, but they have their downside—especially in a centralized country whose social practices find their roots in the salons Balzac already described two centuries ago. Then as now, court culture is primarily an education in jealousy and resentment, all the more so, perhaps, when the preferential treatment one looks for presents itself in the guise of Socialist equality, as certainly was the case in Paris in the eighties. Words, then, end up meaning the opposite of what they stand for. For overambitious young men of dubious origin and unsure of themselves, such a gap between what is and what seems can open abysses of anger.

By the beginning of the nineties, in any case, the luster of the Ministry of Culture was fading, along with the Socialists themselves, and a crowd of young, resentful men of Soral's generation who had failed to make their way started to emerge in the French media world. Determined to settle scores and spit out their rage, they saw themselves as the leftovers of the party. All had a soft spot for nationalism or Stalinism or extreme-right fascism—or anything, really, that looked like the very opposite of the cosmopolitan culture that, in the age of globalization, the ruling left had come to represent.

As for Soral himself, his anti-Jewish awakening seems to have occurred as early as the mid-eighties, when, having written a relatively successful book on fashion with a co-author who happened to be Jewish, he saw his partner presenting their book on TV, by himself. "A Jew who took all the credit had manipulated me," he later said. "From this day on, I studied the Talmud and the history of Zionism and realized that treason and communitarianism were at the heart of that culture."[5] To set oneself to studying the Talmud out of a personal falling-out certainly betrays—if the story is true—an indisputable, passionate energy. That or sheer madness.

THE MORAL DILEMMA IN EXTREME-RIGHT CIRCLES

In any case, in April 2002, when Jean-Marie Le Pen got through the first round of the presidential elections, Soral had left the shores of the cultural left and was sailing into National Front territory. It was the first time since World War II that a nationalist leader had risen so high in Europe. Extreme right-wing militants from all over Europe traveled to Paris that spring to get a sense of the new vanguard. That this breakthrough was an indirect consequence of the terrorist attacks on New York and D.C. seven months earlier was clear. Terror created a new context in which the National Front could indeed strive. There was also the perceptible joy that the attack on New York generated in some extreme-left circles, among former Communists and among anti-American right-wing extremists as well— a joy from which admiration for the jihadists was not entirely absent, despite their religion. Soral appeared in the entourage of Le Pen and his daughter Marine just in time to take part in the deep, heated debate that ensued. To summarize it bluntly, it went like this: Should Muslim anger against "the empire" be seen as a good thing in the nationalistic fight against globalism, and if so, should the National Front court French Muslims as potential voters? Or, to the contrary, should the extreme right support Israel—and the United States—in the Western fight against Islamic anti-modern barbarity?

And, if so, what to do with the anti-Semitic heritage from World War II and beyond from Maurras? That debate, in fact, had been in the works for years, thanks to a current known in France since the seventies as La Nouvelle Droite. But the new context made it a burning question.

Born in the seventies, the French New Right was in many ways a reprise of both Urbain's identity politics and Maurras's emphasis on "the real country." It stipulated that, to defend the "authentic" cultural traditions and customs of the old continent against the Americanization of the world, Europe alone was too weak. The new enemy, globalization, born after World War II out of the defeat of fascism, was all too familiar: Burke's "sophisters, economists, and calculators," best embodied by vulgar, cosmopolitan Jews but backed, this time, by a new, imperialist power. In order to face it, old fascist and nationalist ideological baggage had to be rerouted, paradoxically, toward an alliance with some of the former colonies in the third world that had developed a nationalism of their own. A philosopher and historian named Alain de Benoist was the leader and main thinker of that camp, and he remains today the most influential intellectual among the French conservatives who actually read books. In fact, his influence extends far beyond his own camp to reach former leftists.

Born in 1943, de Benoist had started his career in 1960 as a literary critic at *Lectures Françaises,* a Parisian review founded by the journalist and former politician Henry Coston, who, in the thirties, had run for the legislative elections of Algeria on an anti-Jewish ticket. During the war, Coston had been vice president of the Association of Anti-Jewish Journalists (L'Association des Journalistes Anti-Juifs) before being appointed by Marshal Pétain as the head of the *Information Bulletin on the Jewish Question (Le Bulletin d'Information sur la Question Juive),* the official press organ of the Bureau of Jewish Affairs (le Bureau des Affaires Juives), in charge of spoliations and deportations under the Vichy regime. In the early sixties, when de

Benoist joined *Lectures Françaises,* the review also published the first Holocaust deniers (all of whom happened to be French).

To the literary pieces he wrote for Coston, de Benoist added several texts defending the French Empire and pamphlets in support of the Secret Army Organization (l'Organisation de l'Armée Secrète, or OAS), the extreme-right terror militia fighting the Arabs in Algeria during the War of Independence. He also co-wrote a book in defense of apartheid, *Rhodésie, Pays des Lions Fidèles—Rhodesia, the Loyal Lions' Country*—with a foreword by Rhodesian prime minister and white supremacist Ian Smith. All this was consistent with his intellectual background. And yet, in the early 2000s, when the debate over Muslims started in extreme-right circles, de Benoist was long since known for slogans such as "Europe and the third world together" and "Let us decolonize to the end!" He also stood for, among other regimes, Castro's Cuba and Khomeini's Iran.

The reader who detects common ground between this journey and the world of the fascist and pro-Palestinian Gilles Munier, described in chapter 1, would not be mistaken. De Benoist, in fact, collaborated with Jeune Europe, Munier's movement founded by Jean-François Thiriart, the former pro-Nazi Belgian activist during World War II, and Thiriart had been the first to articulate the notion according to which, for the nationalists and fascists in Europe, the political and existential alternative to both bastardized capitalism and rootless Communism—the USA and the USSR—was to be found in an alliance with the new nationalist movements and governments born out of the former colonies in the third world. This was the thinking behind Jean Genet's articles in favor of the Palestinian and Black Panther causes in the first place. Since 1979, de Benoist, for his part, had been more Iran-oriented. In 1985—the year the Ministry of the Interior issued the Jacques Berque report claiming that the French offspring of migrants should turn their attention toward their parents' religion instead of trying to integrate into the consumerist society—de Benoist wrote, in his own review, called

Éléments, an op-ed piece on Islam in which he quoted Berque and drew logical conclusions from Thiriart's reasoning:

> On both sides of the Mediterranean, and in spite of what separates them, Europe and the Arab world face a similar situation. They must unite, to disentangle themselves from the grip of the two superpowers, and maintain their identity by acceding to a modernity of their own, which does not consist in being absorbed by the modernity of others. The cultural fermentation now boiling in the Arab world announces without doubt what will be the major fact of this ending century: the claim of popular collective identities against the dominant systems that destroy them. This is why "the awakening of [political] Islam" is not in our eyes a threat. Rather, it is a hope.

Four years later, when Salman Rushdie's *Satanic Verses* was judged blasphemous by the Iranian regime and a fatwa was launched from Tehran against Rushdie himself, de Benoist suggested in his review that the release of such a book could only be the result of a Western plot to discredit the Iranian regime.[6]

GHOSTS OF OLD RUSSIA

For better or worse, Paris remains the international lighthouse of intellectual ambitions. In 1989, as the Cold War began to fade and the eastern frontier opened, one man so admired de Benoist that he came all the way from Russia to Paris several times to meet him. Back home, that man set up an ambitious journal dedicated to geopolitics and Russian culture, christening it with the same name (but in Russian) that de Benoist had used for his own magazine: *Elementy.* That man, who, under de Benoist's influence, would soon become the founder of the nationalist, anti-Semitic, and messianic

Russian movement called Eurasianism, was Alexander Gelyevich Dugin, today Putin's chamber philosopher—and one of the main influences on Steve Bannon.

His father had been an officer in Soviet intelligence, as was his grandfather. As for him, born in 1962, he had spent his youth in Moscow fighting "the system"—in his case, the Communist one—inside a secretive group called the Lujinski circle. Members of the Lujinski group were all young, self-taught men who, like Soral in Paris during the same period, spent their time reading and discussing intensely. In contrast with Soral, however, their favorite subject was not Communism. No, what they loved debating was mysticism, paganism, the knights of old, Russian Orthodox Old Believers, and Russian "authentic" identity. Islam was not absent of such a mystical landscape, either. One of the founders of the Lujinski circle, a Gueïdar Djemal, would later travel to Tajikistan to found the Islamic Renaissance Party and is today the head of the pro-Putin Islamic Committee of Russia.

The KGB arrested Dugin in 1983 for anti-Communist activities, but perestroika was on its way, and soon he was out of the woods. Back in the Lujinski circle, his main activity then consisted of translating authors he thought worthy of attention. One was René Guénon, a French mystic and spiritualist of the early twentieth century who converted to Islam in Egypt—an heir of sorts to Ismayl Urbain—and another the Italian dandy and anti-Semite fascist of the 1930s Julius Evola, whose latter-day fans also include Steve Bannon and whose most famous book, *Revolt Against the Modern World,* published in 1934, calls for the end of egalitarian democracy, the return of the sacred in politics, and the establishment of a social order based on the Indian—"Indo-European Aryan," in the fascist parlance—caste system.

The young Dugin translated these writers, then the Cold War ended, Communism collapsed, and—in search of intellectual mentors—he began traveling west.

"EURASIANISM" AND THE DISRUPTING
OF WESTERN DEMOCRACIES

De Benoist was not his sole encounter. The second step of his initiatory journey took him to Rome to meet an acquaintance of de Benoist's, Claudio Mutti. The two men knew each other from their turbulent youth at Jeune Europe. Mutti was—and is—an essayist who, some thirteen years earlier, had supervised an Italian translation of *The Protocols of the Elders of Zion* to which, for good measure, he had added several of Evola's articles on "the Jewish question." In 1985, after his arrest by Italian police in the dismantling of a neofascist terror group called Ordine Nero (Black Order), Mutti converted to Islam, taking the Muslim name Omar Amin—the very name the SS officer Johann von Leers, mentioned above, had used for his own conversion in Egypt thirty years earlier—to honor him.

The third personality Dugin had to meet in order to complete his initiation could only be the mentor to the first two men: the former head of the Friends of the Greater German Reich and founder of Jeune Europe, Jean-François Thiriart himself. Then aged sixty-seven —he would die three years later—Thiriart was a veteran of the Cold War, and his vision of things could only be deeply shaken by the collapse of the USSR and, above all, by what he saw as the absolute domination of the USA over the world. To his theory of an alliance between European nationalists and third world movements against the two superpowers, he had to add a new stage. It would take the form of a call for a pact between former fascists and former Communist regimes in order to create a united front across the continent that would ultimately take power. This "Euro-Soviet Empire," as he called it, was the sole force, in Thiriart's mind, that could win the political and cultural identity war against this new form of American imperialism called rootless globalization and worldwide neoliberalism. During the 1990s, this theory would come to be known in intellectual and media circles across the continent as "the red-brown alliance." One of its most dynamic bases would be France.

Did this idea also allow Dugin to reconcile his turbulent, half-nihilist punk youth with the Communist heritage of his father, which he had first rejected? In any case, it seems to have provided him with the answer he was looking for. Back in Moscow, he constructed his own ideology, Eurasianism—a term that had had its brief luster among exiled White Russians of the 1920s fleeing the Russian Revolution but had since been forgotten. Dugin picked it up, so to speak, among the rubble of the Berlin Wall to give it a new meaning.

In 1991, in Moscow, Dugin began to set up regular roundtables with several figures of the European New Right, most notably de Benoist. They met with department heads at the Military Academy of the General Staff of the Russian Armed Forces. (The first issue of *Elementy*, released in April 1992, includes a transcript of such a gathering.) These reunions were made possible by Dugin's status as a protégé of the commander of the General Staff academy, General Igor Rodionov, who became defense minister in 1996–97. That year, with the active help of other high-ranking Russian military figures, he published his first major book, *Foundations of Geopolitics*, in which he advocated for a program of destabilization and disinformation spearheaded by the Russian special services against the West. The United States in particular was targeted. The purpose, wrote Dugin, was "to provoke all forms of instability and separatism within the borders of the United States . . . To encourage all kinds of separatism and ethnic, social, and racial conflicts, actively supporting all dissident movements—extremist, racist, and sectarian groups . . . It would also make sense simultaneously," he added, "to support isolationist tendencies in American politics."[7]

In 1997, when *Foundations of Geopolitics* was published, the book had such a warm reception among military leaders that, according to the Russian investigative weekly *Versiya*, Dugin took part in the writing of the Russian National Security Blueprint. Four years later, he would be one of the most outspoken defenders of the conspiracy theory according to which 9/11 was the work of the American government itself.

In *Foundations,* Dugin furthermore suggested the building of a "continental Russian-Islamic alliance" against "Atlanticism." Dugin had Iran in mind, but for him, "the entire Islamic zone represents a naturally friendly geopolitical reality." The "fundamental principle" overarching this alliance is "the principle of 'a common enemy.' The rejection of the supremacy of economic, liberal market values . . . represents the common civilizational basis, the common impulse which will prepare the way for a strong political and strategic union" between what Dugin calls Eurasia and regions in the third world, especially Muslim ones.

These ideas were right out of Thiriart and de Benoist's playbook.

"SATANISM AND DEGENERATION"

The seemingly rational tone of the above should not mislead anyone. With Dugin we have entered a world of superstition, fanaticism, and mystical madness of which we will soon encounter the Muslim iteration. It is worth, then, giving a hint of what exactly Eurasianism is, or rather, of the worldview that supports it and of the tone with which Dugin presents his ideas—assuming, that is, that one can summarize in a few lines the extreme mental confusion laid out by each of his volumes, the French translations of which have forewords by either de Benoist or Soral. It goes more or less like this: Exhausted by decades of individualism and postmodernism, the West has lost the spiritual means of its autonomy. The end of history simply registered that fact as the Cold War ended. Yet this death is also a promise of resurrection. For America is nothing if not, to quote Dugin, "the island reappeared on the historical stage only to accomplish the fatal mission of the end of Times"—in other words, Leviathan.[8] In the nineties, America's apparent victory only announced the final battle that would see its demise.

For Dugin, then, the geopolitical situation is but the last episode to date of an ancestral cosmic drama where nothing less than the human soul is at stake. Two types of societies clash, and they are irreconcilable. The bad one, whom Dugin calls in his jargon *thalassocratic*, is governed by the fluctuant seas: it is "Atlantist," that is to say, always changing, untrustworthy, mischievous, engineered by commerce and impure exchanges of all kinds, individualistic and hostile to hierarchy. The other one, the good one, *tellurocratic*, is just the opposite: rooted in the earth, and especially in the Russian-European soil, it is of a single mind, and its values are the values of the knights of old. Its mindset is Russian Orthodox, Muslim, and Socialist in spirit. Its roots run deep in a tradition of vertical hierarchy that everyone must serve, against his own feeble individual interest, because this hierarchy leads to God. One may identify here a trace of Maurras's dichotomy between "the legal country" and the real one.

According to Dugin, in the twentieth century, the last battle between these two worlds was fought by Hitler—leader of the People from the North and the East—against the internationalist, merchant Jews. Muslims were not absent of this fight, either: "According to a Shiite tradition," he writes, "the sacred blood of the five imams is attracted to the magnetic poles, that is to say to the North. This is why some [among the Muslim Ummah] do not reject the idea that Hitler was a hidden imam."[9]

Yet Hitler was but a prophet, and the real messiah is still to come. He is, of course, Russian, for Russians have a messianic destiny, and their transcendental significance is panhuman.

As for the goal of the ultimate war to come, it is simple. To save himself from damnation, man must "come back to the Being, to the Logos, to a new Middle Age. For all the content of modernity is Satanism and degeneration. Its science, its values, its philosophy, its art, its society: All this must be wiped out."[10]

"KALASHNIKOV EDITIONS": FRANCE IN THE NINETIES

All this may sound rather removed from Soral and Dieudonné, but it is not.

In the early nineties, France was entering a bleak period. After World War II, General de Gaulle and the Socialists had both, in different ways, entertained a narrative according to which, despite the Vichy regime, France was unambiguously among the winners and, despite the dismantling of the empire, remained as powerful a country as ever. Born in the cradle of the Cold War, that narrative had survived in large part thanks to the atomic bomb and to France's "Arab policy," but in the years following the fall of the Berlin Wall, Socialism and Gaullism, the two pillars of the country's political identity, began to crumble as well. Due to a central mode of governance, which had its roots in the Ancien Régime and in the specific weight of the Communist Party in French politics since the Cold War, France was the one country in Western Europe that bore similarities to the countries of the Eastern Bloc, particularly Russia. The parallel, needless to say, goes only so far, and France never experienced, even remotely, the violence into which Russia plunged in the early nineties—let alone the gulags of the previous era. But the two countries share an anti-modern fiber, a taste for lyricism and revolution, and an attraction to nihilism, and both lend boredom an existential importance. (Emma Bovary can be seen as a French Anna Karenina.)

In any case, while a new liberalism seemed to spread worldwide, the debt France had accumulated to finance its social system during the prosperous years caught up with the country. Meanwhile, under Jacques Chirac's leadership, Gaullism appeared senile, transfixed by the global changes, and corrupt beyond repair, while Socialism, represented by super-rich personalities such as Dominique Strauss-Kahn as finance minister, looked like capitalist globalization in disguise. Corruption seemed to corrode not only politics but language itself, and the old political vocabulary appeared to have lost any discernible meaning. This was when the French philosopher Jean Baudrillard, who for years had claimed the "death of the event" — in a consumerist society saturated by mass media, nothing really new can ever happen — acquired the status of a prophet, and when Michel Houellebecq started to publish his novels on planned, mass sexuality as the sole horizon of the coming century. In such a context, Thiriart and de Benoist's "red-brown" theory sounded less like a fascist invention than the framing of the current zeitgeist. People in intellectual circles began to praise philosophical *negativity* as a necessary answer to the new global order. Anything was better, it seemed, than what was imposed on the world by the new empire. Regardless of their past affiliation, what was left of the ideological rebellions of previous centuries against the bourgeois order should unite.

Added to this mindset was the complex relationship to the Occupation years that France imposed on itself in the nineties. As early as 1991, it was revealed that President Mitterrand — the man who'd brought the left to power — was a lifelong friend of René Bousquet, a high-ranking civil servant during the war who had been responsible for the famous Vel' d'Hiv' roundup, during which thirteen thousand Jews were arrested in two days in July 1942. Now we learned that Bousquet had partly financed Mitterrand's 1981 campaign. The scandal was pernicious because Mitterrand stood firmly by Bousquet in the name of friendship and blamed the press, even as Bousquet was being indicted for crimes against humanity. In 1993, before the trial could take place, a lonely, failed writer and an outcast of sorts, Christian Didier, shot him dead at home. (Later sentenced to five years, Didier died of cancer.) The Barbie trial, some years earlier, and the Papon trial, some years later, bookended the period, only ten years after the release of Claude Lanzmann's *Shoah,* for the first time since the war that the French public became fully aware of the specificities of the fate of the Jews in the country during the Occupation years. In the official culture, however, this realization translated into a *"devoir de mémoire"*—a duty to remember—that soon became asphyxiating and reinforced a desire for transgression.

Meanwhile, exotic characters such as the Russian writer and former Communist Eduard Limonov, who split his time between Paris and Moscow, where he'd set up the National Bolshevik Party with Alexander Dugin, became the rage among intelligentsia. In the magazine I was working for at the time, for instance, he could show up priding himself for having spent time in Serbia with Milošević's militias, shooting in the street. Not that he was the only one, either. Two hours away from Paris by plane, the Balkan wars were actually a trendy hot spot for anti-liberal intellectuals boasting of being politically incorrect and in search of a new battlefield. They weren't alone in this. In the *cités,* young Muslims, too, traveled on their own to Croatia to join the Muslim brigades set up and financed there by the Saudis—and by Osama bin Laden.

In retrospect, that search for a politically incorrect stand against the society of spectacle finds its most disturbing example in the person of Stéphane Charbonnier, who, under the nickname Charb, would die from the Kalashnikov bullets shot by the Kouachi brothers when he was chief editor of the weekly *Charlie Hebdo,* during the first attack of the terror wave in early January 2015. In 1991, Charb was a hardcore Communist Party sympathizer. (He remained so more or less all his life and, on his request, "The Internationale" was sung at his burial.) In 1991, two years after the fatwa against Salman Rushdie, Charb wrote two different columns in a hard-up fanzine named *La Grosse Bertha.* One was called "Charb Does Not Like People," and the other, bafflingly enough, "The Fatwa of the Ayatollah Charb." One year later, he joined several cartoonists in relaunching *Charlie Hebdo*—a magazine that had had its hour of glory in the seventies and stood as a symbol of a more joyful era in France, an era when liberal prosperity and full employment in real life went hand in hand with dreams of Marxist revolution in culture. Once the new version of the magazine was on its way, Charb and his friends sat down in search of a name for the managerial company that would handle it, a name that would reflect the guerrilla-like culture war they intended to launch. Later, that name would change to the more benign "Rotary Press," but when they first registered the company, it was under the name "Kalashnikov Editions."

What kind of imaginary world was thus convened? But, of course, nobody thought seriously that words had any power to influence reality any longer: we were living, after all, in the society of spectacle where nothing could happen.

Curiously enough, that mindset may well have been prophesized in the early days of the Cold War by Simone de Beauvoir, in the sequel of the speech she gives to her character Scriassine in *Les Mandarins,* already quoted in the foreword of this book. After having mocked the French for being unable to know whether they won or lost the war, Scriassine goes on and focuses on the intellectuals:

> French intellectuals are at a dead end. Their art, their way of thinking, will retain any meaning only as long as a certain civilization can maintain itself. [But] progress in science and technology, economic changes, are going to shake the world so that even our ways of thinking and feeling things will be revolutionized ...Among other things, art and literature—these two sources of French prestige—will be outdated.[11]

These lines were published in 1954. Do they not constitute a cruel but convincing explanation for the pull of the Communist Party in French culture—an influence that lasted until the mid-eighties? Is it too much to say that, after the Vichy regime, the party answered an anxiety among French intellectuals, allowing them to find relevance in a new, changing world, even at the price of a lie? And is it far-fetched to argue that, on the right, France's fading imperialism was fighting the same fight for survival — trying to build up a third-worldish "Arab policy" to ensure a posthumous life for the empire?

In any case, in the nineties, as the global order seemed to be taking hold and Scriassine's prophecy was becoming truer than ever, what had appeared to be a solution was again in shambles. As Philippe Muray, one of the most talented essayists in France, wrote in 2000, in lines that both echo Scriassine and appear involuntarily prophetic: "What are we to become without general strikes, without riots, without fanatical kamikazes killing themselves en masse? All these makeshift expressions of history, they were still a kind of solution. They didn't happen. The Barbarians let us down. Godot abstained himself. The planes did not fall."[12]

Well, they were just about to.

VOTE-CATCHING IN THE *CITÉS*

It was this insurrectional spirit that allowed for the breakthrough of Le Pen in April 2002. There is almost a foreshadowing of the 2016 U.S. elections in this event: that the moderate left-wing, liberal candidate, Lionel Jospin, would win was pretty much a given in the same way Hillary Clinton was practically inside the White House even before the first round. Instead, Jospin lost the first round to Le Pen, in large because, not unlike Hillary Clinton, he had been judged too much on the side of what the French call *la gauche caviar* and Americans call "the limousine left." As a consequence, left-wingers — unknowingly acting out the red-brown rapprochement — simply refused to vote for him, casting their ballots instead in favor of a multitude of micro-leftist formations, splitting the vote and opening the way for the National Front.

By then, however, the red-brown alliance theorized by de Benoist and Thiriart and boosted by the depressing cultural broth of the nineties had been put to the test. While fueling fear and support for the National Front in a growing segment of the French public, the terror attacks in New York and Washington had also raised the aforementioned dilemma within the far right: In light of the new terror age, were the reactionary tendencies inside the Muslim world to be supported against global capitalism? Or, to the contrary, was Israel to be defended—not as the country of cosmopolitan Jewry, but as the leading edge of Western nationalism against the barbarians?

I had the chance to witness a direct manifestation of this political stretching in French extreme-right circles when, in the spring of 2000, a writer by the name of Renaud Camus (no connection with Albert) published his journal, in which he lambasted "the Jews"—for being too dominant in French culture and for not being able "to fully understand the French tradition." Because Camus was a disciple of Roland Barthes and of the poet Louis Aragon—and because, as should now be clear to the reader, French conservative trends transcend political affiliation—the journal was praised in the left-oriented press without anyone focusing on these lines. Because I was the editor of the literary section in *Les Inrockuptibles,* a trendy cultural newsmagazine, itself on the left, the tedious task of exposing the anti-Semitic passages fell to me. The unhealthy debate that ensued to determine whether or not Camus was anti-Semitic lasted for three months, with everyone in Paris (or so it seemed) taking sides, sometimes in quite an unexpected way. (The philosopher Alain Finkielkraut sided with Camus, and was taken to task for it in *Le Monde* by Claude Lanzmann.) The point, in any case, is that one year later, in the wake of 9/11, the same Camus turned into an ardent Zionist and a fierce anti-Muslim while becoming, at the same time, the official writer of the National Front.

Alain Soral went the other way. A former Communist, he began to travel to Moscow at Dugin's invitation in the early 2000s. In time, he would write the foreword for the French edition of

Dugin's book *The Fourth Political Theory* while making it onto the cover of de Benoist's *Éléments*. In 2004, when he got in touch with Dieudonné, he was operating for the National Front as an adviser on social issues and the problems of the *cités*.

There was a sense in the party that, despite its racist DNA, the National Front could reach a significant fraction of the Muslim voters who, being born and raised as French, could feel threatened by the more recent waves of immigrants and therefore embrace Le Pen's credo. Muslim conservatism on family matters and gender issues was thought to carry some potential. In January 2014, the Day of Wrath march would prove this intuition to be true, at least in part.

The irony, of course, is this: the "liberal" side of the party, from which emanated this idea of prospecting the *cités* in search of new voters, immediately clashed with the anti-Semitic rhetoric that was considered the best means for accomplishing it. Impersonated by Soral, the "Dugin side," so to speak, of the National Front worked with the assumption that the anti-Jewish bias would best seduce the electorate in question. Hence the call to Dieudonné.

Needless to say, sources of financing played their part as well: by Dieudonné and Soral's admission, Tehran at least partly financed the short-lived Anti-Zionist Party they put together in 2009 for the European elections. Coincidentally—if it is indeed a coincidence—the nine-million-euro loan granted by Russia to the National Front five years later, in 2014, transited through a small bank called the First Czech-Russian Bank, an establishment said to be close to Putin and to service Iran trade facilities.[13]

By the same token, the trips Soral and Dieudonné made to Syria in those years coincided with the activities of Marine Le Pen's long-time friend and moneyman Frédéric Chatillon, whose advertising agency, Riwal, managed the National Front's communications for years while a subsidiary company called Riwal Syria was under contract with Bashar al-Assad's government.

There is hardly a doubt, then, that between the mid-2000s and

2015 at least, through personalities like Alain Soral and with the support of Russia, the NF tried to build a united front of conservatives that would extend from the traditional French extreme right to some areas of the Muslim population. That front coalesced around questions such as gay marriage and "globalism" and found its momentum during the Day of Wrath march in January 2014, which led, two months later, during the municipal elections, to the complete demise of the left across the country. It was also during that same march that anti-Semitic slogans were heard in the streets of Paris for the first time since World War II. Meanwhile, anti-Jewish aggressions rose from that month on, to reach the astonishing level of eight hundred—two a day—by the end of the year. Ironically, then, this attempt toward a "non-racist approach" on the part of the National Front, its desire to reach a hand toward the world of the *banlieues,* helped to give way to the worst anti-Semitic campaign France has known. The inevitable question, of course, is: Were Soral and Dieudonné right to use anti-Jewish biases as a tool to reach the *cités?*

THREE
"The Little Prince of the Maghreb"

H e was thirty-four years old when we met, in the spring of 2016, an unemployed nurse whose internship at the Pitié-Salpêtrière Hospital, in Paris, was briskly cut short the week the *Charlie Hebdo*/Hyper Cacher slaughter occurred. The victims had been shot by his own ex-disciples and were brought into the very unit he was working in that day.

"I understand, I do," he said in the Bastille café he chose for our appointment. "The hospital knew of my past from day one, but when something like that happens, not to want me around is only natural."[1]

Back in 2003, barely twenty-one but looking more like fifteen —a pale, almost gray silhouette with something androgynous in his adolescent, almost elf-like features—he would go from his day shift as a maintenance employee to the Adda'wa Mosque, in the Belleville quarter, once a week. It was one of the biggest mosques in Europe, with three to five thousand believers every Friday, and to the youngest fraction of these he would deliver his teaching, a commentary on the Three Fundamental Principles of Muhammad bin

Abdul Wahhab, along with praises for Al Qaeda in Iraq and entreat-ies to the youth to join the jihad there.

Photos from that era show him at the peak of his stardom in Belleville: a red-and-white *keffiyeh* tied up on his head, hair down his shoulders, sunglasses half hiding the soft face, and his body dis-appearing under an Afghan *shalwar kameez,* somewhat impressive in spite of, or because of, the obvious frailty, a character out of a Wil-liam S. Burroughs novel. Farid Benyettou is his name. Among his most dedicated students were Chérif and Saïd Kouachi, then aged twenty-one and twenty-three, the future killers of the *Charlie Hebdo* journalists. "Each time he spoke, it just felt like the truth," Chérif Kouachi, the younger one, said at their trial in 2008, three years af-ter their arrest for having set up the first network in France to send jihadists to Iraq. The Kouachis held Benyettou in such high esteem at the time that they had even started pressuring their sister, Aïcha, to divorce her husband and marry him instead. (She refused.)

How did they meet?

"Chérif Kouachi wanted to leave for Iraq soon, and, what I taught being considered good preparation for such an enterprise, someone I knew asked if the Kouachi brothers could follow my teaching," Benyettou explained. "I said yes, sure, no problem. Why not? Then they showed up at the mosque. As simple as that."

"Someone you knew?" I asked.

"Yes," he said.

"Someone who stayed in France, who's in France to this day?"

"Yes."

"This was during the war in Iraq. People would come to you, regular people, and they would recommend friends or acquain-tances willing to go fighting, because they thought your religious training would fit their project, give it maybe some legitimacy? But they themselves, these people acting as go-between, although they did not oppose the general purpose of jihad, they wouldn't leave? They stayed?"

"That is correct."

"And what happened to them? Do we know? Did they change their minds? Are they still around?"

This, Benyettou said, he did not know.

He was short, had a sallow complexion, uncombed black hair, and a thin, curly beard at the tip of his chin. He wore a colorless, dusty jacket—it was a bit difficult to picture him as the physical instructor of the "Buttes-Chaumont network," as the police called the gang, after the park of the same name, the Parc des Buttes-Chaumont, near which Benyettou lived with his parents at the time, a few minutes away from the Belleville mosque. According to the investigation, he used the park as a makeshift military training ground of sorts between 2003 and 2005, preparing jihadis for the trip to Iraq to kill Americans.

Benyettou shrugged. "That is what the press and the cops said," he commented, with a pale, dismissive smile. "But even the judge at the trial did not take that seriously. It is Chérif Kouachi who had come up with this idea of running in the park—it had nothing to do with anything, he just thought it would be good for me to train a little. Fact is, very soon after we began to run, the cops arrested us and that put an end to it. I don't even know why they bothered arresting us in the first place."

The arrest may have had something to do with Benyettou introducing his joggers one day to a mysterious man who allegedly provided them with rough sketches on the handling of a Kalashnikov. The drawings were exhibited by the prosecution at the 2008 trial, as evidence of the military nature of the training. Not particularly convincing, though. A few sketches . . . a few runs in the park . . . a religious teaching displayed by a kid who looked so young that journalists covering the trial nicknamed him the Little Prince from the Maghreb. "Please, draw me an AK-47"—did it make any sense? The sketches were said to have been drawn in the middle of the street, in full daylight, by an enigmatic sketch artist who had just come out of the Métro and reentered it in a blink. Again, a scene from a Burroughs novel.

This was the 2000s. That some of Benyettou's disciples had indeed ended up on the Iraqi battlefield, that three of them were killed there in 2004, was seen by the judge as well as by the press almost as a coincidence, the inconsequential result of childish impulses meeting adult reality.

And, maybe because the connection with something as serious as a war was hard to envision, nobody paid that much attention to the incident Chérif Kouachi said had triggered his awakening to jihad. He claimed he had been unfairly dismissed from some shitty job by "a Jew" some years back, that this was what had made him understand how the world really worked when it came to Muslims. Answering the prosecutor who was underlining this as an obvious sign of his anti-Semitism, Chérif Kouachi's lawyer brushed off the argument as "an obvious exaggeration." And while Benyettou was sentenced to six years, Kouachi got only a few months, and expressed his more sincere regrets as the verdict was announced. He had been, he said, the victim of a group dynamic he had no control over. That dynamic had led him to project a courage he never possessed, so he actually was grateful to the cops and to the tribunal that sent him to prison, off the street, free from the spell of fear and temptation he'd fallen under.

Today Benyettou still defines himself as a practicing Muslim, but he has stopped any kind of radical teaching, and he condemns the *Charlie Hebdo* killings, as he does all terror acts. He says that his first doubts about his actions came in prison. While waiting for his trial in jail as a DPS—*détenu particulièrement surveillé,* or closely monitored detainee—between 2005 and 2008, he was looked up to by cellmates as a sort of "emir," and he began to secretly listen to music—which, according to his own teaching, was *haram*—and to study math and history at the prison's library. Once freed, in 2009, his first move was to put his *shalwar kameez* back on and go straight to teaching at the mosque, but he soon realized that things had changed and he progressively distanced himself from the most radicalized among his pupils. The final divorce with Salafi jihadism happened in 2012, when, in the aftermath of the killing of three Jewish children in Toulouse — more on this below — these same pupils asked him to teach them the *hadith* that sanctioned the killing of children. It was then, he says, that he fully realized how wrong his teaching was. He cut his ties with the mosque, began looking for professional training, chose to become a nurse, and that's how he ended up at La Salpetrière hospital, where his past brutally caught up with him in January 2015. He resigned from the hospital and, aware of his moral responsibility, joined an association specializing in "de-radicalization," handled by a Muslim anthropologist.

Benyettou's assessment is probably genuine. There is no reason to doubt his commitment to de-radicalization, and the account he gives of his own journey to come to terms with Islamism rings true. He also acknowledges Chérif Kouachi's fierce anti-Semitism — an anti-Semitism that led Kouachi to harass some of Benyettou's Jewish neighbors each time he came to visit. The difficulty here is that the picture of the Buttes-Chaumont gang we are left with through his testimony does not radically differ from the ones journalists and judges were offered in 2008 — namely, a bunch of lost, discriminated underdogs who played together in the park and somehow, because of Benyettou's influence as much as of the wrong path they had taken, ended up, in some cases, on a Middle Eastern battlefield and, in others, inside *Charlie Hebdo*'s offices. Things, however, appear to be more complicated.

THE SYRIAN AGENT

Aside from the Kouachi brothers, one of Benyettou's first disciples in 2001 was Boubaker El Hakim, twenty-three. El Hakim was French, born in Paris, of Tunisian descent, and worked as a salesclerk in the Monoprix supermarket chain, the French A&P. El Hakim was the first of Benyettou's devotees to actually travel to the Middle East — not to Iraq, where the kids ultimately planned to go, but, curiously enough, to Syria, with the intention of completing his religious training. It was there, as police investigations have revealed, that he was recruited by Syrian intelligence as early as 2002.

How the connection originated between a bunch of lost proletarian kids from the Belleville quarter and a Syrian religious center with ties to Syrian intelligence is unknown to this day. As in many other episodes in this book, the role played by the Syrians in El Hakim's subsequent journey remains unexplained.

In any case, traveling back and forth between Damascus, Iraq, and Paris from then until his arrest in 2005, El Hakim was able to handle logistics for the inexperienced jihadists of the Buttes-Chaumont gang once they arrived on-site. He thus came to have considerable influence over the other "joggers." Adding to his aura were the interviews he gave in Iraq in 2003 to the French national radio outlet RTL, in which he displayed a childish enthusiasm in freestyle rap: "I'm from Paris, Nineteenth [Arrondissement]! To all my pals in the Nineteenth, I say come over! Come over to jihad! Me, I'm ready to blow myself up! Throw dynamite and *boom-boom!* I'm from France! I'm from Belleville! Americans, we're gonna kill! We'll kill everybody! *Allahu akbar!*" (That these sentiments could be aired on French national media at all, while synagogues and Jews had been under pressure since 2000, is a good indication of the mindset in the country at the time.) El Hakim was also the real "coach" in those training sessions in Parc Buttes-Chaumont, for which Benyettou provided the religious-ideological justification, and there is every reason to believe that the man who sketched the Kalashnikov drawings was, in fact, him, not the mysterious stranger the gang pinned the blame on at their trial in 2008. This raises the obvious question of what Benyettou knew of El Hakim's activities and connections at the time.

At that same trial, El Hakim was sentenced, like the rest of the group, to seven years for conspiracy. Having already served half that time, he walked free in 2011, and almost immediately he flew to Tunisia, where the overthrow of Zine al-Abidine Ben Ali's autocratic regime had just given rise to what has been known ever since as the Arab Spring. Needless to say, the hope that this movement would expand and help spread democracy in the Arab world was, for most of the regimes, a concern.

More freedom, however, meant less police surveillance. El Hakim's idea—or his instruction—was to use these new freedoms in Tunisia to better undermine the regime that had just allowed them. And that is exactly what he did.

The local branch of the Libyan terror group known as Ansar al-Sharia, which he set up in no time, had the progressive lawyer Chokri Belaïd executed that same year. In Tunis in 2013, he personally gunned down, in full daylight, a Tunisian left-wing representative named Mohamed Brahmi. El Hakim is also thought to have given the green light for the massacre at the Bardo National Museum, which claimed twenty-two victims in Tunisia the following spring.

"Kill anyone," he advised future French jihadists in a propaganda interview published on *Dabiq,* the ISIS online magazine, in the spring of 2015. "Don't waste your energy looking for difficult targets. Kill every infidel in France."[2] According to the journalist David Thomson, El Hakim had joined ISIS at the beginning of that year and had been appointed head of international operations. The part he may or may not have played in the synchronized attacks of November 2015 in Paris is unknown, as is the extent of his links with Syrian intelligence at the time. In December 2016, he was killed by an American drone strike.

So Benyettou wasn't simply the tentative instructor of a bunch of losers and amateurs who progressively lost control. He was the religious mentor to the very first group of petty criminals who started out in France in the fall of 2001 as seekers of transcendence and identity, then carried on as would-be jihadists and ended up becoming some of the most spectacular terrorist sociopaths of the following decade, whose actions would be felt in France and abroad. The connection that at least one of them had with a foreign intelligence service, namely the Syrian, and to what extent Benyettou may have known about it, remains a mystery to this day. But another point still deserves examination.

THE ALGERIAN CONNECTION

Benyettou grew up the third of four children in a large six-room apartment in the Nineteenth Arrondissement of Paris. His father, a maintenance worker, had settled there after coming from Algeria in the 1970s, and his mother did not work. His teaching position at the mosque, according to his own telling, happened almost by chance.

One day in 2001, when he was still in high school, spending his free time after class studying Islam on his own, someone came to him and offered him the job, as he recalled:

> My family was religious, but in a simple, traditional way. And as I reached adolescence, I felt the need to learn more. So I began to study alone. I did meet some religious people once. Salafi people, Algerian men — it was at a family wedding in a *cité* in 1996. I was impressed by their piety; they struck me as the real thing, and I asked them for books to read in order to advance toward perfection. But I did not stay with them. I preferred to study at home, by myself. Here in France, you see, the preachers have no real training — they're autodidacts, most of them, and that was even truer for me. I just read a lot. But the word spread that I was serious, so someone came to me one day. He told me that since 2000, new people had been coming to the mosque en masse — young-

sters, kids who mostly knew nothing of religion. And wouldn't it be great if I could lend a hand with the teaching there, as I was myself young and could understand them better while being so well read at the same time. So I went. And I realized that, although they had entered religion very recently and indeed knew nothing, the zeal in these youngsters was such that they already considered themselves to be learned men. They were consequently very, very judgmental toward the traditional imam, for whom they had barely any respect at all. But me, yes, they respected. Because I provided Salafi teaching of the kind they were looking for. So I thought, *Yes, I can be useful. I can teach them something.* That's how it happened. As simple as that.

Except that it wasn't. After Farid Benyettou's arrest in 2005, investigators searched the family's apartment. They found no fewer than twelve hundred religious books in Arabic and as many audiotapes — hardly the material of the "simple, traditional family" Benyettou says they were.

There is every reason to think that the arrival of this material coincided with that of a man named Youssef Zemmouri, who in 1996 traveled to France from Algeria to marry Asmahou, Benyettou's sister. He moved in with the entire family in the Buttes-Chaumont apartment, the young bride covering herself with a *niqab* according to her new husband's instructions. Since Benyettou claims he had his decisive encounter with Salafis "by chance" that very year at a wedding, one can deduce that the Salafis in question were none other than Zemmouri and his friends. Benyettou was sixteen years old at the time.

By then, as it turned out, Zemmouri already appeared on an Algerian most-wanted list as a member of an organization called Groupe Salafiste pour la Prédication et le Combat, or the Salafist Group for Preaching and Combat (GSPC). The GSPC was a dissident organization of the Groupe Islamique Armé (Armed Islamic Group), the GIA, one the most violent terror organizations in Algeria at the time. (After the civil war ended, the GSPC mutated into Al Qaeda in the Islamic Maghreb.) In such a context, the marriage between Zemmouri and Benyettou's sister seems likely to have been an arrangement to provide the husband with a safe house and a hiding place away from the Algerian military police and intelligence. It is possible that Benyettou's parents acted out of personal conviction or as a repayment for some kind of debt, or both. Two years later, in 1998, Zemmouri was arrested and charged with plotting a terror attack against the World Cup, being played that year in France.

Zemmouri would not have been the first among the FIS operatives of the period to enter French territory at the time, some even as political refugees. Many showed up during those years, with the task, first, of setting up Islamist networks and using France and Europe as a base to provide weapons, money, and future mujahideen to the cause in Algeria, then performing attacks in France itself. People like Kamar Eddine Kherbane, co-founder of the Front Islamique du Salut—Islamic Salvation Front—or FIS, who arrived in Paris as early as 1990 straight from Peshawar, Pakistan, and is now living a peaceful life in Algeria; people like Anwar Haddam, the main speaker at the Islamist meetings touring France in support of the Algerian killers, who in 1992, after being expelled by Paris, was granted political asylum in the United States as a host of the American Muslim Council, an organization financed by the Saudis; people like the engineer Mohamed Kerrouche, later arrested and charged with terrorism. And also less high-ranking, anonymous men who traveled to France as political refugees or simply through family ties and marriage, like Benyettou's brother-in-law, Youssef Zemmouri. Together they boosted the "Salafi revolution" that changed Islam in France and, turning mainstream in less than a decade, became the best provider of answers to that significant fraction of the discarded French Muslim youth that was getting in touch with its own alienated rage.

The previous chapter focused on the networks emanating from the French New Right, which, driven by its anti-modern stance and its fascist heritage, began targeting the *cités* in the early 2000s with a political offer based on anti-Semitic propaganda, with the hope of attracting a new electorate there, on the one hand, and with the prospect of being sponsored in doing so by foreign operatives such as Iran, Syria, and Russia, on the other. The difficult question of how accurate their calculation was, however—whether or not a corresponding *demand* for such an offer existed in the *cités* at the time—has to be addressed, but in order to do so, we must first look into this *other* offer, the Algerian-Salafi one, which preceded the extreme right's by ten years in the *cités* and changed Islam in France. It is necessary, in other words, to travel back in time, and across the Mediterranean, and settle in Algeria for a while.

Algeria, the first colony of the modern French Empire, the place where the French imperialist narrative was shaped—where, in a sense, it all started. Algeria, where, in the early nineties, after years of rampant social and economic crisis, Islamists and a corrupt government clashed and the country plunged into an extremely brutal civil war that, by the end of the decade, would claim a total of 200,000 victims, mostly women and children.

To get a sense of what happened, and how it affected France, in addition to interviews I conducted with witnesses of the era, I will be relying here, for chronology and quotes, on the following books: *La Nébuleuse Islamique en France et en Algérie,* by the Algerian journalist Hassane Zerrouky; *Histoire Secrète de l'Algérie Indépendante,* by the Algeria journalist Mohamed Sifaoui; and *Chronique des Années de Sang,* from the former agent of Algerian intelligence Mohamed Samraoui: three travel guides, so to speak, to lead us along the blood-soaked trail that brings us to the current terror wave inside France.

FOUR
The Algerian Factor

lgeria began to unravel in the fall of 1988, one year before the Berlin Wall crumbled—we're back, once again, to the end of the Cold War. The crisis, though, had deeper, localized roots.

In 1962, the year it became independent, the country rivaled Cuba as an international emblem of the third world battle for freedom and against imperialism, and, as in Cuba, the USSR came almost immediately to the aid of the country. In a handful of years, as a result, the Front de Libération Nationale, the FLN, which had been the party of resistance against the French, purged itself of inner opposition and came to rule the country alone, with the help of the army, through a system pretty much in accordance with any republic of the Eastern Bloc: free speech limited; democratic and ethnic minorities repressed, in this case the Kabyle Berber people; arbitrary arrests and torture; exile and assassination of political opponents; favoritism and bribes. A planned economy made a free market and consumerism impossible, while an oligarchy free to monopolize the enormous resources provided by the oil and gas trade diverted public money through a system of front companies and straw men, spending their fortune in the capital of the former empire where they lived part of the time—and where, thanks to France's "Arab policy," France's industrialists and politicians were no strangers to that system, either. As for the French public, despite the percentage of Algerian migrants in the country, it was blind to all this and simply saw Algeria as a tourist destination.

By 1980, corruption plagued the FLN Party and state and local administrations. The Algerian economy was in deep recession, with unemployment reaching 20 percent nationwide, while half of the population was under thirty-five. Religious conservatism prevailed in the rural areas, the cities were the subject of another sort of moralistic propaganda, a Socialist one, and the mix of the two resulted in an intense atmosphere of bigotry from which only a minority of intellectuals among the urban population were able to escape. For the rest of the country's inhabitants, lack of money stopped people from traveling, anarchic urban development created a major housing crisis and, in cities like Algiers, forced families to live together in small, cramped apartments. The nation had become an open-air prison. The sole distractions were football and the mosques.

During the first years of that decade, however, young Algerians were able to find an outlet for their unrest in underground networks set up with Saudi money, operated by the Muslim Brotherhood, and unofficially tolerated by Algerian intelligence. These networks conveyed Muslim volunteers to Afghanistan to fight with the Taliban against the Russian invasion. The link between that fight and the rebellion against the domestic situation was all the more natural since the USSR backed the ruling FLN Party in Algiers. No one knows the exact number of young men sent during the 1980s from Algeria to a structure in Peshawar, Pakistan, called Beit al-Ansar, financed and managed directly by Osama bin Laden, where they received military and ideological training. The Algerian consulate in Pakistan, however, reports 2,800 visas officially delivered between 1985 and 1989, to which must be added the hundreds of travelers who transited through Saudi Arabia under the pretext of a pilgrimage to Mecca. Once the war was over, these young men simply returned to Algeria.

In the meantime, an intelligentsia with close ties to the Egyptian Muslim Brotherhood began to advocate "the completion of the Algerian revolution" that had begun in 1962 with the departure of the French. The revolution, they claimed, was a three-stage missile. Stage one had been independence from the French Empire; number two was economic growth, which, despite appearances, was a success, providing that Algerians understood how to manage their country; and number three, which would teach them precisely how to do that, was the identity revolution. What they meant by this was the setting up of an "Arabization" program for Algerian society altogether. Pretty much in accordance with a state identity policy, it implied the giving up of "neocolonial values," such as French language and French education, as well as equality between women and men, considered a Western practice. As for the government, it had to redeem itself from its corrupt, Socialist sins by adopting Muslim measures. Only this, they claimed, would solve the social and moral crisis Algeria was going through. Because of its anti-imperialist flavor, this current, which called itself "the Arabist movement," found some support on the other side of the Mediterranean in Paris, where left-wing journalists and politicians saw in its religious aspect nothing more than an expression of authentic culture: something less dangerous than fanaticism, but, precisely for that reason, something genuine that only neocolonial minds would dare to counter.

The man who ruled over the FLN and over the country from El Mouradia presidential palace in Algiers, was Chadli Bendjedid. He had been elected in 1979 with 99.4 percent of the ballots. As always in such a situation, this lack of parliamentary opposition only boosted intrigue and rivalries inside the circles of the powerful. Chadli's predecessor, Houari Boumédienne, was so wary of his entourage that, once diagnosed with Waldenstrom's disease, a rare form of blood cancer, he had chosen to travel to Moscow to be treated there by incompetent doctors rather than be taken care of at home. After his death, in 1978, the council of the unique Party FLN, composed of apparatchiks and high-ranking officers, had appointed Chadli in large part because he had served under Boumédienne's orders during the War of Independence and was thought an obedient, malleable man. Yet, since he had entered El Mouradia, Chadli, aware of the way he was perceived, had embarked on a series of maneuvers to extradite himself from that web of advisers who thought they could control him. Instead he was trying to build up his own circle. For this, he needed the street.

Apart from "the Arabists," the most important opposition in the country at the time came from the Kabyle Berbers. In 1980, the Kabylie region had seen the birth of a "Berber Spring"—a cultural and political movement calling for the end of repression against ethnic and cultural minorities and for pluralism and democracy. But the main leaders of this movement were considered traitors and lived in exile, which meant that Chadli could not ally himself with them without undermining his own power and appearing to be a traitor himself—not in a country like Algeria, where, despite or because of the corruption, it seemed that all that remained to sustain the population's pride was religion and a virulent nationalism, inherited from the revolutionary past. "Algeria is an Arab and Muslim country," Chadli declared in 1980, in response to the Berber Spring, in a statement that Ismayl Urbain would certainly have approved. By saying so, he had just aligned himself with the Arabist camp.

In 1981, the French-Arabic bilingual educational system in place since independence was thus banned from schools in favor of an exclusively Arabic one. Three years later, the liberal, "Westernized" family code was repealed in favor of a set of laws legalizing polygamy and repudiation and limiting women's rights.

But this was not enough for Chadli, who also had in mind a series of economic reforms that, pretty much like those introduced to

Russia in the nineties, under the pretext of liberalizing the country, would allow him and his clan to better control the finances and resources of the state, to their own advantage. To accomplish that, he first had to marginalize the political commissars of the Socialist FLN who, along with the generals of the Algerian army, had the power to stop him. Operation Potemkin, as the plan concocted by Chadli and his clan was called, referring to the Eisenstein movie, consisted of stirring up a series of limited social protests across the country: he would use the social anger to create a controlled political crisis by which, with the apparent support of the street, he would get rid of the FLN barons and their allies in the army.

Operation Potemkin was launched on September 19, during Chadli's annual speech on social issues. "In some countries," he declared in front of a dumbfounded audience, "citizens do not hesitate to take to the streets in order to defend their own interests when prices are too high." His message was received loud and clear. Three weeks later, on October 4, in the middle of the night, the popular neighborhood of Bab-el-Oued was in flames. In the morning, around 100,000 demonstrators invaded the streets, curiously devoid of any police force. Among them mingled agents provocateurs from the military intelligence, sent by Chadli.

But another secret service, controlled by the FLN barons who had understood Chadli's maneuver, was there, too. Armed, in plain clothes, and driving unmarked cars, they began to shoot at the crowd. This was when Operation Potemkin turned to chaos. As the first bodies fell, the anger of the crowd became uncontrollable, ministries were ransacked, and Chadli had no choice but to call the very generals he wanted to get rid of. Under the guidance of the minister of defense, General Khaled Nezzar, tanks and helicopters deployed in the capital and fired without restraint. In five days of protests, Operation Potemkin ended up with five hundred dead, thousands wounded, and arrests by the dozens, which resulted in either disappearance or torture. The population had been the victim of the palace's inner war.

The main political force to come to the rescue of the demonstrators with medical support, by transforming the mosques into makeshift hospitals, was the Islamists. Soon afterwards, they regrouped into one party, the Front Islamique du Salut (FIS), or Islamic Salvation Front.

In February, unmoved and unrestrained, President Chadli went according to plan. He announced a new constitution, which, in effect, ended the one-party rule in place since 1962 and authorized political pluralism. Local and national elections were announced in the two coming years: Chadli looked like a liberal. In Paris, the French applauded. (In Moscow, meanwhile, Gorbachev, implementing his perestroika program, was launching a new Congress of People's Deputies through new elections as well.)

Among the newly legalized political parties that Chadli intended to use to his benefit was the brand-new FIS.

As stated by one of its thirty-five founders and its leader, Ali Belhadj, in the inaugural speech he gave at the Ibn Badis Mosque, in the Algiers suburb of Kouba, on March 21, 1989, the FIS's goal was "the establishment of an authentic Islamist society dedicated to the mission to save the Algerian people, humanity and civilization."

In an interview he gave to the daily Algerian paper *Horizons* two days later, however, Ali Belhadj clarified what, for him, salvation meant: "There is no democracy, because the sole source of power is Allah, through the Koran, not the people, and when the people vote against God's law, it is nothing but a blasphemy, and in such a case, you must kill them all."[1]

"IN ORDER TO CLEAN UP THIS COUNTRY, WE ARE READY TO LIQUIDATE TWO MILLION"

The violence announced from day one by Belhadj became real for the Algerians as soon as the municipal campaign began one year later, when unveiled women were randomly attacked in the streets and political rallies ransacked. Whether this violence was necessary at all is debatable, since the FIS was indeed popular. In any case, on June 12, the day of the municipal elections, it won 54 percent of the ballots, becoming the leading political party in the country.

The year and a half that followed, up until legislative elections, saw the cities administered by the Islamists introducing a series of civic reforms unheard of in Algeria. The corruption of the FLN's civil servants was denounced and banned, local social services and welfare were reformed and improved, and "Islamist markets" were set up in public places for the poor and needy. Women, of course, paid the price: they were forbidden to go to beaches, and the *hijab* became mandatory. As for the parabolic antennas that allowed people to receive French and Western channels, they were dubbed "paradiabolic" and their use forbidden.

The 1990 Gulf War was another occasion for the FIS to demonstrate its strength. The movement launched a general strike in support of Saddam Hussein, successfully blocking banks, administrations, and high schools across the country. Back from bin Laden's training camps, Afghan veterans set up paramilitary parades in public places: in schoolyards, soccer fields, and beaches. Meanwhile, on Fridays, FIS militants surrounding the mosques forced regular Algerians to follow the group's religious practices regardless of their own, personal choices.

On December 23, 1991, three days before the legislative elections, the guest star at an FIS rally in Algiers was a man called Saïd Mohammedi. Mohammedi is of interest in our story because he provides a link between the several worlds explored in this book. Born in 1912, a veteran of the War of Independence and a minister of the first government of Socialist Algeria, he was also a deeply religious man, and during World War II his faith had led him to enlist with the 13th Waffen Mountain Division of the SS Handschar, the all-Muslim Nazi legion founded in May 1942 in Croatia by the grand mufti of Jerusalem. On December 23, 1991, during the FIS rally, Saïd

Mohammedi said this: "The day of the elections will be the day of separation between the miscreants and the Muslims. We will win because it is written in the sky, and you will be the first liberators of Palestine. We will get rid of neocolonial forces and of all those who want to smother Islam. In order to clean up this country [Algeria] and build an Islamic state, we are ready to liquidate two million of its inhabitants."[2]

The project was clear, and it was public: an Islamic state would emerge in Algeria from a massive blood sacrifice that would purify the country of its neocolonial values—after which Algerians would march to free Palestine from the Jews.

Three days after that speech, in the first round of the elections, the Islamists won 46 percent of the ballots, giving them 188 of the 430 seats. The FLN, the party in power since independence, received only 23.5 percent—16 seats—and the rest was shared among minority democratic groups. The abstention rate was 41 percent; only 24 percent of the registered electors had actually voted. The FIS, now the first party in the country if the abstention rate was disregarded, could set its sights on an absolute majority after the second round. "Algeria has reconnected with its authentic Islamic identity," one of its leaders, Abdelkader Hachani, told the French newspaper *Libération*. At the Essuna Mosque, in Bab-el-Oued, a few days later, he added this—which, the references to Islam notwithstanding, could have come from Dugin, de Benoist, or Maurras: "Our fight is the fight of Islamic purity against democratic impurity . . . Democracy is championed by the West on the pretense of defending freedoms, the freedoms of the homosexuals, which brought us Communism, Marxism and Capitalism, all systems that enslave man where Islam liberates him."[3]

While rumors were spreading of secret negotiations between President Chadli and the Islamists to create a coalition government, the army decided to step in. On January 11, on the grounds that the elections had been "neither free nor honest" and that their results could "end the constitutional regime," General Nezzar forced President Chadli to resign, the elections were canceled, and the army seized power. Immediately, the FIS denounced a coup d'état perpetrated by "an Islamophobic international conspiracy"—the usual code name for Jews and Americans. On February 2, a fatwa issued by the FIS declared jihad mandatory for every Muslim. This jihad was to target not only the army or the agents of the government but "all those in power and democrats who oppose the observance of divine prescriptions, who encourage fornication through music, dance, nude women, sexual mixing, evening gatherings on the beach . . ."[4] The war was on.

THE BLOODBATH

Meanwhile in France, FIS operatives had begun to settle. France was of special importance for the FIS because of the number of Algerians living there, which made the country a potential staging ground for smuggling weapons and money, but also because of its symbolic weight as a former empire. It is a golden rule in any given country that the more corrupt the political class, the more it needs to reassert itself publicly by displaying all the manifestations of patriotism. In Algerian political culture, being "pro-French" or "sold to the French" is the ultimate insult—along with being Zionist—and even though virtually all politicians in the country have an apartment in Paris, there's no better way to prove one's patriotic credentials than to come down on France. (When he began to distance himself from the FLN apparatchiks in the early eighties, President Chadli was thus labeled pro-French, which is one of the reasons he leaned on the "Arabization program" in the first place.) Similarly, in order to prove its revolutionary nationalism, the FIS had to adopt an anti-French rhetoric very early on.

A fifteen-point program targeting migrant populations in France had thus been issued by the FIS in Algeria as early as the spring of 1990. It claimed "the necessity to protect the migrants from racism and Islamophobic campaigns in the host countries [and] to defend the right for the migrants to an Islamic education." In other words, an infiltration program. The same year, an association called Fraternité Algérienne en France was created, the purpose of which was to serve as a front for the FIS, which had no legal representation in the country. As soon as the violence began in Algeria, rallies in support of the Islamists were set up by the Fraternité in suburbs around Paris such as Sartrouville, Nanterre, and Bobigny and in cities like Lille, Roubaix, Lyon, and Marseille, where the group could rely on a web of local associations. (Ironically, the model for such a network was the web of *"amicales"* and cultural associations used for decades by Algerian intelligence to police the migrants.)

Islamist propaganda and anti-French diatribes were the rule during these meetings, where leaflets distributed to everyone accused Paris of collaborating with the army in the repression of the Muslims. The truth, however, was quite different. President Mitterrand, understanding that the end of the Cold War implied reforms and changes, had supported Chadli from the start in the hope that those changes would thus remain under control. Caught short by the riots and the repression, an embarrassed French government had supported the electoral process and, after the military seized power, allowed the FIS militants to settle in the country, sometimes as political refugees. At the same time, however, France tried to maintain good relations with Algerian intelligence, in order to spy on the Islamists. In short, France was trapped in the crumbling of its own "Arab policy."

Meanwhile, from the North of France, FIS militants began to spread to the UK. By the mid-nineties, through an organization called the Algerian Community in Britain, modeled after the Fraternité, they had established a base in London from which they supervised Islamist activity throughout England, the North of France, and Belgium.

Retired police captain Sammy Ghozlan, who at the time was appointed to the city of Lens, near the Belgium border, remembers: "Once a month, buses appeared behind the Lens Stadium and were filled up by a combination of Muslims and converts. They drove to Calais and from there would take the ferry to England. There was a mosque in Brixton in those days where they received ideological training."[5] This Brixton mosque in fact hosted Abdullah al-Faisal, a Salafi preacher later expelled from the UK for advocating the murder of Jews, Hindus, Brits, and Americans. (He is now said to live in Jamaica.) Regular congregants included Zacarias Moussaoui, the sole Frenchman among the future plotters of the 9/11 attacks.

But in this pre-Internet era, England also served as a base for the Islamists to communicate on what was going on in Algeria. And what was going on was this.

"They started to kill people that no one would stand for," recalls the sixty-year-old Algerian sociologist Marieme Helie Lucas, today the co-founder of the news website Secularism Is a Women's Issue. Helie Lucas lived through the whole of the Algerian civil war and saw many of her friends killed at the hands of the FIS and its armed branch, the Groupe Islamique Armé (GIA). "They began with outcasts. Socially discriminated or isolated people. Known gay poets, for instance, were among their first victims. Female schoolteachers were also quickly targeted, especially when they worked in small, backward villages where no help could be provided to them."[6]

Soon after, more systematic killings ensued. "Algerian London-based fundamentalist newspapers announced in advance what category of the population was to be hit and destroyed," Helie Lucas says. "One day there were 'the journalists,' for instance, another day 'the artists' or 'the intellectuals.' Then it simply was the women. The threats issued in England were carried out in Algeria, and the crimes were claimed, again from London. Now, if your life depends on it, you can stop being a journalist—but how do you stop being a woman? So women became the main target partly because they were the easiest one."

A few examples: On November 8, 1994, in the outskirts of the village of Sidi M'Hamed were discovered the bodies of Saïda, sixteen, and Zoulikha, twenty-one. They had been abducted with their mother three days earlier, to be used as temporary wives by the Islamists. Both had been raped before having their throats slit. The mother's body was discovered a few days later.

On March 13, 1995, at 8 a.m., six bearded men armed with Kalashnikovs and a saber entered a classroom of the high school of Oued Djer, a small town thirty-five miles from Algiers. Three of them jumped on Fatima Ghobane, fifteen, whom someone had denounced for not wearing a *hijab.* Her hands tied behind her back with barbed wire, she was dragged into the courtyard, where she was laid down before one of the killers raised her head and cut her throat with the saber.

On June 18, five women, aged fifteen to twenty, were decapitated at Oued Fodda, ninety miles from Algiers. On August 20, nine wives of the communal guards of a small village called El-Grareb were killed with knives.

But as the civil war intensified, targeted killings began to degenerate into indiscriminate butcheries. Whole trains were attacked by GIA commandos, and all their passengers massacred. By the middle of the decade, the frequency as well as the magnitude of the killings reached such a bloody pitch—an attack every two days, on average, between two and three hundred victims each week—that to give a complete rendition of the period is simply impossible here. The scenario, anyway, was always the same: an army of bearded men wearing Afghan tunics would seize a village or a little town or a suburb, blow up the doors with explosives, select women to keep, and butcher the rest of the inhabitants in the worst possible ways. Here are a few examples:

On the night of July 27, 1997, at Si Zerrouk, a neighborhood in the town of Larbaa, near the Atlas Mountains, electricity was abruptly cut off and, as a series of explosives blocked all access to the roads, a hundred GIA men carrying guns and lamps entered the streets. They selected and abducted the women, killing fifty-one people and wounding ninety.

One month later, on August 29 at 10:30 p.m., two hundred Islamists entered the south Algiers suburb of Rais, blowing up doors with explosives, entering each house, and burning it down after gathering the inhabitants together in the street. Then, to cries of *"Allahu akbar,"* they butchered the unarmed civilians with axes, knives, and guns. The death toll that day climbed to three hundred, among them thirty babies. Rais, like most of the places thus destroyed, had voted against the FIS five years earlier.

Almost a month later, on September 22—and after three other "minor" massacres had taken place in the country—150 men entered Bentalha, another Algiers suburb filled with the wrong voters. As a survivor testified to the press, "They had lists of names. And as babies, infants and women were being slaughtered in a flood of blood, their neighbors waited their turn in an extreme state of hysteria and terror." Again the death toll was three hundred.

On December 30 at 6 p.m., finally, a total of 517 people were slaughtered in a synchronized attack against the four villages of Kherarba, Sahnoun, El-Abadel, and Ouled Tayeb, mainly with knives and axes. Half of them were women and children. According to the correspondent from the journal *Liberté,* who managed to visit the site afterwards, "most of them had had their throat cut, had been decapitated, some dismembered. Children had been killed by being thrown against walls."

By that time, however, France had already been the subject of a series of attacks. Once in jail, the perpetrators would become the mentors of the first jihadists of the 2015 terror wave. As for Farid Benyettou, the future religious mentor of the Kouachi brothers, it was at this time that he turned to Salafism. As he told me, the bloodshed occurring in his parents' country did not trouble him. In his mind, the army itself, with the moral support, if not with the direct help, of the French, had perpetrated the killings of innocent Muslims. Islamists were innocent.

FRANCE, "FIRST ENEMY OF ISLAM"

Why did the Islamists think this way? Why did they involve France in the conflict? As we've seen, France had welcomed the Algerian elections won by the FIS, and even allowed the Islamist militants to take shelter on French territory. The images of the Algerian army firing on the crowd in the riots preceding the electoral process had furthermore caused real trauma in the French political class — especially, perhaps, among the left, many of whom still entertained friendly relationships with the Algerian ruling class of the FLN, and for whom the realization that their friends could shoot demonstrators in the streets — and in front of all the cameras — was insufferable.

The idea that the "authentic" heirs of the War of Independence were not in the government any longer but in the street, among the people who voted for the Islamist FIS, and that therefore these Muslims should be supported against a military coup was widespread in France. Jacques Chirac, who replaced Mitterrand at the Élysée Palace in 1995, was of the same mind. That Islamism was less a religion politicized than the cultural expression of the people was consistent both with the imperial tradition toward Islam that Urbain had helped to establish and with the current French debate over the migrants' children who protested for their civil rights — and to whom the government answered by praising their so-called cultural heritage.

Farid Benyettou was therefore far from alone in the belief that the massacres in Algeria were, in fact, performed by the army rather

than by the Islamists. Most of the French press at the time expressed
doubt about who the real killers were.

These doubts became known on both sides of the Mediterranean
as the "Who kills whom?" theory. They were nourished by classical
counterguerrilla techniques as they were practiced, without particular scruples, by the Algerian army at the time: death squads mir-
roring the Islamist militias to kill Islamist sympathizers; fake Islamist
agents infiltrating Islamist networks; disinformation on a grand scale;
fake denunciations of Islamist leaders as government agents in order
to create inner divisions; and so on. The army also took advantage of
the civil war to kill several democratic opponents, attributing those
crimes to the Islamists themselves, who then had to deny that they
had anything to do with them. In short, everybody killed everybody,
and everybody lied about it.

But because of the paradoxes of the colonial past, and because of
the post–Cold War environment, the French public and the French
government tended to believe, and to sympathize with, the Islamists
more than with the Algerian army.[7] So, again, why did the Islamists
list France as the "first enemy of Islam," as they phrased it?

As explained earlier, part of the problem was Mitterrand's history and personal involvement as minister of justice during the War
of Independence, in the sixties. This past weighed very heavily on
everybody from the French left to the Algerian government—but
especially on the Islamists of the FIS, who were looking to present
themselves as the true heirs of the national revolution and could not
begin to admit any kind of closeness with a figure as closely connected with imperial repression as Mitterrand was.

This connection had been made very clear as early as 1991 by
the FIS leader Ali Belhadj: "My father and his brothers have physi-
cally expelled the oppressive France from Algeria in the sixties, and
I, along with my brothers, we dedicate our lives to banning the
French intellectually and ideologically with the arms of the Faith.
We want to be finished with these venomous partisans. So that Al-

geria can again become master of the Mediterranean Sea, according to the line preached by the Koran, the Sunna, and the lives of our pious ancestors."[8] (Note, in passing, the lack of any feminine reference in this summarizing of the War of Independence, during which, in truth, Algerian women played a crucial part.) The first attacks against the French in Algeria following this statement occurred three years later, in 1994, with the bombing of a neighborhood of French expats in Algiers, an attack that the FIS labeled, in its subsequent statement, an action against "French Crusaders and Jews."

These lines are important because they link a political issue — the relationships with France — to the notion of authenticity and purity, on which there can be no compromise.

The seeming paradox is that Islamists were turning against a French power that supported the electoral process that they had won. The implication of that support, however, was that Paris's influence was not for naught in the elections themselves. France, in other words, was still France: the country of the Enlightenment and of the Declaration of the Rights of Man, it succeeded in playing its traditional civilizational role even in the midst of a grave crisis in Algeria. This was Mitterrand's stand, and, ironically, Islamists could not have agreed more. They, too, saw democracy and elections as a Western creation — in this case, that of imperial France — except that it was the *reason* why they despised it and hated France for importing it. Whichever political force won the elections aligned itself with the enemy.

As one of the FIS's killers, Abdelkader Layada, said: "We reject this religion of the democracy. We state that political pluralism equals sedition. It was never our intention either to participate in the elections or to enter the Parliament. Besides, God alone can legislate."[9]

Of course, by such reasoning, the Islamist leaders of the FIS had to work hard to avoid their followers' concluding that the FIS's credibility itself rested on a process they did not acknowledge as valid. It was an impossible double language. How could they state that they rejected elections while at the same time protesting that their electoral victory had been stolen from them? They fought for the acknowledgment of their legitimacy in a process to which they denied any legitimacy. A way to solve the issue was hate.

In extremist movements, *authenticity* counts more than anything else: to say something and to do it should be one and the same. Words uttered out of sheer propaganda soon acquire a life of their own, from which the militant cannot disentangle himself. Soon, that combination of words and actions becomes more important than rationality or self-preservation. Paranoia, then, becomes for the militant the only reasonable shelter—the only way to maintain control over what's going on. Paranoia, to put it another way, is the unavoidable consequence of authenticity.

This explains, I believe, the vital necessity for the Islamists to list the French government—which lets them settle in France and use France as a rear base—as their enemy, along with the Algerian army, against all logic and self-interest. It did not just make the FIS the legitimate heir of the War of Independence; it also allowed the Islamists to hide their proximity with the "decadent," "homosexual" democracy that had given them their legitimacy. The author of the bolt-loaded bomb attack in the Saint-Michel subway station that killed eight and wounded 117 on July 25, 1995, Smaïn Aït Ali Belkacem, who would become one of the inspirations for the *Charlie Hebdo* killers twenty years later, said as much at his trial in 2002: "France is the first enemy of Islam, an accomplice of the shameful massacre of mujahideen in Algeria. Stop calling us terrorists. It is you who are the terrorists, for you try to impose on us your depraved behavior." Among other manifestations of this depraved behavior were, of course, the very elections that the party had won.[10]

THE FIRST TERROR WAVE

Given such logic, attacks on French soil were unavoidable. They began as soon as 1992, as the French debated who really was responsible for the killings in Algeria. Two converts named Christophe Caze and Lionel Dumont, regular attendees at the FIS-controlled Mosque Archimède, in the city of Roubaix, near Belgium, left the city with eight Muslim-born friends and traveled to the town of Zenica, Bosnia. There they befriended Fateh Kamel, a notorious FIS operative, said to be an Afghan vet, who now lives in Canada. Kamel led a mujahideen group that aimed to create an Islamic state in the Balkans. The Balkan wars, which were raging at the time, are the other side of that story, as Islamic volunteers in Croatia and Bosnia benefited from the same networks of weapons and money transiting through former Communist countries in Eastern Europe, to Belgium and France, as the FIS benefited from in Algeria. Depending on the Islamist group, the money came, in greater or lesser degrees, from the Saudis and from bin Laden. (Still in place in 2014, those networks served to provide their Kalashnikovs to the men who would attack *Charlie Hebdo* the following year.)

After two years of fighting Caze, Dumont and his gang came back home, where, under the nickname "the Roubaix gang," they started a series of ultraviolent robberies, using rocket launchers against banks and department stores with the intention of financing jihad with the loot. Caze was killed, and the group dismantled, during an operation by France's counterterrorist RAID unit against the gang's safe house in March 1996. Dumont, however, managed to escape, reaching first Singapore and then Malaysia, where he joined the Jemaah Islamiyah group, later responsible for the Bali attacks of October 2002, which killed 220. He was finally arrested in 2003 in Germany, and sentenced in 2007 to twenty-five years in prison.

In the gang's safe house, police found leaflets and newspapers proving that the Roubaix gang had ties to the FIS and the GIA. But the interior minister, Jean-Louis Debré, acting on the direct orders of President Jacques Chirac (who had replaced Mitterrand but shared his politics), denied any connection in front of the cameras. "It has nothing to do," he said, "with Islamism or with terrorism. We will not go further than that."

Around the same time, 350 miles to the south in the Lyon suburb of Vaulx-en-Velin, a kid by the name of Khaled Kelkal, born in 1971 in Mostaganem, Algeria, and recruited by the FIS through the Fraternité Algérienne en France, was activated. On the FIS's orders, Khaled Kelkal first assassinated an imam in Paris, then attacked a police station in the Lyon suburb of Bron, and set up no fewer than five attacks in France, in what became the first terror wave on French soil. The most spectacular of these was Aït Belkacem's bomb at the Saint-Michel subway station.

Kelkhal was killed in a spectacular shootout with RAID on September 29, 1995, at dusk, in a small village near Lyon called Maison Blanche. Because of the specificities of the French atmosphere in France and the persistent denial of the part played by the Islamists both in Algeria and in France, he was immediately consecrated by the media as a social hero, a victim of social discrimination, and a symbol of the disgruntled children of the migrants. To this day, the role played by the FIS in his recruitment remains forgotten by most, and his attacks are seen as acts of French rebellion.

In other words, it was during this decade that the seeds of the present situation were planted. Whether out of guilt (for having supported the Algerian FLN for so long) or out of blindness (when confronted with its migrant youth), France had relied on its own orientalist imperial narrative in order to explain to itself a situation that was, in fact, on both sides of its borders, entirely new.

Now forgotten, because it failed, one of the attacks planned by Kelkal deserves a special note. It involved a car bombing in front of a

Jewish school called Nah'alat Moché, in Villeurbanne, close to Lyon, on September 7. Directly engineered by Kelkal himself, this plot was designed to maximize casualties, as the car was placed right in front of the door that each of the seven hundred schoolchildren — aged two to fifteen — had to pass through when leaving school. But the timing was wrong. The school day in France ends at 4:30 p.m., and the car exploded at 4:35, when Kelkal might have expected the kids to be walking through the door. As it turned out, most of them were still packing up, and the bomb injured only a few parents waiting at the door. In order to have done maximum damage, he should have set the bomb to detonate at 4:40. Nobody mentioned it. Kelkal was killed three weeks later and the story faded away.

FIVE
Words and Blood

ADRENALINE RUSH

t is now time to come back to France today, and to the question left unanswered: Were Soral and Dieudonné right to bet on anti-Semitism to rally the French *cités*?

At the turn of 1990, as the Cold War began to fade and the two pillars that had supported France's political identity since 1945 crumbled—and as an endemic economic crisis persisted, along with an enduring discriminative system—various anti-modern narratives were on display among the disgruntled segment of the migrants' offspring trying to make sense of their growing resentment.

One was played out from the early 2000s on by the comedian Dieudonné, under the guidance of the essayist Alain Soral, in the shadows of the "red-brown" alliance theorized by the New Right and its correspondents in Belgium and Russia.

Another had already been on offer since the early 1990s, thanks to FIS networks—and to their half allies and half competitors, the Muslim Brotherhood—who, in less than ten years, successfully engineered the Salafi revolution in Islam in France. As Farid Benyet-tou told me: "When I first began to teach at the Adda'wa Mosque in 2001, I realized how things had changed since I got interested in Salafism five years earlier. At the time, I was alone. Now all the youth came looking for Salafi teaching. The imams who had not adapted were totally over the hill. Which was why they had called for me in the first place."

This last statement raises the question of the *demand*. Suddenly, at the turn of the new century, kids of Muslim background entered the mosques in significant numbers in search of Salafi teaching, the more politicized the better. But what triggered so sudden a rush of adrenaline? Why did it work so well and so fast? Was it 9/11? Was it the Middle East, the collapse of the Israeli-Arab negotiations known as the Oslo peace process and its coverage by the press? *Which was it?* I asked Farid Benyettou. What trend of heroism seemed grandiose enough to enlarge their lives, redeem the humiliation of their working-class fathers as well as their own? Having failed, many of them, at school, and the ones who had not, having hit the glass ceiling of the French social system; dating girls either much too free or not enough, and themselves not knowing which was worse; split between what they wanted and the humiliation of wanting it; ending up at thirty working part-time jobs or being unemployed, and living with their parents still, in *cités* that were both the mark of their social infamy and the cherished home they always returned to; leading a life constantly watched and gossiped about by friends, neighbors, and the cops, and themselves watching and gossiping in return—these young men were condemned, in short, to an existence of daily frustration in a country that was once an empire and of which they now were, ironically enough, citizens, born into and raised by families who'd chosen to settle there and work their guts out, and for what? Which of these factors suddenly triggered their anger, made them listen to

Dieudonné's speeches on TV, and go to hear the likes of Benyet-tou's sermons at the mosque?

"About 9/11," answered Benyettou, "they could not care less. It would never come up in the conversations." But Palestine? "Oh, yeah, sure. Palestine is why they came to me in the first place. They were very sensitive to what was going on there. Also, most were twelfth graders who had experienced some sort of a breakup with the way religion was practiced in their families. They had no real respect for the imam in place, either; they saw him as an incompetent man, there to mechanically perform the prayers and nothing more. Me, by contrast, they could speak to."

Benyettou's trademark article of clothing at the time was his red Palestinian *keffiyeh*. He had picked the color carefully, had started to wear it as a headband in 2000 as a sign of solidarity with what the international press called "the second intifada," and which translated on the ground, in the Middle East itself, into the first major wave of suicide bombings and blind terror of the century. This *keffiyeh* was what had first brought him success among the youth searching for dialogue at the mosque. It was the "anti-Zionist" rallying emblem they were looking for.

There is no doubt that this massive arrival at the mosques of a youth looking for leaders who could focus their rage into words they could identity with coincided with the first anti-Jewish aggressions in the country. Logic, then, would lead us to assume that these two phenomena are one and the same — that political propaganda works mechanically, that the authors of anti-Semitic aggressions were Islamists obeying slogans, or at the very least religious militants of the Palestinian cause. But is it really the case?

The first murder of a Jew in Paris in those years happened in November 2003, in this same multicultural neighborhood of Belleville, just a few hundred yards, as it happens, from the Adda'wa Mosque, where Farid Benyettou was teaching — and yet, it seemed to have nothing to do with politics.

AMBIGUITIES OF THE FIRST MURDER CASE

Edith Piaf was born in Belleville, at Tenon Hospital. Once a bastion of the post-Commune proletariat world, Belleville is where the Communist Party's headquarters was erected, under the direction of the Brazilian architect Oscar Niemeyer, in 1965. A symbol of modernity and the vanguard at the time, the building now stands almost unnoticed in an area full of cool Chinese restaurants and less cool Chinese prostitutes, of greasy kosher and halal snacks lined up on the same dusty sidewalk, of African food markets, synagogues heavily guarded by police, and mosques and Islamist bookstores watched closely by French intelligence. Across from the building is the beginning of the Rue Louis Blanc, where the murder occurred. The victim was Sébastien Selam, then twenty-three, and his killer was his childhood friend Adel Amastaïbou, the same age.

Both lived in a seven-story building at the corner of the Place du Colonel Fabien and the Rue Louis Blanc. Sébastien's mother, Juliette, had settled there in 1985 after Sébastien's father's death, when Sébastien was only five. There he met Adel, the only son of a self-effacing father working as a waiter in a Champs-Élysées pizzeria and an unemployed but energetic mother—so energetic, in fact, that she sometimes had to be confined to the Maison Blanche Psychiatric Hospital. "But other than that," testifies Juliette today, "she appeared perfectly all right, a nice, warm, generous woman who never hesitated to climb the three flights of stairs separating our two apartments to bring some couscous to share."[1] The two women, both of whom were born in Morocco and settled in France as children, felt a common bond. So did Sébastien and Adel, who, skipping school together, learned the wild streets of adolescent life in cosmopolitan Belleville in the early nineties.

By the end of the decade, Sébastien, eighteen, was trying to establish himself as a DJ. Through family contacts he entered the world of some trendy nightclubs downtown, like Les Bains Douches, only twenty minutes from Belleville but a completely different Parisian landscape. Adel carried the mixing boards for Sébastien's performances, and it seems he also used the opportunity to provide drugs on the side to the upper-middle-class clientele, mostly working in fashion and media, who partied at Les Bains Douches. What exactly drove them apart was never clarified. Maybe it was the drug dealing, maybe social discrimination against Adel, or maybe it was Adel's answer to the tribal feeling uniting the Jewish and Israeli DJs performing in the club — or a mix of all of the above, or maybe something entirely different still. In any case, after a while, Sébastien's producer and colleagues at Les Bains Douches — annoyed by what they called Adel's "resentful" attitude — told Sébastien that his friend was no longer welcome.

The two slowly began to drift apart. Adel pursued a path of petty delinquency, which he had already started, while Sébastien was spotted by the European DJ star David Guetta and, under his guidance, began making a name for himself in Paris as well as in hot spots like Ibiza, Miami, and Tel Aviv. At twenty, having rechristened himself "Lam C" (Selam in reverse), he was on his way. In 2001, he signed with a major U.S. record company, and soon there was a brand-new Audi to show off in the neighborhood. By 2003 Lam C was planning to move to Miami for good and to bring his mother with him. "He had already bought the tickets, and we were more than happy to leave here when that thing happened," says Juliette.

During either the fall or winter of 2000, Adel's mother began sneaking into neighborhood buildings to pull out the mezuzahs that traditional Jewish families, of which there were many in the area, hang on their doorposts. She tore them off and tossed them away in the gutter. During the same period, she also became known for mumbling in the streets. People who heard her said she cursed the Jews. The Selams were by no means her specific target, even though, living in the same building and knowing each other as they did, they soon became the easiest and most consistent one. Juliette Selam says that one day Adel's mother slit the throat of a live rooster in the building's corridor and left the animal to bleed and die on the Selams' doormat. She had cast the evil eye.

But even though this harassment went on for the next three years on a more or less regular basis, it did not totally undermine what remained of Adel and Sébastien's friendship. Less regularly, perhaps, given Lam C's hectic life, and maybe with some uneasiness on both their parts, given Adel's mother's strange behavior, they still saw each other. Adel was sometimes in trouble with the law; sometimes he also had to be institutionalized for a short while, in the same psychiatric ward where his mother got treatment. Each time, says Juliette, Sébastien made a point of visiting.

On November 20, 2003, Sébastien was to perform at Le Queen, one of the most famous gay nightclubs on the Champs-Élysées. (The homosexual dimension of the story was one of the many points entirely passed by in the investigation. With the exception of the two mothers, no feminine presence is discernible.) Another pal of his, also Muslim, named Marwan, was to play Adel's part that night as bodyguard and gear wrangler, transporting Lam C's mixing table and records. They arrived in Sébastien's Audi on Rue Louis Blanc that evening around 9 p.m. Juliette was out having dinner with friends, so Sébastien gave Marwan his apartment keys and instructions to go to his room and get the equipment in order and start wrapping up the vinyl selection for the night while he drove the car to the parking lot. He would be there in no time.

Marwan complied, Sébastien drove the car away, and, according to what was later reconstructed, he found Adel at the entrance of the parking lot, looking preoccupied. On a sign of his friend, Sébastien stopped and invited him to get in, and the two friends vanished underground. Some fifteen minutes later, witnesses saw Adel springing out of the parking lot with blood on his clothes and in a state of ecstasy, yelling, "I killed my Jew! I'll go to heaven! Allah guided me!" Surprisingly enough, given her own mental issues, it was Adel's mother who had the presence of mind to immediately call the cops after her son ran to her to break the news. In an act of uncontrolled fury, he had stabbed his friend with a kitchen knife in the chest, in the throat, and, more strangely, in the eyes.

Whatever the real motivations for the murder may have been, it is the killer's narrative that matters here. Interviewed for psychiatric evaluation while in custody soon after, he repeated at first what he had said right after the murder—that he had killed "his" Jew and would be rewarded for it by going to heaven. His statement was duly recorded by the psychiatrist, a woman who deemed him mentally sane at the time of his crime. Anti-Jewish hate, she said, was the motivation for his actions. Her conclusion was backed by Adel's criminal record, which, it turns out, showed, in addition to several arrests for robbery, an arrest for randomly beating a rabbi in the street. Everything was clear. But clarity sometimes leads to complex issues.

Like his mother, the investigation also revealed, Adel had been diagnosed years before with paranoid schizophrenia. Both the mother and her son were under a thorough medical protocol at home to regulate their condition—a condition severe enough in Adel's case, it seems, that knives had been completely removed from the Amastaïbous' home; before committing the crime, Adel had had to borrow one from the neighbors. That detail suggested planning. At that time, however, he had also not been taking his medication for weeks.

During the years of legal procedure that ensued, Juliette Selam and her lawyer, Axel Metzker, fought to have Adel Amastaïbou tried for murder. In order to do so, Metzker attempted to prove that the psychiatric condition Amastaïbou and his mother had been diagnosed with, and for which they had been treated for years, was a hoax. Pretending to be mad, pleaded Metzker, was, in fact, the best proof that Adel Amastaïbou was indeed an Islamist militant and an anti-Semite: it was a manifestation of what is called in Islam *taq-*

iya, or deceiving the unfaithful in the name of the true faith. Two years after the murder, after the dismantling of the Buttes-Chaumont gang in 2005, when Farid Benyettou's story became a subject for the news, Metzker also tried to link Amastaïbou with the nearby Adda'wa Mosque. That the context in the neighborhood had played a part in the murder sounded only logical.

But, of course, you don't establish the sanity of a person through the symptoms of his mental illness. There were years of medical prescriptions and hospital records to attest to the reality not only of Amastaïbou's state but of his mother's as well. Both had been diagnosed, the mother for severe depression and paranoia, Adel for paranoia and delusions. As for the mosque, as far as was established, Amastaïbou had never set foot inside it, nor had he followed Benyettou's teachings.

So Metzker's strategy failed. In the end, Amastaïbou was considered non compos mentis: Adel's consciousness was "altered at the time of the act," a notion that in French law makes one unfit to be tried.

This is not all. Right after his custody interview, Adel had been handed over to the very Maison Blanche hospital that had treated both him and his mother. The medical team there favored regular contact with his family environment as a means of helping to improve his general state. A part-time hospitalization was arranged, which resulted in Adel's coming back home every weekend to visit his mother, in the very building where the murder had taken place. That he could come across his victim's mother at any time on the stairs did not seem to be a concern. For more than two years, through her lawyer, Juliette repeatedly protested and asked the social services to help her find another place to live. In 2005, however, it was the killer and his mother who were moved away, to an apartment on the other side of Paris, where, to the best of my knowledge, they still live today. Juliette, on the other hand, still lives where her son was killed.

During the following decades, similar ambiguities would arise in other murder cases involving Jewish victims, most notoriously in the Ilan Halimi story, recorded above, in the Sarah Halimi case in April 2017 (of which more will come later), and, to an extent, in the Mireille Knoll murder, a year after that. Another repeated theme is that Jewish associations and their supporters would fight hopelessly in order to prove that the perpetrators of such hate crimes were militant Islamists and terrorists, only to be denied by the facts. And yet, not to see a connection between the ideological narratives presented above, which nurtured terror acts, and these impulsive crimes that defy explanation seems impossible. So what is the connection?

WORD VIRUSES

In the fall of 2015, I met with Smaïn Laacher, an anthropologist and sociologist at the Pierre Bourdieu school who has written several books on migrant culture. "Sociology" has become a magic word on both sides of the Atlantic — and even more so, perhaps, in France, under the shadow of Pierre Bourdieu, who, since his death in 2002, has joined the long list of "human science" prophets whom French academia all too regularly produces, out of nostalgia for its past intellectual dominance. But Smaïn Laacher is different. Born in France to Algerian parents, at a time when Algeria was still a French territory, he was raised with both languages, which makes him an Arabic-speaking French national, a cosmopolitan, and not a migrant, and it is the acknowledgment of this biographical pluralism in his own writing that, I believe, accounts for the quality of the nuanced and complex books he has written on difficult subjects such as, to quote some of the titles, *Violence Inflicted on Women in Migrant Populations* and, more recently, *Sacredness and Public Freedom in the Arab World*.

France was deep into the 2015 terror wave when we met, and it says something about the tensions pervading the country that even someone as scrupulous as Smaïn Laacher had been dragged against his will into a public debate and a trial for libel. The debate, of course, was about anti-Semitism.

Its main protagonist was Georges Bensoussan, a sixty-five-year-old historian who is currently a lead editor at the Shoah Memorial in Paris. In 2002, while anti-Semitic brutalities were rising across the country, Bensoussan had broken into the French media landscape under the pseudonym of Emmanuel Brenner as the editor of an anthology called *Les Territoires Perdus de la République* (*The Republic's Lost Territories*). With the exception of two government reports that had been shelved, *Les Territoires* was the first account by teachers and high school directors set in the French *cités* testifying to the anti-Semitism, sexism, and racism that plagued them. Although the book had been a hit, it had also stirred controversy, with Bensoussan being listed by the left as a "new reactionary" and a French "neocon." But Bensoussan's book also found serious defenders in the intellectual and media world. One was the Algerian writer Boualem Sensal, who, having witnessed the Algerian civil war firsthand, had been one of the first to ring the alarm bell against Islamist networks in France. Another was the philosopher Alain Finkielkraut.

On October 10, 2015, Bensoussan was invited to *Répliques,* the radio talk show hosted by Finkielkraut on France Culture, the French NPR. The occasion was a documentary titled *Profs en Territoires Perdus de la République* (*Teachers in the Republic's Lost Territories*), set to be aired the very evening of the same day, featuring an interview with Laacher. During the course of the show, Bensoussan—speaking of "the Muslims" rather broadly—said: "Today we are in the presence of another people inside of the French nation, and as a result a certain number of democratic values that structured our nation are now regressing. There won't be any integration as long as we do not get rid of this atavistic anti-Semitism, which is concealed as a secret.

Just let me quote an Algerian sociologist, Smaïn Laacher, who with great courage just said as much in the documentary. 'It is a shame,' he said, 'to maintain this taboo that in Arab families in France, and everybody knows this but nobody wants to say it, anti-Semitism is suckled along with mother's milk."[2]

The next day, the "Algerian sociologist" in question, Smaïn Laacher, issued the following statement: "I have never said nor written anything of this ignominious nature. How could anyone believe even for half a second that in these families, anti-Semitism would be passed on by blood? My work, my positions, and my public engagements all stand for my relentless efforts against any form of essentialism, even should it be involuntary. I never assumed that a biological order could be the first rudiments of a religious, ethnic, or national hate. This purely fantastical quote must be seen as a naive, if cowardly, attempt to enlist me on one 'side' against another."

Two things especially angered Laacher in Bensoussan's phrasing, he told me. One was the reference to him as an Algerian sociologist. "Why Algerian?" he said. "Because I look like one? Because of my name? Of Algeria I know almost nothing. Each time I have to go there to do research, I have to get a visa like any French citizen. I was born in France, I'm French, probably more so than Bensoussan will ever be." (Bensoussan was born in Morocco.)

The second point that infuriated Laacher was, of course, the dwarfing of his research and theories into a vague metaphor about poisoned milk. What he actually said in the documentary, which Bensoussan had carelessly paraphrased, was this: "This anti-Semitism [in the French Muslim narrative] is already planted into the domestic space. It quasi-naturally rolls off the tongue, planted into the tongue." He went on: "When parents want to reprimand children, it is enough for them to call them *Jews*. OK, every Arab family knows that. Not to see that this anti-Semitism is first domestic is a monumental hypocrisy."

In the autumn of 2015, when we met, Laacher had just filed a libel complaint against Bensoussan. It would take a year before the two men's lawyers put together an official press release in which Bensoussan, maintaining his "freedom of interpretation," would recognize that he had misquoted Laacher's interview, and Laacher and Bensoussan would agree to let the matter rest. In the meantime, however, the Muslim association Collective Against Islamophobia in France (CCIF) and the International League Against Racism and Anti-Semitism (LICRA), an anti-racist French institution created at the time of the Dreyfus affair, had both seized the opportunity and filed a complaint of their own, suing the chief editor of the Shoah Memorial for "incitement to racial hatred." Although Bensoussan would be found not liable in February 2017, the story exposes the high level of tension in France.

While the differences between what Laacher actually said about "rolling off the tongue" in "the domestic space" and Bensoussan's off-the-cuff summary of anti-Semitism being imbibed with "mother's milk" may seem like a variety of French academic hairsplitting, it may help us begin to elaborate an answer to the question above.

Laacher's primary concern is the language — one's tongue — and part of the confusion comes from the fact that, in French, the same word — *la langue* — denotes both language and the physical organ. So Laacher's analogy does have a physical connotation. This was what led commentators such as Bensoussan to their essentialist interpretations. But Laacher defends his stance against that.

"The language one is raised in," Laacher says, "the tongue he is taught to speak as an infant, is one of the defining components of his subjective identity that will never go away."

But language, for Laacher, is a paradoxical thing. It is the tool an individual needs to master in order to express himself at his most singular; but it's also the instrument through which the collective — call it a tribe, a people, or a nation — frames that individual into a set of values, beliefs — and biases. In that sense, languages aren't simple systems of combined words haphazardly dispersed through geography. They are existential, structural systems of understanding loaded with history. Unbeknownst to the individual, the words one uses carry with them a vision of the world. The author of *Naked Lunch,* William S. Burroughs, believed that words were like viruses, carrying diseases, affecting one's behavior. Laacher concurs. He maintains that words transmit beliefs and notions that one is unaware of, and it may take years of serious education before one is able to recognize them, distance oneself from the biases they imply, and access one's own subjectivity. Laacher insists that *every* culture is thus structured—not just the Muslim one.

I had called him wondering whether his theory might not help to explain, to a point, the murder of Sébastien Selam by his childhood friend—if it might not provide the missing link, in other words, between a collective context hostile to Jews and whichever more individual intimate motivation may have been at play—but also, more generally, whether it might not shed light on the nature of the *demand* to which the Dieudonné and Salafi narratives were the offer. By way of an example, I submitted to Laacher the following story.

"YOU WANT THE JEW TO FUCK YOU"

In the first days of July 2014, in Vaulx-en-Velin, outside Lyon, a young deputy mayor in charge of sports, by the name of Ahmed Chekhab, was secretly taped by the manager of the local athletic club he was talking to while assessing violent anti-Jewish remarks.

On the recording, one could hear him saying, with a drawl, "How can you do this to me? I'm a Muslim just like you! But you prefer dealing with the Jew! That's what you like, don't you? You don't like it when people like you are in place and wanna help. People of your kind. No. You'd rather have the Jew. You want the Jew to fuck you. You want the Jew to fuck you in the ass, don't you?"[3]

Chekhab was a member of the new Socialist administration of Vaulx-en-Velin, which had taken over three months before that incident occurred, in March, during the municipal elections, and "the Jew" he was referring to was Philippe Zittoun, a man from the previous administration who had held Chekhab's position overseeing sports at City Hall for years. From the clip alone, one could not tell what the disagreement was about, but the raw anti-Semitic hatred was unmistakable.

"This is a perfect illustration of someone who speaks the collective language instead of expressing his own subjectivity," argued Laacher when I brought up that story. He went on:

A language is the collective component through which the individual expresses himself. It speaks us, if you will, as much as we speak it. And it never speaks randomly; it is always meaningful. The language, as it were, speaks us as much as we speak it, and in doing so, collective values and feelings, which is what anthropology calls a culture, are being passed on. Of course, this includes the passing on of collective negative feelings and passions as well, such as hate. To insult someone, in that regard, can act as a reminder of what you belong to. A reminder, also, that to be singular or to drift from the norm of the group you belong to is not allowed. In the Arab language we say "*al-ye-hudi!*" which means "The Jew! The Jew!" each time we want to mock someone. But as a rule, none of this is specific to the Arabs or the Muslim culture. Every group in the world has at its disposal a stock of expressions, and a group of figures it holds in contempt. It would be very easy to reconstruct the trajectory, the universe of words one has internalized through which one has learned to name and categorize certain foreign groups as targets. But of course, to go from that to the murder of representatives of that group requires a more conscious activism, and a political will.

I traveled to Vaulx to meet Ahmed Chekhab a few weeks after my encounter with Laacher. It was November 12, 2015 — coincidentally, the eve of the coordinated terror attacks in Paris.

At the Lyon railroad station, I was welcomed by the local LICRA representative, Patrick Kahn, an Ashkenazi in his early sixties, who had unruly, curly black hair and the rapid-fire speech of a man in a hurry. We got into his car and drove past the Rhône River toward the low-rise buildings of the *cités* that constituted the Mas-du-Taureau district of Vaulx, where Chekhab was born in 1985. It was there, five years later, that the first serious streets riots erupted in a French suburb, and there as well that, as recounted above, the main operative of the 1995 terror wave launched by the FIS in France, Khaled Kelkal, grew up.

As we drove, I noticed on the sullied white surface of a peeled building a tag that had obviously survived the municipal campaign of the previous year. It said: SOCIALIST PARTY = ISRAEL. This made little sense to me. Patrick had to explain, rather counterintuitively, that it was a left-wing slogan emanating from the local Communist Party.

Communists, he went on, had had control over Vaulx's City Hall ever since the 1920s. This was by no means an exception. Many of the working-class suburbs of France had turned Communist between the late 1890s and the 1920s, even before the party became the second most powerful political force of the country after World War II. But since the virtual disappearance of the white working class in Vaulx, and after the end of the Cold War, the party found itself deprived of both its ideological and its demographic base and, as a result, the municipal team began to rely more and more on "the Palestinian argument" in order to remain in touch with their electorate. As with Soral and with the Salafis, whether they were right about this or whether they created or at least enhanced a potential demand remains debatable. In any case, Vaulx was far from being an isolated case during the post–Cold War decade. In the Paris suburb of Saint-Denis, for instance, the Communist mayor's team set up humanitarian trips to Gaza repeatedly, as did nearby Montreuil. In Bagnolet, a quiet middle-class suburb bordering Paris, City Hall, whose leadership was also Communist, signed a sister-city agreement with, of all places, the Palestinian refugee camps of Sabra and Shatila. Disgruntled Muslim kids growing up in France in the nineties and in search of a narrative that could justify their rage by blaming the country, the Jews, or both did not have to look far. In the fall of 2000, Vaulx-en-Velin itself was twinned with Beit Zatoun — a small Christian town on the West Bank, near Bethlehem — and, as of this writing, it still is.

SOCIALIST PARTY = ISRAEL: That tag that had survived the municipal campaign of March 2014 went along with the rest. It was also connected with the right-wing Day of Wrath demonstration three months earlier, and an echo of its anti-establishment creed was audible in the background of such a slogan. (Local politicians in some of the suburbs used anti-gay rhetoric to claim that Socialists were controlled by the atheist-pedophile Zionists who had implemented gay marriage to undermine Muslim families in the first place.) In Vaulx, then, the target of such a slogan would have been the candidate for the Socialist Party, Hélène Geoffroy, one of the rare Socialists in the country during the 2014 municipal elections to have actually won, despite the climate.

Yet the mystery, to me, was that Ahmed Chekhab, the young Socialist who had been recorded raging against the Jews, was a member of *her* team — the team that was the *target* of the anti-Jewish attacks — while Philippe Zittoun, on the other hand, "the Jew" of Chekhab's diatribe, was a member of the previous one, the one that had tried to use anti-Semitism to its benefit.

In addition to all this, in January 2014, six months before Chekhab was recorded, that same Zittoun — still sports deputy at City

Hall—had received in his official mailbox drawings showing him hanged by the neck, a silhouette dangling at the end of a rope, and labeled "Zittoun the Jew." The sender was never identified.

"I WANNA DEAL WITH REAL THINGS!"

I met with Chekhab at City Hall after a fastidious two-hour presentation on the politics of the new administration delivered by the first deputy mayor, and soon we set off to a nearby, empty café. We sat separated by a small, square red Formica table and ordered two espressos. Then he looked me straight in the eye, and the first thing he told me was "I am not a racist. I am not an anti-Semite."[4] He had a compact, round, solid body and a pale half smile that seemed to disappear at times in the fog of his face, and he moved and spoke very slowly.

His recording had been posted online in July 2014, immediately starting an uproar that reached the Socialist Party, of which both he and Geoffroy were card-carrying members. It took two months for the party executives in Paris to reach a decision, but by the end of the summer Chekhab's membership was suspended. Yet in Vaulx-en-Velin, Mayor Geoffroy stood by him, refusing to let him go. In October, Vaulx's City Hall announced, in response to the scandal, that it was setting up a "plan to fight racism and anti-Semitism" in the city, a plan that was to include public debates, cultural encounters between Jewish and Muslim youths, commemorations of the Holocaust, conferences "on memories," and so on. And who was appointed to head this program? Ahmed Chekhab.

As LICRA's local representative who had first come up with the idea for the program, Patrick Kahn had had to swallow the news. "I first opposed Chekhab's appointment, of course," he told me. "But Mayor Geoffroy made it very clear that the option was either the plan with Chekhab or no plan at all. To see the Jews leave Vaulx under pressure throughout the previous decade had been a shame and a personal defeat, and I saw Hélène Geoffroy's victory as an opportunity. If Chekhab's appointment was what it took to change things . . . Look," he added with obvious embarrassment, "I did not intend to be the Jewish excuse to anyone."[5]

Apart from him, however, that somebody proven to be the author of flagrant anti-Semite statement remarks could, *as a consequence,* be promoted to manager of a civic structure dedicated to fighting anti-Semitism seemed neither absurd nor ironic to anyone.

Rather, it was a "pedagogic measure," to quote Mayor Geoffroy in the interview she gave me before I traveled to Vaulx. For at such a place, she explained, not only would Chekhab be able to teach tolerance; he'd be in the best position to learn it himself. Who better than a sinner, after all, to knowledgeably teach redemption?

"You need to understand that we work with real people here," she told me, "basic citizens whose contradictions reflect the condition our society is in. Chekhab publicly apologized for what he said. By doing so, he audaciously seized what was, at its core, a very complex issue for him, too. Furthermore, he was born in a socially disadvantaged neighborhood, fought hard to get out of it and build a life for himself. He received diplomas, bought an apartment, and today he works with us. And I say, if we do not accompany these kinds of people every step of the way, if we let them go after the first mistake they make, then what? Why not give up right away!"[6]

But as convincing as this social concern may sound, other factors — political factors — were also at play in Geoffroy's decision to stand up for Chekhab and make such an appointment. Factors she did not mention.

This may be a good place to explain for the U.S. reader the phenomenon of the French *"cité"* — a word for which there is no American equivalent, since the places it refers to are so specifically French. The closest would probably be "projects," except that in France, these projects are blocks of buildings set up in the *"banlieues."* Technically, *banlieues* are the towns surrounding large cities, that is, suburbs. But unlike their U.S. counterparts, the French suburbs were built up in the 1930s, and more massively after World War II, to shelter first poor workers, then the new middle class, and finally, from the 1980s on, the *déclassés*—the new poor and the migrants. A *banlieue* is thus a midsize town that may contain several *cités*.

Given their history, from 1920 until the 2014 municipal elections, most of these *banlieues* were administered by the Communist Party. Municipalities in France have special programs for housing the poor and subsidizing cultural activities, which means that the party had its hand in the cultural lives of these towns and could decide who lived where. During the prosperity years, right-wing municipalities often sent the poorest segments of their own populations to these places, so there was a sort of gentlemen's agreement among the political forces to divide French territory according to social classes and who would vote how. While the western suburbs of Paris, for instance, traditionally voted on the right, the east, north, and southeast would vote for the left. But as the white working class began to disappear at the end of the seventies, and as the Communist ideology started to wane during the following decade, Communist apparatchiks ended up with a particular problem: how to deal with a new population among which there was no memory of the French working-class struggles, such as the legendary Paris Commune of 1871 or even the Popular Front of 1936—two events that had shaped the French collective memory and the identity of the French left? This crisis of identity on the left was aggravated by the end of the Cold War and translated itself on the ground into the search for new strategies and new narratives in order to win votes among a virtually unknown population. Since each of these *cités* has its own name and constitutes a different territory, that task became harder still. As people tend to regroup by family or clan, the toughest of these *cités* are virtually impossible to enter without the proper introduction. They do not, however, correspond to what an American would commonly call ghettos, as they may be ethnically diverse. If *cités* in Vaulx-en-Velin, for instance, are predominantly Algerian, Bobigny, near Paris, contains several dozen ethnic groups dispersed in every *cité* of the town. Every one of these groups relies on its own set of familial and religious codes, often superseded by the connections with the country of origin. Yet all these groups may unite to defend the "honor" of one *cité* against another.

Today, as a rule, the *cités* are populated either by foreigners unfamiliar with the French scene, and deprived of the right to vote, or French nationals, often from immigrant backgrounds, who are disillusioned with politics and live in survival mode, skipping voting altogether unless they find out about an issue they have a personal investment in. Abstention rates, as a result, are huge, and winning or losing a local election is often a matter of a few hundred ballots. Mayors, if only to maintain civic harmony, pick up—and make deals with—the one or two organized groups of activists they can find, whose members have access to corners of the *cités* that officials can't reach. In return, as these groups, now linked with politicians, began to make promises about public subsidies or lodging, they began to acquire a political legitimacy entirely disconnected from what they actually represent. In a sort of feedback loop, this new artificial legitimacy from above ends up giving them real power over the general population—if only because they're rewarded with some appointment or other once their candidate has won.

Because they manage the primary activities in these under-equipped urban spaces, and because they need public subsidies to survive, sporting associations are often one of the main strategic tools in such a system. This places the deputy mayor for sports in a key position in City Hall and makes that job one of the most powerful, and hence most desirable. In the 2000s, Chekhab had set up an association for citizenship, with close links to the former Communist administration, and his own sports club, called UNI6T (as in "unicity," and "uni-*cité*"), was financed with the help of public local subsidies. Yet he never really made it to City Hall. Geoffroy poached him, probably with the promise of appointing him sports deputy, providing he could deliver the few ballots needed for a victory. Which, apparently, he did. "Politics is what I do," he confirmed to me somewhat cryptically. "I brought a lot of young people to vote." The abstention rate in Vaulx during the election that ensured Geoffroy's victory was only 60 percent.

"It hurts me to be called a racist while I've been discriminated against since I was a child," Chekhab went on.

He had grown up the son of a father who had come from Algeria and settled in Vaulx in the early fifties to work in construction, he told me, and who, at the end of the decade, as the War of Independence started in Algeria, had proven himself to be much more than a simple worker. He was also a mujahid, clandestinely smuggling money and weapons from France, through Switzerland, for the FLN. Yet, after Algeria's independence, he stayed in France, where Chekhab's mother joined him and where they had seven kids together, of which Chekhab was the fourth — and the only one to enter French politics. "We lived in the Mas-du-Taureau area. I grew up there trying to understand the revolutionary spirit there is in this zone," Chekhab told me. "It is France's vanguard as far as social struggle is concerned."

He was five when he witnessed the death of the young delinquent by police that started the 1990 riots. "I was playing soccer with friends. Suddenly there was this noise, and when I approached to see, the kid was already lying dead on the asphalt, his bike beside him. I had never seen a dead body before, but I did not feel any fear. Curiosity is what I felt." He was seven when he watched the Mas-du-Taureau shopping center burned down by rioters in 1992; ten when his neighbor, FIS operative Khaled Kelkal, the head of the 1995 terror wave, met his death in a shootout with police. By then his mother had him enrolled in a private Catholic high school in downtown Lyon, Les Brotteaux, which was where he first found out that there were places in the country that didn't look at all like a *cité* or like Vaulx.

How had he experienced the Kelkal story? I asked him. I knew that tension had arisen in the streets of Vaulx-en-Velin the very evening of the shootout, as soon as the news broke. Thirty-six cars were burned that night in the Mas-du-Taureau area alone. Two units of the State Security Police force, the CRS, were deployed in the streets throughout the entire weekend in order to prevent further trouble, while several groups of young men were arrested with Molotov cocktails in their hands. In the neighboring suburbs of Bron, Saint-Priest, Villeurbanne, Vénissieux, Meyzieu — in short, all around Lyon — cars were burned, phone booths vandalized, and, when morning came, tags such as VENGEANCE FOR KHALED and YOU KILLED KHALED BUT WE'LL HAVE THE LAST LAUGH could be found on walls. The confusion between social rebellion and Islamist propaganda as conveyed by the FIS was already complete. There was a lot Chekhab could have said about this, but, either out of social shame or fear of being misunderstood, or out of his own feelings, he downplayed it all: "Well, we followed the news like everyone else in France, and that's it. The story certainly contributed to stigmatize us even more. It certainly didn't help us."

"Us." Whether his family, the neighborhood, the Communist Party, or Hélène Geoffroy's Socialist team, he constantly seemed to speak for and from a group. Where was *he* in all this? Who was he when he said "I," and what did he want for himself?

"Me?" he answered, in what was probably his most sincere statement. "I wanna rise above all of those silly issues, you understand. I want to speak out here, about Vaulx! When I was a child, what mattered for my parents was how to fill the fridge. Not anti-Semitism! Not racism! That's still what I want to talk about. You understand? I want to be a Vaulx-en-Velin representative! Like everyone else! I want to deal with real issues for real people! That's it."

He was perfectly genuine. And yet he had made the anti-Semitic statements, which was why we were here talking in the first place. He had created the incident that was now forcing him to deal with an issue that did not interest him, a question in which, he said, he had no interest. And, if I have to be perfectly honest, neither did I — not especially. And yet here we were. "Look, I never said one anti-Semitic sentence in my life," he answered. "I was not speaking for myself that day when I was taped."

THE VERBAL IMAGINATION OF HATRED

The man who recorded him that day, he explained, was named Majid Diri, and he presided over a small sporting association called the Athletic Club. He and Chekhab had been friends since they were ten years old, Chekhab told me. Diri had grown up a Dieudonné fan. He still was. He had felt gravely hurt when Chekhab joined the anti-Dieudonné Socialists for the 2014 campaign and felt his friend had betrayed "them." Chekhab told me, "One day — it was during the 2014 municipal campaign, and I was distributing leaflets for Geoffroy — I met Majid by chance, and of course I said hi. But as soon as he saw me and saw what I was doing, he began to lecture me. We were in the food market. He began to shout — in front of everybody. He said that working with Mrs. Geoffroy on a Socialist ticket was working for Israel. That it was working with the Zionists. Let me tell you, this gave me a headache. A headache! It really hurt! In the food market? In front of everyone? Do you have any idea what this meant?"

It meant his reputation and honor were at stake. It meant, consequently, that his credibility as a local political operative, his ability to win votes — in other words, his career and social status — were threatened. But then he added: "This was like saying I worked with the French during the Algerian War! Like saying I tortured with the

French during the Algerian War! Me! Me, whose father smuggled money for the FLN!" This, for a moment, left me speechless. So this is what the tag on the wall I had seen earlier implied. Simply distributing leaflets for the Socialist Party was being a Zionist, which was being a French torturer. But what did all this even mean? Wasn't Chekhab himself French? Was this twisted logic the only way for him to be the heir of his heroic father? Was that what honor implied for him? "I wanna rise above all of this," he'd told me. "I wanna speak about real issues, about Vaulx!" But what exactly was reality for him, caught as he was among so many contradictory narratives?

After the municipal elections, on the eve of Chekhab's nomination for the sports office, a meeting had been called at City Hall during which all the sporting-club presidents of Vaulx had dressed Chekhab down. He was too young to be heading sports and its four-million-euro-a-year budget, they said. They also questioned his legitimacy, having been appointed deputy mayor without ever being elected. The next day, the local press, briefed by Geoffroy's losing opponents, reported the meeting, making Ahmed Chekhab its laughingstock for the day. The "traitor" was being punished. Because he had brought votes from the *cités* to Geoffroy, Chekhab was a strategic element inside the new mayor's team. The attack against him could not be left unanswered. Chekhab promptly quit his job as salesman and started lobbying every sports director in town to convince them that he would be as good at the job as his predecessor, Zittoun, had been. Among these sports directors was Diri. And Diri, using the pretext of a money issue—a subsidy that he claimed Zittoun had promised him and Chekhab wasn't aware of—refused to meet. This was the context for the anti-Semitic remarks. After several phone calls, Chekhab showed up unannounced at the Athletic Club and, in the fiery discussion that ensued, launched his tirade. What he said, in effect: *After everything you said to me at the food market, pretending I work for the Zionists, now you don't want to work with me, a Muslim, while you used to work with Zittoun the Jew.* Diri, most likely working with the losing opponents, and knowing what to expect, recorded it. "I was answering him," Chekhab told me again. "Because that sort of thing cannot be left unanswered. I was not speaking for myself. I never said one anti-Semitic sentence in my life."

This last sentence seemed a perfect illustration of Laacher's theory, which is why I offer this story of local petty politics in such detail. In a sense, Chekhab was right: he never said anything anti-Semitic. And yet the words were uttered, the feelings they carried were expressed, through a collective dynamic over which neither he nor anyone else, from what I could tell, had any control. Probably only a few individuals are really, consciously hateful anti-Semites. The majority simply walk about carrying a collective verbal arsenal full of clichés through which they understand the world. But doesn't the worldview this small incident betrays also reveal a complete reversal of what should be expected from a local French representative? If, for Chekhab, members of the French Socialist Party, "Zionists," and torturers of the freedom fighters during the Algerian War are one and the same, what does that imply for him? What does that make him in his own eyes? "There is no radical discontinuity anymore," said Laacher, "between home and the outside environment. Because this environment is all around, like the air you breathe, and it is very difficult to escape it, especially when you interact with the group of reference where the same words are exchanged, along with the same worldview."

How could Chekhab work on a Socialist municipal team at all —let alone as the head of a special program to fight anti-Semitism? And where does the violence underlying such a worldview lead, once rightly framed by an ideological narrative such as that of the FIS?

One year after my visit to Vaulx, Hélène Geoffroy set up a special day to commemorate the first year of the program; it was occasionally interrupted by a handful of Islamist activists and provocateurs.

Although officially head of the program, Chekhab remained totally silent in the face of the protests, unable to intervene, and left Geoffroy to deal with it. (Today the program is virtually dead.)

Of course, none of this implies in any way that Chekhab, as an individual, has any sympathy for the Islamist movements or even for Salafism, but it is precisely the fact that he does not that reveals the depth of the problem. His powerlessness in front of the protests, as well as the narrative he relied on to define himself when we met, suggest that the reason for the success of the political propaganda, whether the FIS's or Dieudonné's, that invaded France's public debate in the 1990s and 2000s leaned on something that was already there—call it a substratum, still unshaped, which may have been the result of France's anti-modern tradition, but only in part. The other part was provided by elements of the collective story through which migrant fathers—particularly, albeit not exclusively, Algerian ones —justify their humiliating presence in France *in their own eyes:* what Smaïn Laacher calls a language.

There were several reasons for what Urbain called, in his writings in the 1840s, "the contempt in which Muslims hold the Jews" in Algeria. One, as we've seen, was that Jews, having been discriminated against by Ottoman law before colonization, tended to see the French as liberators. This was reinforced, from 1865 on, by a decree giving the Jews the political rights Muslims were deprived of through their Muslim personal status, so that, for most Arab Muslims in the country, the Jews and the French became almost one and the same imperialists—"almost" because Jews born in Algeria, now looking like traitors, were even worse.[7] Isn't it tempting to see a reprisal of these representations in Ahmed Chekhab's rhetoric about Zionists and French torturers? To see, in other words, this narrative substratum as a foundation for future political propaganda?

The French anti-modern trend and the remains of the French "Arab policy"; the anti-Jewish biases; the propaganda of Dieudonné/ Soral and the FIS: let us now see how all these elements coalesced during the 2000s—as French media coverage of the Middle East violence echoed part of the "anti-imperialist" narrative and anti-Jewish incidents were on the rise—in two stories: the *Charlie Hebdo* trial and the Gang of Barbarians trial. Both were front-page news in those years, and in both cases, the representation of the Jews turned out to be crucial.

MANIPULATING MUSLIM OPINION: THE *CHARLIE HEBDO* TRIAL

So much has been written on it, so much of it conflicting, that it bears returning to the origins of the *Charlie Hebdo* story.

It started, as one may remember, not in France but in Amsterdam, on the morning of November 2, 2004, at 9 a.m. That was when the polarizing documentary maker Theo van Gogh, forty-seven, was shot eight times in the street. As he lay on the sidewalk, still conscious, half-decapitated, Mohammed Bouyeri, twenty-six, his killer, plunged his knife into his chest, hanging on the body a death threat for Ayaan Hirsi Ali, then a Somali refugee in the Netherlands who had worked with van Gogh on a documentary on the condition of women in Islam.

It was the first Islamist murder in Europe. The anxiety it generated led to the first signs of an epidemic of self-censorship in the cultural world all across the continent. In November 2006, to give only one example, the director of the Deutsche Oper Berlin, Kirsten Harms, decided to cancel a production of Mozart's opera *Idomeneo* to avoid "incalculable security risk." Departing from the original libretto, the staging of the opera presented the severed heads of Jesus, Buddha, and Muhammad placed on chairs. Threats had been received by phone, and, on the grounds that "one should respect sensibilities and avoid hurting a great religious community," Ali Kizilkaya, head of the Islamrat, one of the main Muslim associations in Germany, supported the decision to cancel the show, without any mention of the threats, let alone condemnation of them. It had taken Angela Merkel's firm stand against censorship to finally get the opera rescheduled the following month without incident.

In nearby Denmark, the writer Kåre Bluitgen complained that he couldn't find any artist willing to illustrate his book on Muhammad. In September 2005, as a solidarity gesture toward Bluitgen, and to tamp down the rising fear, the Danish journal *Jyllands-Posten* asked forty-two illustrators to draw their own interpretation of the Prophet Muhammad as an experiment to test fear, and ended up publishing twelve of them on September 30. On December 1, after two months of heated debate and after a complaint of offense was filed by Denmark's leading Muslim organizations, eight of the twelve illustrators secretly met with representatives of the Muslim community to cool things off. The next day, however, a Pakistani Islamist group issued a statement offering a reward to anyone who would kill the illustrators. A few days later, the European Committee for Prophet Honouring, composed of several Danish imams, built a forty-three-page dossier on the cartoons and undertook a trip to the Middle East, in order to gain international support and leverage against *Jyllands-Posten*. In addition to the drawings themselves and Danish articles on the subject, the committee had added three pictures of its own. One of them showed a man wearing a pig mask, with a caption saying, "Here is the real image of Muhammad." The photo was wrongly reported by the BBC, the next February, as having been published by *Jyllands-Posten*. In fact, the image had been picked up from an innocuous pig-squealing contest at a regional feast called La Pourcaillade, held each August since 1975 in the French Hautes-Pyrénées. The two additional drawings — also never part of the original cartoons — showed Muhammad being mounted by a dog and as a pedophile. Whether the imams had intentionally linked these additional images to the Danish newspaper or whether they were understood to be part of the cartoons because they were in their files as evidence of an alleged Islamophobic climate in Europe was never clarified.[8]

In any case, once they began to appear online, these three images infuriated the Muslim opinion worldwide. Mass demonstrations ensued outside Western embassies in Muslim countries, becoming so violent and scary as to generate a statement of apology from the European Council, in Brussels, in the name of the entire continent. This statement, in turn, was seen as a capitulation to fear by several European publications, which, as a reaction, offered to publish the original set of cartoons as they had been printed by *Jyllands-Posten* —that is to say, minus the material that had been added by the Danish imams. Among these magazines and newspapers were three French ones: *France-Soir, L'Express,* and *Charlie Hebdo.*

The first of the three, *France-Soir,* was owned at the time by an Egyptian-Lebanese businessman of Syrian background named Raymond Lakha, and Lakha immediately had the paper's chief editor fired before he could go to press. The second journal was the prestigious weekly magazine *L'Express.* Its owner happened to be President Chirac's longtime friend and financial backer, the armament industrialist Marcel Dassault. The very week the publication was scheduled, Dassault was selling French Rafale planes in Saudi Arabia, with Mr. Chirac acting as the company's chief salesman. From Riyadh, Dassault called *L'Express* chief editor Denis Jeambar and ordered him to kill the story. Forced to comply, Jeambar submitted his letter of resignation the next day. The drawings had not been published. That left *Charlie Hebdo,* by far the least powerful of the three papers, if also the most independent.

Whether Mr. Chirac advised the Saudis to press charges against *Charlie Hebdo* while he was still in Riyadh is not known. In any case, it was not the French Muslims of the *cités* who first protested against the newspaper—then a fanzine they had never heard of— but the Muslim World League, a Saudi-backed entity whose subsidiary in nearby Brussels, the Islamic and Cultural Center of Belgium, was legally represented by Dieudonné's friend and lawyer Sébastien Courtoy. Meanwhile, back in Paris, Mr. Chirac sent his own personal lawyer, Francis Szpiner, to the Grand Mosque of Paris, with the mission of convincing its rector, Dalil Boubakeur, to join the Saudi Muslim World League, which, along with a third association, the Muslim Brotherhood–controlled Union des Organisations Islamiques de France (UOIF), was pressing charges against the journal. The rationale for Chirac's decision to send his own lawyer to the mosque was that plaintiffs needed a moderate voice, so the extremist would not be the only one to speak, and, despite the absurdity of the reasoning—what moderate voice makes an extremist demand?—a reluctant Boubakeur finally agreed. In fact, Mr. Chirac's calculation was simple: friendly relations would thus be maintained with the Saudis, while French Muslims would be shown that their ostensible concerns were taken care of—even though they hadn't shown any particular interest in the cartoons until then.

Mr. Chirac, however, had reasons to be worried about the *cités*. During the previous fall, in October 2005, Zyed Benna, fifteen, and Bouna Traoré, seventeen, fleeing a police identity check, had sought refuge in a local power station, where they met their deaths via electrocution. The case of two police officers who had apparently watched as the boys entered the power station and taken no action to get them out was still pending. (A controversial acquittal verdict would be pronounced, but not until May 2015.) Some of the more severe riots that had ensued "in retaliation," as it were, for these two deaths had erupted around mosques. The burning of cars and clashes with police that continued for the next three weeks had nourished the feeling that France was on the verge of some sort of intifada. Mr. Chirac, then seventy-three years old, was two years away from the end of his second term. He had beaten the National Front three years earlier. His opposition to the war in Iraq had made him extremely popular in the Arab world as well as in the *cités,* and he was not ready to risk this legacy. A state-backed righteous action against a blasphemous magazine seemed the best symbolic gesture to make. It was the stubborn continuation of the policy consisting of transmuting social civil-rights issues into religious ones. So he'd sent Szpiner, his personal attorney, to the Grand Mosque and to court. But did Szpiner intend to win?

The two-day *Charlie Hebdo* trial started in February 2007—two years after the riots in the suburbs and one year after the murder of Ilan Halimi, described in the opening of this book. Despite the somber context, it looked like a scene out of a Milos Forman movie.

Anyone attending the hearings was struck by the light, joyful atmosphere, slightly childish even, that reigned in the courtroom. Simply by stepping into the room, you knew exactly who the good guys were. They were the cool ones. Star journalist Philippe Val, who was then *Charlie Hebdo*'s editorial director and editor in chief, and as such had added some luster to the declining magazine during the previous years, appeared on the stand, tall, elegant, and funny, always right in his thinking and hopelessly French in the self-satisfaction he displayed for being so; the essayist Caroline Fourest, one of the best-known columnists at *Charlie Hebdo,* looked like the star student, and everyone could (rightly) praise her courage and her feminism in her fight, despite threats, against both Islamist networks and the French extreme right; chief editor Charb, of course, was there, as were lesser-known members of the team who had not been exposed to the light of public admiration in years or, in some cases, ever. And all appeared on the witness stand as determined as they were relaxed, humorous, and smart—as were their star lawyers, starting with the sophisticated dandy Georges Kiejman.

In short, *Charlie Hebdo* had become trendy overnight. Letters of support for the fanzine poured in at the hearings from all across the political spectrum, from the Socialists (François Hollande, then secretary-general of the party, came in person) to the presidential candidate Nicolas Sarkozy and even the National Front; from literary stars like Philippe Sollers and Julia Kristeva to Claude Lanzmann and Bernard-Henri Lévy. When he was not exchanging friendly jokes with Francis Szpiner, Georges Kiejman recited each famous name supporting *Charlie Hebdo* with such obvious and proud delight that he seemed to be reciting the *Who's Who* at a cocktail party. If you were in the city, to put in an appearance was more than a moral obligation: it was the place to be, an intellectual frenzy that only Paris can produce. And yet — or, rather, because of this — it was also a real, serious debate, involving global questions and French values. A French production where French philosophical issues such as secularism and the heritage of the Enlightenment would be re-energized with lightness and grace — at the obvious expense of the World Muslim League's lawyers, who looked during the hearings like the Stalinists of old: lost in their own seriousness, all honor wounded and deprived of any hint of humor.

So did Szpiner, acting for the Grand Mosque on Chirac's behalf, intend to win? Could Mr. Chirac appear as the president under whom censorship would prevail in France? Of course not. The risks were nil — or so it seemed.

Interviewed outside the courtroom between sessions, the philosopher Élisabeth Badinter might have been the only one to express a sense of the tragic undercurrent running beneath the comedy that was going on inside the courtroom. "To me," she said to TV reporters, "the people at *Charlie Hebdo* are heroes. Because they know — we all know today, and this is no fantasy — that something really awful can happen." But nobody listened; nobody really realized — maybe not even the *Charlie Hebdo* team itself. Then again, why should they have? Brilliant jokes burst forth, smart analysis springing up on all sides. It looked like the resurrection of what the French call "the spirit of May '68," i.e., the last collective manifestation of a youthful insurrectional spirit that, after so many decades of boring compliance with the state-sponsored court culture, everyone was understandably nostalgic for.

But then something happened. The trial ended, a verdict was announced, and the spotlights were turned off. Soon Szpiner found himself on a new mission for Chirac—representing Ilan Halimi's mother at the Fofana trial, where Jews would end up being vindicated. And as for the magazine's star bylines, they cashed in their new social glamour and left for more secure and prestigious positions. The less well-known Charb replaced Val as the head of the paper. Paris went back to ignoring *Charlie Hebdo.*

In the Dieudonné circles, among Muslim militants, and in the *cités,* however, the story didn't end. People scorned what they saw as a bourgeois theater production staged by a clique of corrupt intelligentsia. Not only were Muslims the only ones *not* to laugh in the courtroom; they were, in fact, the ones laughed *about.* They'd been had. The French president himself had advised them to take action. But to what end? To be ridiculed. If they had not heard of *Charlie Hebdo* before, people in the *cités* now knew everything there was to know about the magazine—and more.

And here is the interesting point. While absolutely nothing in the story of the cartoons, nor in the *Charlie Hebdo* team or in the trial itself, was in any way related to Jews, Zionists, Israel, or any topic or entity that might remotely be considered Jewish, Muslim opinion following the trial responded to it by referencing the worst episode in Jewish history. In classrooms when the subject came up, on Muslim blogs and websites, as the cartoons of Muhammad were criticized and raged against, the drawings were not compared to cartoons of Christ or of Moses—they were compared to mocking the Shoah. *Why can one mock the Prophet and not the six million?* it was asked. *Why can you mock what we believe in while we don't have the equal right to laugh about your religion, which is the Holocaust? Is this not yet another sign of the double standard between Muslims and Jews in France? Isn't this proof that* Charlie Hebdo *is in fact Zionist-controlled, and the whole thing one more plot to humiliate us?* Of course, not ev-

ery Muslim blog or *every* classroom in the *cités* in the aftermath of the *Charlie Hebdo* trial adopted this line—there *was* no line, in fact, and it would be perfectly possible to find many examples of people there thinking otherwise. But a narrative was born, one that was boosted by Iran's decision in November 2007 to set up in Tehran an annual competition for cartoons about the Shoah as an "answer" to the cartoons of the Prophet. In his show at the Main d'Or theater, and on tour, Dieudonné dutifully echoed the parallel between the cartoons of Muhammad and the untouchable "faith" in the Shoah, thus spreading the notion across the country. Coincidentally or not, Tehran began to sponsor Dieudonné and Soral's short-lived Anti-Zionist Party soon after. In return, that narrative fueled anti-Jewish incidents in a significant enough number to suggest an abrasive climate. That was when the death threats began at *Charlie Hebdo*. Once again, the twists and turns of a senile French Arab policy and perverse right-wing and Islamist propaganda had collided with the rampant clichés of a dormant narrative. Now the issue had taken on a life of its own.

In the following years, Charb and his colleagues thought the best way to respond to the rising volume of death threats they received was to answer them by doing what they always had done, to the best of their ability: publishing cartoons even though, in the eyes of their (soon to be ex-) leftist friends, this was beginning to make them look cynical—were they trying to surf on the fame the trial had brought them? Or were they now so "obsessed" with Islam as to turn "Islamophobic," and therefore to be avoided? The death threats became part of daily life at the magazine. Security systems were installed, guards were posted. In 2010, when a bomb destroyed the office of the magazine, there was no particular outcry, and very little interest among intellectual celebrities in reviving the issue. Some, such as the young essayist Rokhaya Diallo, claimed that *Charlie Hebdo* was simply trying to make money, which suggested that the journal's team had planted the bomb. The general feeling was that the staff of *Charlie Hebdo* had more or less asked for it. In other words, they had become Jews.

THE GANG OF BARBARIANS TRIAL

It was two years later, in 2009, that the trial began for the self-proclaimed Gang of Barbarians, whose members had abducted, tortured, and killed Ilan Halimi in 2005, as recounted above. Not only did the trial offer yet another example of the inability to deal with this mix of individual pathology and collective narrative encountered in the Sébastien Selam case, but while media, police officers, lawyers, prosecutors, and judges all did their best to demonstrate that Ilan Halimi's fate had had "nothing to do" with anti-Semitism, the hearings began attracting attention from many segments of the population with questionable motives and mindsets.

At Mr. Chirac's request (France has a long tradition of political interventionism in judicial affairs), Francis Szpiner was assigned as the lawyer for Ilan Halimi's mother, Ruth. As soon as the hearings started, he spewed righteous anger, in front of every camera in the country, against the state prosecutor at the trial, Philippe Bilger, whose father had been a Nazi collaborator during World War II. His leniency against Halimi's killer, claimed Szpiner during the hearings, proved him a "biological traitor." Boasting about his personal contacts with President Chirac, he added that, if the verdict disappointed him or his clients, he'd do whatever it took to get a more suitable sentence on appeal.

The result, needless to say, was devastating. In the media as well as in public opinion, the Jews appeared as a powerful community that saw itself above the law and was able to get what it wanted from the state. During the four months of the trial, newspapers published op-eds denouncing the communitarianism of "some" who, by "systematically manipulating" the facts—i.e., claiming anti-Semitism where there was none—took "the risks of raising one community against the other." Meanwhile, at the Main d'Or theater, as Dieudonné was playing his sold-out show *Mahmoud*—a reference to Iranian president Mahmoud Ahmadinejad—he joked about *Charlie Hebdo* and interviewed the terrorist Carlos from his jail cell. Carlos's lawyer, as it turned out, one Isabelle Coutant-Peyre, fifty-seven, had converted to Islam to marry her client in jail and had volunteered to represent Youssouf Fofana, the leader of the Gang of Barbarians and the one most responsible for Ilan Halimi's death—a narcissist sociopath of the first order who, while on the run after the murder, had given an interview to a TV crew from the Ivory Coast, where he had sought refuge before being extradited; who, from jail, had tried to sell his memoirs to *Paris Match* and spent the hearings insulting everyone. After some months, Coutant-Peyre resigned from Fofana's defense team, but in between, she had influenced him enough for him to start transforming his instinctive hate of the Jews into a more structured ideology. Sentenced to life imprisonment, he turned into a devout Islamist. (For years after his condemnation, his name would be invoked by perpetrators of anti-Jewish acts, for whom to "do an Ilan Halimi" became a common phrase. In 2011, Coutant-Peyre, for her part, announced that she had been hired by the Iranian government to launch legal proceedings against U.S. movie studios for features said to misrepresent Iran. For good measure, Coutant-Peyre is also a legal counsel for Dieudonné.)

Finally, there was the prosecutor himself, Philippe Bilger, whose father, Joseph, had indeed been one of the most important leaders of the Deutsche Volksgemeinschaft (DVG), the German People's Community, which was the Lorraine counterpart to the Nazi Party in the North of France, and had been sentenced to ten years of forced labor in 1945. Paranoid Szpiner was right about that. Born in 1943, Bilger had grown up in the shadow of his father's shame, and, by his own admission, it was his sentencing, which he found unjust, that had inspired his own decision to become a judge. Coincidentally, a few months before the gang's trial started, Bilger had published a book in which he favorably portrayed his father as a sort of modern Creon, torn apart, like Sophocles's character, by conflicting duties and a moral "dilemma" during World War II—as if there was indeed any dilemma to have in the years of the Nazi Occupation. The mental world in which Bilger lived appeared several times during the hearings as he denied that, apart from Youssouf Fofana, any anti-Semitism existed among the gang. But maybe the most telling was a minor incident on the margins of the hearings, the day Ruth Halimi appeared on the witness stand. In a flood of tears, she concluded her testimony with a statement claiming that the murder of her son was a sign that "the Shoah was starting all over again." This was, of course, an expression of her grief. But Bilger did not exactly see it that way. He then took the liberty to comment on it that very evening on his blog. It was only two words, but in their coldness, they spoke volumes: *"Restons calme"* ("Let's keep calm—let's not exaggerate").

Indeed, as a new decade was about to begin, and as the process of incubating hate was now complete, this could have been the answer of the country at large regarding the ordeal Jews had gone through since the early 2000s.

SIX

A Revelation and a Denial:
The Toulouse and Montauban Killings

TARGETING THE BEST

The only thing the Ozar Hatorah school of Toulouse was known for until March 2012 was its reputation for excellence. To this day, its students still have a 100 percent pass rate at the *baccalauréat* national secondary school exit exam, 87 percent of them scoring grade A.

The Ozar Hatorah network, of which the school is part, was created in the aftermath of World War II by an American philanthropist of Syrian background, Isaac Shalom, who'd emigrated from Aleppo to the Lower East Side of Manhattan in 1910, made money in the *shmatah* business, and, after 1945, contemplating the state of affairs of the Jews, decided to dedicate his wealth to the creation of Jewish schools first in Israel, then in North Africa, and, after most of the Jews from the Maghreb were thrown out of the Arab countries and settled in France in the early sixties, in France as well.

Although it was the third of its kind after Lyon and Sarcelles, the Toulouse Ozar Hatorah barely deserved to be called a school when it first opened, in 1983, in a private apartment in downtown Toulouse, with no more than eight students. It took the arrival, in 1992, of a rav from a Moroccan family of well-reputed rabbis — the charismatic Yaacov Monsonego and his wife, Yaffa — to change that. Yaacov and Yaffa Monsonego were in their thirties when they settled in town. Taking the reins of Ozar Hatorah, they decided to try to turn the small school into an ambitious institution that would be recognized nationally as a center of academic excellence.

"Such a project required determination, faith, and a great deal of energy," the school's deputy, Anne Werthenschlag, explained to me, "but mostly it required good recruiting. For to get the agreement of the state, you needed to have more students, and in order to have more students, we needed an excellent educational team. So Mr. Monsonego looked for dedicated teachers regardless of their religious background. Teachers who believe in what they do, who think of their work as a vocation and have in mind, like us, the interests of the students above all. That was, and still is, the key."[1]

Today the curriculum follows the Ministry of Education guidelines, to which ten hours of Judaism per week are added. Freedom of thought and freedom of opinion are welcome and encouraged in class. How "religious" does that make the Ozar Hatorah school of Toulouse, then?

"It is more like an experiment," Werthenschlag said. "We provide the children with a kind of teaching and a kind of life they keep with them afterwards. And it produces results. The school has a structural financial deficit that forces us to call upon the alumni for donations. We've been able to raise some sixty thousand euros per year that way. From all over the world, former students want to help, because they feel they should give something back. This mutual commitment is what explains how Mr. and Mrs. Monsonego succeed in waking up every morning despite what happened. It helps to understand how they walk through that gate."

Anne Werthenschlag is a tall woman with a distinctly French elegance and charm mixed with a discreet but energetic authority. She is an observant Jew, but she displays no outward signs of religious practice. A notary by trade, she stumbled into the job at the school in 2010, after she'd left Strasbourg, where she was born. "The vagaries of life," she soberly comments on her moving to Toulouse. "I had small children and was in search of a job that would leave me room to practice my Judaism. The opportunity showed up, I took it."

Of the killings here, she speaks only reluctantly, and when she does, she refers to them as "what happened." "What happened, happened," she says, for instance, with a controlled voice that keeps sentimentalism at bay. "It was, of course, a shock. One's never prepared. Even the police cars protecting the gates of the synagogues at certain points in our Jewish history here in France"—a reference to the security measures that have had to be taken regularly for Jewish establishments since the first terror attacks in the early eighties— "even the fact that, in a way, it has always been here, this threat . . . You know? You go to the shul, you say to yourself, 'Well, the police are here.' So what? Surely, if it happens at all, it'll happen elsewhere. But even more surely, nothing will happen at all. The feeling of normalcy lives on for a long time even in abnormal conditions."

But once that feeling's gone?

"Well, let me tell you a story. Maybe ten days after it happened, we had our first dinner at the school with the students. There was the rav, Mr. Monsonego, some professors, and me, and one of the professors made a speech. He said, in essence, that after carefully studying the question, he thought we should be very careful because, as a rule, it's in the three months after an attack that a second one is likely to occur at the same spot. And my first thought hearing that was: He's crazy. First, this is an irresponsible statement to make in front of already traumatized children. Second, it didn't make sense. We'd been hit once; how on earth could we be hit a second time? But if I was right on the first point, of course, on the second I was wrong, at least partly. Because we could. In three days, in three months, in three years: the truth of the matter is that we had as many chances to be hit as anyone else — and maybe a bit more, because we'd been exposed."

Werthenschlag refers here to the many threats and insults that the school received through letters, emails, and even phone calls, along with numerous words of solidarity, after the attack. Two years later, in 2014 — a year, as I said, decidedly full — a man would take pains to post a picture of himself doing the infamous *quenelle* in front of the school, and in July somebody would throw a Molotov cocktail at the building.

But in the Jewish French world, the school was far from alone in experiencing a backlash after what had happened. "Why is it that Jews, when something happens to them, always make such a fuss of it all?" a lawyer acquaintance of mine asked me the following day. "Do they protest when non-Jewish children are being murdered that way? What is it that's so special with you guys? Don't you realize that's why it's happening?" Soon I found myself losing control, too, as I explained to her that it was precisely that: other children usually did not get killed that way in the streets. At least not in a Western democracy. At least not since World War II.

"I refuse to give up," Anne Werthenschlag went on as we walked in the courtyard of the school. "If we give up, what then? Are we going to run away and live in a foreign country? What about the ones who can't? You have to work in order to make the children succeed the best they can. To make them dream the way they dreamed before it happened. This, to us, is the most important. We can't let ourselves be demolished. We can't let our educational project be destroyed by what happened."

The school's most remarkable feature is its lack of ostentatiousness. A quiet courtyard surrounded by three low-rise buildings sheltering, on one side, the classrooms and administrative offices and, on the other, the cafeteria where we'd just had lunch and the shul where most of the students were still gathered when the killer showed up. From outside the dark gates, nothing distinguishes this particular address from the rest of the quiet middle-class La Rose-raie neighborhood of pavilions and flowers. Only rarely did pedestrians stroll by on the sunny sidewalk that day. There was no wind, and the deep-green leaves on the frail trees added to the feeling of complete calm and stillness.

The only sign of "what happened" was the new higher walls and barbed wire over the gates. After the attack, when they were installed, Werthenschlag had asked if those wires and walls couldn't be transparent. When I first heard that detail, I thought of it as a touchingly naive question, a slightly ridiculous excess of delicacy — but now, looking at those gates and walls, listening to her, I was of a different mind.

I thought of that other wall: the label "Orthodox," given by the press to the school in their coverage of the incident. *An Orthodox Jewish school attacked.* Yet 95 percent of the teachers were not Jewish. (Incidentally, despite some pressure from their families, all of them stayed at the school afterwards.) "Orthodox" is hardly an innocent word in a country where *laïcité,* the French version of secularism, is as ideologically charged as ever. I began to wonder whether this was not what all of this was really about. To confine an original experiment within the walls of a restrictive identity, to assign those people to an imagined Jewish tribalism that French opinion could blame the killings on. I wondered if the discretion of the school, its refusal of ostentatiousness, even Werthenschlag's reluctance to tell the tale of "what happened" — if this was not, in fact, an elegant resistance to clichés, a way to remain free and in charge. "I close my eyes," said Werthenschlag, "and I hear the children laughing in the courtyard, and it is like I am in any other school."

What happened on March 19, 2012, at the Ozar Hatorah school really began one week earlier, on March 11, in the south part of town, with the murder of Imad Ibn Ziaten, a French officer of Moroccan origin in the 1st parachutist regiment who had posted an ad on a website to sell a motorcycle. A buyer had declared himself, an appointment had been made. But when Ibn Ziaten showed up, instead of buying the bike, the anonymous person shot him in the head with a .45-caliber gun. Witnesses saw the killer fleeing on a black scooter.

Four days later, early in the afternoon of March 15, in front of an ATM machine in the nearby town of Montauban, three other soldiers—Abel Chennouf, a Catholic, partly of Algerian descent, Mohamed Legouad, a Muslim, and Loïc Liber—were shot a total of thirteen times with the same weapon. (Liber was the only one to survive, though he was paralyzed.) This time, video cameras captured a young man, face hooded by a black helmet, riding a black scooter. Because all of the targeted soldiers had Maghrebian origins, the authorities directed their search toward extreme-right racist circles—a lead that would later prove to be one of the many blunders of the investigation.

"My son was in sixth grade and my daughter was going to the Gan Rashi school—the annex of the Ozar Hatorah for small children," Anne Werthenschlag told me. "Every morning before I took my son to school with me, I would drop off both my daughter and Mr. Monsonego's daughter, Miriam, eight years old, at Gan Rashi, and Mrs. Monsonego would bring my daughter back in the evening. But that day, my daughter was sick. So when I brought my son to the school and little Miriam made a move to get into the car, I said, 'No, sweetheart, I'm sorry, I can't take you today. I'm calling your dad right away to arrange another car to pick you up.' She stayed with a professor, Rav Sandler, and his children, and I left."

The events that unfolded less than five minutes later have been widely reported: how the man on the scooter, helmet on his head and a GoPro camera fixed to his chest, parked his scooter right in front of the gate; how he pulled out a Parabellum nine-millimeter and fired several bullets, hitting first Rabbi Sandler, then his sons Gabriel, three, and Aryeh, six (as the video surveillance would later show, one of the children crawled toward his father when the killer shot him); how he chased Miriam Monsonego into the courtyard of the school, hitting, in passing, Aaron "Bryan" Bijaoui, fifteen, who was trying to help the little girl run from her killer; how he grabbed her by the hair, put his weapon to her head, and pulled the trigger, but the weapon jammed, forcing the killer to give up his nine-millimeter for a .45 ACP, with which he shot the child at close range. Then, with the courtyard now empty and no other target in sight — the synagogue's lack of identification probably saving the children gathered inside, as the killer did not identify the building — he got back on his scooter and disappeared, leaving behind one dead adult and three dead children. A street video camera filmed him proudly wheeling away on his scooter. Aaron Bijaoui, although seriously wounded, survived.

Nicole Yardéni, the local representative of the council of French Jewish organizations at the time, was home having breakfast when her cousin called to break the news. "He knew because he had his two children there," she told me. "But I actually had to make him repeat the sentence three times. 'There's been a shooting at Ozar Hatorah.' I literally did not understand what that meant."[2]

Yardéni is a warm, strong middle-aged woman. On the scene, she says, what she found the most striking was the silence. The parents at the end of the street massed behind police fences, not allowed to get in, their faces grave, their bodies immobile, with no way to know who was hurt and who was safe. Inside the school, the bodies still lay in the courtyard, and everybody waited for the investigative team to proceed. Children had been transferred from the shul to the refectory, and no one was allowed out. And nobody said a word.

The police let her pass because of her status. She says that when she entered the refectory, she faced the children, not knowing what to say, and the first thing that came to her mind was a sentence in Yiddish: *"Schwer zu sein a Yid."* She knew it from her father, who was one of the last remaining German Jews to have actually witnessed Kristallnacht before his family fled Germany. She adapted it, adding a few words of her own in French: "I'm sorry you're so young to learn it, but now you know what it is, at times, to be a Jew."

Reference to past history was inescapable. In the dignified, poignant statement she would give that evening, Yardéni said she had a thought for her mother-in-law, who had lost a son and a daughter in the Shoah—a mention she says she regretted afterwards.

Exiting the refectory, she saw Monsonego, unable to stand, carried by someone, and that was when she understood that her task in the coming days, as head of the French Jewish council, would be to act as "a screen" between the school and the general public—a public made up of the press, the police, and the many politicians threatening to flood in. For the presidential campaign that would put François Hollande in power was in full swing in 2012, and the two main candidates—Hollande and incumbent president Nicolas Sarkozy—already were on their way. Soon they would be followed by Benjamin Netanyahu. (Among the French political leaders, Marine Le Pen, from the National Front, was the only one not to come, nor even to make a phone call.)

"When Mr. Monsonego flew to Israel to bury his children," said Anne Werthenschlag, "he gave me the keys to the school—he put me in charge. That freed me from all the questions. It all became about logistics. What to do with the students in the dormitory? We had to send them back home in terrible condition: one of them was wounded, others had heard, sometimes seen, what had happened. Fortunately, the rectorship sent a team of psychologists to help, and by and large, all the authorities helped us very efficiently."

Messages of sympathy came in from all over the world. And two energetic women were in charge. "My only concern," Nicole Yardéni told me, "was to place that tragedy in the national context. Jewish children had been killed, for sure, and I had no doubt as to the anti-Semitic motivation. But who had done this did not inter-

est me in the slightest. I thought if we ever knew, I'll never pronounce his name. Psychological explanations, sociological explanations, none of this interested me. What mattered was what this
tragedy meant for the country."

But what did it mean for the country at that time?

A FLOOD OF WORDS TO COVER THE PANIC

It is not too much to say that as soon as he was identified and killed
by police, Mohammed Merah, the twenty-three-year-old killer of
Algerian descent, born and raised in Toulouse, became an object of
obsessive fascination in the Muslim community as well as in France
at large, overshadowing any feeling of empathy for the Jewish victims.

That week of the Ozar Hatorah incident, I was invited onto
France Culture twice, on unrelated themes. The first of the two
broadcasts took place, coincidentally, the morning of the killings. I
was the only one there to mention what had happened at all; during the second show, two days later — coincidentally, the day of the
killer's death in a shootout with the RAID elite section — everyone
in the studio was debating *him:* What had triggered his violence?
Nobody asked about the victims and their families.

Meanwhile, the minute of silence declared nationwide for the
dead children in all French primary and secondary schools was
countered on at least two occasions by teachers who felt they should
list the killer among the casualties — the minute of silence was to be
for him, too, or else not at all, for surely he was a victim of the system, and it was important for remembrance to be balanced, to not
favor one "side" over the other.

Two weeks after the slaughter, *Le Monde* went as far as to
commission and publish a front-page short story authored by a

French writer of Algerian background named Salim Bachi, titled "I, Mohammed Merah."[3] It was a fictionalized account that purported to get *inside the head* of the killer. The story presented Merah as (to quote the author) an isolated rebel, a "little brat" victim of France's social and racial discrimination. Three months before the killings, the same author had published a novel called *I, Khaled Kelkal,* dedicated to the GIA operative in Vaulx and head of the 1995 terror wave, and based on the same narrative principle. Despite my own intervention—as a contributor to the newspaper, I received Bachi's piece beforehand and argued for an hour over the phone with the chief editor of the literary section, trying to persuade him to kill it —*Le Monde* published the new piece without any more regard for the victims' families, even though some of them may have been subscribers.

For the left—where France Culture and *Le Monde* stand politically—the emergency was not so much to exonerate the killer as it was to save France's Muslims from any prejudice that might result from Mohammed Merah's actions. *Do not generalize!* became the standard watchwords. Needless to say, the subtext was also about saving the left itself, or at least the part of it that had denied for years that any structured, violent anti-Semitism could pervade a significant fraction of the French Muslim youth. In a sense, it was a continuation of the Selam/Ilan Halimi dilemma but turned upside down, so to speak. Whereas in 2003 and 2006, the killers were too mentally unstable to "really" be anti-Semites, now, to the contrary, Merah's anti-Semitism was seen as the incontestable sign that he was precisely that: a deranged loner. Albeit a single aberration, however, Merah was also the fatal, sociological product of the discriminative "neocolonial" French system. The esteemed intellectual Tariq Ramadan, who had close ties to the Muslim Brotherhood and was then at the peak of his influential popularity in France, kindly provided the rationale for that somewhat self-contradictory narrative on his blog, where, denouncing the crimes, he nonetheless presented the killer as "nice ... a teenager with an affectionate heart ... a poor boy ... victim of a social order that had condemned him beforehand, him and millions like him, to the margins, and whose story sends France to its own mirror."[4] (Why the social environment could be so determinative when it was French, while not at all as soon as the Algerian Muslim background was concerned, was not even discussed.)

But, to be fair, the theory of Merah's exceptionalism was by no means exclusive to the left. More crucial to the pervading atmosphere in the country was the public prosecutor François Molins's statement on March 21, shortly after Merah had been killed: "No information indicating any connection between Merah and an organization on French territory was available to any intelligence service." He was followed three days later by a full-page interview given to *Le Monde* by the head of the Central Directorate of Internal Intelligence (DCRI), Bernard Squarcini, who, in spite of the fact that the investigation had barely begun, defended with complete confidence the idea that Merah was a "lone wolf." In fact, it was this interview that popularized the notion.

Because the killings had attracted international attention, the lone wolf theory soon traveled across the Atlantic. On March 23, 2012, the *New York Times* published an op-ed by the French political scientist Olivier Roy, stating with the highest certainty that Merah "was not known for his piety: He did not belong to any religious congregation; he did not belong to any radical group or even to a local Islamic movement. A petty delinquent, psychologically fragile, he ... found in Al Qaeda a narrative of solitary heroism and a way, after months of watching videos on the Internet, to achieve short-term notoriety and find a place in the real world."[5]

That reasoning went a long way. In France, the anthropologist Dounia Bouzar, a former student of Roy's, used it to set up the first "deradicalization" unit, Le Centre de Prévention des Dérives Sectaires Liées à l'Islam (the Prevention Center of Sectarian Excesses

Connected with Islam), which became, that year, the exclusive partner of the French government on the subject and would remain
so until the wake-up call of the synchronized attacks of November
2015. In the English-speaking world, even after the *Charlie Hebdo*
massacre, the American journalist Adam Shatz would assume the
same reasoning, arguing on the *London Review of Books* blog that
the Kouachi brothers, the killers of the journal's team, were "products of the West ... It's unlikely they could have recited more than
the few *hadith* they learned from the ex-janitor-turned-imam who
presided over their indoctrination. They came from a broken family
and started out as petty criminals, much like Mohamed Merah, who
murdered a group of Jewish schoolchildren."[6]

Mohammed Merah's murder spree has given birth, paradoxically,
to a narrative in which Islamist networks are nowhere to be seen. Its
general conclusion was summarized by Olivier Roy's *Times* piece:
"People like these are difficult to spot precisely because they do not
belong to a network of militant cells."

"UNTIL THE DEATH OF ALL OF US"

In the days following Mohammed Merah's death, however, his
brother Abdelkader, then aged thirty, was charged with conspiracy
with terrorist intent and accessory to murder, and incarcerated at
Fresnes Prison.

Mohammed's body had been stored, meanwhile, in the morgue,
and his mother, Zoulikha Aziri, fifty-five, was called by the authorities to identify the body. Apparently unable to comply, perhaps overwhelmed by emotion, she had sent her brother Hamid, Mohammed
and Abdelkader's uncle, to perform the task. At Abdelkader's request,
it seems she had also asked Hamid to take pictures of the corpse.

On October 4, 2012, Kader received a visit from Zoulikha in jail.
The following conversation, which occurred in Arabic, was taped

by the wards, on the investigative judge's instructions, translated into French, and added to the accusatory file I managed to gain access to.

ZOULIKHA AZIRI: You see, my heart is oppressed. I'm worried about you.

ABDELKADER: Why?

ZOULIKHA AZIRI: I'm worried about you.

ABDELKADER: But I am well, Mama.

ZOULIKHA AZIRI: I pray to Allah that he helps you to put up with it.

ABDELKADER: Don't you know what Merah or Merat means?

ZOULIKHA AZIRI: I know. Merat, it is "heritage."

ABDELKADER: And "gift"? How do you say "gift" in Arabic? In classic Arabic. You say *"hadia."*

ZOULIKHA AZIRI: Yes, *hadia.*

ABDELKADER: By Allah, Mohammed, he made me the greatest gift there is!

ZOULIKHA AZIRI: Praise to Allah! What if you were to have a child and your child turned out just like him? What if your child became like his uncle?

ABDELKADER: *Inshallah!* What a success if he became like him! I would call him Mohammed Abu Yusuf, *inshallah.* [Abu Yusuf was Mohammed Merah's nom de guerre.] . . . You didn't want to see him at the morgue, it was difficult.

ZOULIKHA AZIRI: I couldn't. It was so insufferable.

ABDELKADER: Did you tell them to take pics?

ZOULIKHA AZIRI: Of?

ABDELKADER: Of Mohammed, Allah's mercy be upon him.

ZOULIKHA AZIRI: I told Hamid. I told him, you see, that Abdelkader wants to have pictures of his brother. Allah brought him back in front of us shining, you hear? They say he was never killed. He fell.

ABDELKADER: He sprang like a lion . . . The lawyer, he told you

he's going to visit, right? *Inshallah,* tell him to bring me Mohammed's autopsy report. All his pictures when he fell. His
head, how many bullets he took and all.

ZOULIKHA AZIRI: Ah!

ABDELKADER: How the autopsy was performed and all.

ZOULIKHA AZIRI: Ah! . . . It's all in pictures and all.

ABDELKADER: A whole file like that!

ZOULIKHA AZIRI: Allah is the greatest, *inshallah.*

Two months later, on December 18, Zoulikha Aziri visited again,
accompanied this time by Abdelkader's wife, Yamina. The conversation about the pictures resumed. (In French jails, visiting rooms are
one space where detainees and visitors can hug each other.)

ABDELKADER: [*speaking of the shootout between his brother and the
RAID squad, which ended with Mohammed being killed by a sniper
as he was trying to jump from his balcony*] So fast he was, so quickly
he shot! *Ta-ta-ta-ta!* They believed he had two guns! The one
aiming from afar [the sniper], he shot him, and the bullet ex-
ited. He had three wounds here, two here, and a shot, Allah be
praised, between the fingers!

YAMINA: You know them all by heart, ha ha!

ABDELKADER: I saw them! I saw them!

ZOULIKHA AZIRI: How so, you saw them?

ABDELKADER: He was naked, they took pictures of him.

ZOULIKHA AZIRI: Naked? He was naked?

ABDELKADER: Yes, naked!

ZOULIKHA AZIRI: The darling! He is gone now, and so are you.
You are dear to me. All my children are dear to me, you hear?

ABDELKADER: He is dearer. Me, I am dear, but he's dearer.

ZOULIKHA AZIRI: Yes, yes! He's been upgraded a little, whether
you want it or not. Ha ha!

ABDELKADER: [*Suddenly bursting into tears and hugging his mother*]

Of course! Upgraded a thousand times! [*To his wife*] I love him more than I love you! It's true! I love Mohammed more than everything! That's how it is! [*To his mother again, who hands him a handkerchief*] Don't you worry, Mama, I'm happy, I swear I am. More than all those people outside.

ZOULIKHA AZIRI: He visited me two nights ago. He appeared in a white towel. People said the perfume he wore has no existence down here. It was a perfume of which people spoke. They asked, "Who is this Mohammed, and where did he get such perfume?" He was wounded. And I asked him, "Who hurt you, Mohammed?" And he said, "A woman, Mama. She hit me with a drill."

ABDELKADER: I saw him.

ZOULIKHA AZIRI: Hm-hm.

ABDELKADER: He was sitting on a chair. I asked him, "What is the purpose of heaven?" And he answered: "Right now, I am driving." And I woke up and I wondered, "What does 'I am driving' mean?" And, in fact, Allah the Magnificent says the souls, they come like birds under the throne of the Merciful, they—

ZOULIKHA AZIRI: They swirl!

ABDELKADER: They swirl! Wherever they want. So, in fact, he drives the birds!

ZOULIKHA AZIRI: He drives the birds! Oh, they say they feed on the best dishes, you hear?

ABDELKADER: Ha ha ha!

ZOULIKHA AZIRI: And until the death of all of us, and at the end of the world, we will stand in front of Allah and he will marry them with the *houris* [virgins]!

ABDELKADER: He's got the *houris* now!

ZOULIKHA AZIRI: Now! Right now! Swear by Allah!

ABDELKADER: Yes, right now. He's not in the grave. He's in heaven!

ZOULIKHA AZIRI: Ah! And he's got the *houris* with him!

ABDELKADER: He's got the *houris* and he does the shameful act

with them. He does everything! [*They both laugh.*] Let us praise
Allah! He's got a wife, he's got everything, he eats!

ZOULIKHA AZIRI: They say he's got many!

THE SCAPEGOAT

This dialogue gives us a glimpse of the world from which Mohammed Merah sprang. Let us shed some light on this world.

The "darling" who, because he killed three soldiers, a rabbi, and
three Jewish children, is said to appear gloriously in his mother's and
brother's dreams and perform "the shameful act" in heaven; the little
brother whom Abdelkader loves, he says, even more than his wife,
so much so that he is dying to obtain pictures of his naked corpse
from the morgue, to contemplate in his cell, along with the autopsy
report detailing his every wound — this youngest son of the Merah
clan was, in truth, the scapegoat of the family.

One day in 2003, as one among many stories go, the future killer
of the Ozar Hatorah school, then aged fourteen, was slapped several times by Abdelkader, who then tied him to the bedpost in his
room, put a motorcycle helmet over his head, and hit him on the
head with a broomstick for two hours. He then forced him to eat
rotten food he'd retrieved from the trash bin. Despite, or rather because of, that kind of sadistic treatment, Mohammed conceived for
his big brother such a mix of passionate attachment and estrangement that this feeling is today seen as his primary motive for en-
listing, in 2006, in the Salafi gang that French intelligence calls "the
Artigat network" (after the region where it was formed), which Abdelkader had joined as far back as 2003, the very year of the broomstick incident — a network that, according to authorities and intellectuals alike, did not exist at all.

Confirmed by several reports from social services that were included in the criminal file, this torture session in 2003 was reported by the oldest of the Merah brothers, the renegade Abdelghani, in his book *Mon Frère, ce Terroriste* (*My Brother the Terrorist*).

Prior to this, however, it was Abdelghani who was the most violent of the siblings, hitting everyone around, his wife included, in a family that appears to have been entirely wracked by physical abuse and parental perversion from the start.

It seems that the reason why, in such an environment, the future killer Mohammed occupied the worst position was simply that he was the youngest, and therefore the weakest, though also, apparently, the brightest. The first warnings of his maltreatment at home were registered by the social services when he was four. When he was twelve, in 2000, a report given to the social services by the vice principal of the high school he attended speaks of "a child in grave danger: It is most urgent to intervene in the familial environment. For in light of his intellectual capacities, Mohammed could well turn into a very dangerous teenager."

Nothing, it seems, was done.

During Mohammed's adolescence, the dynamic of ardent attachment, estrangement, and reconciliation that characterized his relationship with his brother Abdelkader was already in full swing and would remain unchanged until Mohammed's death. For us, the aftermath of 9/11 appears to have been a key moment, because it indicates that hate *preceded* militancy. According to all the testimonies, his own included, Kader, though not yet an Islamist, burst with joy when he learned of the attacks in New York and D.C.—so much so that he started to yell, "Bin Laden! Bin Laden!" in the streets and seriously envisioned having the Al Qaeda leader's name tattooed on his forehead. Given the impracticalities, he asked his friends instead to call him from now on Grand Ben Ben, in reference to his new hero (after the French spelling, Ben Laden). Mohammed, who copied him in everything, took the name Petit Ben Ben.

In 2011, after a story of estrangement and reconciliation, Mohammed went to visit Kader in Cairo, where he was studying Islam at Al-Azhar University, and by the time they were back in Toulouse, in January 2012, two months before the attacks, they were inseparable. Abdelkader was present when Mohammed stole the Yamaha Tmax scooter that he would use for the killings.

As one does not find biographical elements such as these in every family, regardless of the religion they may profess, stories like the Merahs' present us with a narrative paradox.

Once upon a time, the novelistic approach used exceptional stories as exemplary cases from which to draw general lessons. The murder of the student Ivanov by the radical group Narodnaïa Volia, led by Serge Netchaïev, in Moscow in 1869, for instance, gave Dostoyevsky the material for *The Demons,* in which he "generalized" in order to expose some of the darkest corners of the Russian mind, prefiguring the Communist dictatorship fifty years in advance, the same way Flaubert "generalized" in *Madame Bovary* the deadly boredom in the French province from a real case of suicide, and Fritz Lang's movie *M* tells of the rise of Nazism through the seemingly disconnected story of a pedophile murderer in Germany.

But we live in an algorithmic age, which says that exceptionalism cannot be meaningful — statistical curves are. Pathological stories such as the Merahs', therefore, offer too rare a sequence of events to hold any sociological or political lesson at all about the Muslim world. It is from such reasoning that the lone wolf theory proceeded — politics and the need to cover the blunders of the investigation notwithstanding. Whereas the novelistic approach used to intuit general truths from unique cases, offering pathological exaggerations of the norm, statistical generalization forbids any possible extrapolation from the particular, or even from minor variations. The statistical approach, in other words, normalizes and decontextualizes, whereas, by focusing on the multifaceted individual journey, the novelistic view both particularizes and historicizes.

A DYSFUNCTIONAL FAMILY IN ITS HISTORICAL CONTEXT

What is really telling in people like the Merahs is how the random-
ness of their private troubles merges with historical events to produce who they are — who they can't not be, what we used to call
fate. Isn't there more than a coincidence in Mohammed Merah's
date of birth, October 10, 1988? That very same day, on the other
side of the Mediterranean, in downtown Algiers, there was unfolding the largest of the social demonstrations, repressed in blood by
the regime's army, as described above, that gave the Islamists their
popularity and would lead to civil war less than two years later. In
the living room of his Toulouse apartment, while his wife was at the
hospital giving birth to Mohammed, the boy's father, Mohammed
Merah Sr., was applauding the demonstrators in front of his TV set.

Five years later, in 1993, with the civil war and the massacres now
in full swing, Abdelghani and Abdelkader followed the elder Merah
to his native village of Oued Bezaz, Algeria, for their summer vacation. Oued Bezaz was a rough, dilapidated hamlet tucked away in
the mountains, some sixty miles from Oran, and fully supportive
of the Groupe Islamique Armé, the GIA, which, as we've seen, was
the armed wing of the Islamist Salvation Front, FIS. Abdelghani was
sixteen, Abdelkader only eleven, and all around them, their father's
cousins smuggled weapons for the Islamist commandos.

Mohammed Sr. had lived there until the early sixties. Then, after Algeria became independent, he had begun to travel to France.
While the new oligarchy in Algiers was getting rich through pe-
troleum contracts with the West, the USSR-sponsored FLN, which
was in power, favored a state economy, forbidding free trade and
making the daily domestic demand for consumer goods impossible
to satisfy. That situation led to the emergence of a popular practice
known on both sides of the Mediterranean as *trabendo,* from the

word for contraband—a black market between the newly independent country and its former colonizer, which played a huge part in the developing of immigration. People like Mohammed Sr., called *trabendistes,* would come to France to buy cheap consumer goods and would sell them for five to ten times the price back in Algeria. Mohammed Sr. began his activity with spare parts and later, at the end of the nineties, added drug trafficking.

The total number of children he's fathered remains unknown. The estimates vary between fifteen and twenty, but, to this day, none of the members of the Toulouse branch of the family are able to give a complete list of their half brothers and sisters. What is known is that the patriarch had already had a wife in Oued Bezzaz when Zoulikha Aziri appeared in his life, in 1975. They got married in May of the following year, and after their first children were born— Abdelghani in 1977 and Souad, the first daughter, in 1979—Zoulikha and Mohammed Sr.'s first wife lived with their respective children under the same roof, in a small house of clay and stone, with no electricity or running water, hating each other, while the husband was away. He'd come back only once a year, for two to three months, the time during which he sold off the junk merchandise he'd brought back with him from France. In the early eighties, Zoulikha managed to convince him to let her and her children travel with him and settle in Toulouse for good, and that is how they came to live in France.

Anti-Semitism ran deep in the family, long before the children turned toward Islamism. As Mohammed Sr. did his best to teach his children not to assimilate, they would refuse to celebrate Christmas, on the grounds that—as he had told them—"a Jew wanting to kill the Prophet once hid behind a fir tree."

Mohammed Sr.'s hostility to his own family life in France soon translated into violence. He picked up the habit of hitting his wife and children with fists, feet, a leather belt, and antenna wire. Into this milieu were born Aïcha (1980), Abdelkader (1982), and, finally, the future killer Mohammed (1988).

With time, the domestic violence became so bad that Zoulikha ended up moving to a shelter for battered women for a few months in the early nineties, before asking for a divorce, on her brother Hamid's advice—something that, at the trial, most of her children reproached her for, especially her daughter Aïcha.

With the divorce, in 1993, Mohammed Sr. left the house, and it was during this period that he began to take his sons with him to Oued Bezaz for the summer, and to add drug trafficking to his *trabendiste* activity. The violence of the father stopped, and yet this was when things really started to turn to hell in the house.

Indeed, once freed from her husband's tyranny, left alone, with no income, in a country that seemed to offer endless freedom, Zoulikha, then in her mid-thirties, seems to have lost it completely. She encouraged her children to shoplift, brought men home, and, if we are to believe Abdelghani, set up at least one orgy at home with a girlfriend and two men, in front of her children.

By this time, which coincides with the first social service reports about Mohammed, she already was in the habit of hitting her youngest and weakest. Her favorite tool for this was electrical wire.

Pathology attracts pathology. From a middle-class, quiet, Catholic background, against which she had just rebelled, entered the frail brunette Anne Chenevat. She was sixteen in 1994, the year she met seventeen-year-old Abdelghani, and the two began a love affair. Soon enough, Abdelghani decided to introduce her to Zoulikha, and "the first time she saw me, she spat on my face and called me a dirty Jew," Anne Chenevat testified at Kader's trial, held in November 2017 at Paris's Palais de Justice.

She spoke with a very quiet and soft voice. Then, with a distinct undertone of apology, she added: "I'm not even Jewish! My biological granddad was, but I barely knew him. I did not see him more than twice in my life!" It was Abdelghani himself who had passed to Zoulikha what appeared to be compromising information on his paramour.

Yet, despite this welcome, Anne Chenevat married Abdelghani, and both ended up living with the rest of the Merahs for a while in the family's apartment. ("You're not so bad for a French," Zoulikha told her, in what seems to have been an apology, perhaps even a sign of affection.) During that period, Anne would spend her evenings watching TV, coiled up on the sofa against Abdelkader, who protected her when Abdelghani returned home, drunk or high or both, to beat the shit out of her as he beat up everyone else who was around. She was seven months pregnant.

Then Kader rebelled. It was 2003, the year of the torture session. Violence, it seems, was the main way to gain power over Zoulikha, officially the sole parental authority at home. ("She always stands with the most violent," one of the sisters testified at the trial.) Perhaps eager to maintain his prominence in the family, Abdelghani took Mohammed to the cops to press charges against Kader for maltreatment, but once in the police station, Mohammed backed off—you simply don't snitch on your own brothers. Soon after, in a sort of familial coup, Kader stabbed Abdelghani seven times in the chest, missing his heart by less than an inch. He took over, and from then on, says Chenevat, "he, too, started to call me a dirty Jew. But I didn't really take it personally; I think to insult me was his way of reaching his brother. This was a common enough insult in the family anyway. And everybody, also, called me a dirty French."

THE NETWORK: A "LONE WOLF" IN THE HEART OF INTERNATIONAL TERRORISM

In 2011, Abdelkader had enough authority in the family to set up his mother's marriage with a man he knew, Mohamed Essid, a Tunisian naturalized as French, whose son was a jihadist named Sabri Essid, who later left for Syria. Like Kader himself, both Essids belonged to the Artigat network. Sabri Essid was close with Mohammed Merah, enough so that in 2012 he was one of the pallbearers at Merah's funeral. In March 2015—two months after the *Charlie Hebdo*/Hyper Cacher killings and exactly three years after Merah's slaughter—the Islamic State issued a video showing Essid in Syria, praising the Hyper Cacher attack and promising that ISIS would soon march "on Jerusalem." Like his family, Mohammed Merah, the so-called lone wolf, appears to have been part of a network whose branches extend internationally.

The former director of French domestic intelligence (DCRI) in Toulouse, Christian Balle-Andui, showed up at the hearings for Abdelkader's trial in October 2017. He was a model of competency. Sometimes on the verge of tears, he detailed very thoroughly the extent of everything DCRI Toulouse knew about the Islamist network in that city in the years prior to the Ozar Hatorah slaughter.

In early 2000, he explained, the Artigat network was structured around two cells. One, the more ideological, was set in the La Reynerie neighborhood, in the south of town around a mosque called Bellefontaine; the Artigat men half competed and half collaborated with their rivals from the Muslim Brotherhood for control of the group. The other bridgehead was located in Les Izards, the neighborhood where Mohammed Merah lived, in the north of town, where there was a high concentration of dealers and delinquents. This second bridgehead was centered around Mohamed Essid, the man Zoulikha would marry at Abdelkader's request in 2011. "Essid's a complete fanatic and a very violent man," testified Balle-Andui to the court. Essid, he added, specialized in recruiting delinquents. The idea behind such recruitment was that delinquents, being still ideologically unformed, would better confuse French authorities.

At La Reynerie, the main figure was Fabien Clain, a charismatic six-foot-tall, 220-pound man who'd been born in 1978. Clain mentored Mohammed Merah in the final stages of his journey, and later, in March 2015, would leave for Syria with his family. As his name indicates, he is a convert. He and his brother Jean-Michel started out as deeply devout Evangelical Christians on Réunion Island, a remnant of the French Empire situated in the Indian Ocean, 450 miles east of Madagascar. Disappointed with Christianity and in search of mystical meaning, they discovered Islam in its violent Salafi form only after they came to France, at the very end of the 1990s, and came into contact with Mohamed Moujid Amri, a Tunisian with Islamist convictions, who would be arrested in 2016. Clain read about Islam extensively and learned Arabic, a language he now speaks fluently. At the Toulouse Sunday market, to make a living, he sold, in addition to halal products, religious books. The books came from Brussels, where they were printed by the Belgian Islamic Center, the Muslim World League–affiliated group that was suing *Charlie Hebdo* at the time, and whose lawyer Sébastien Courtoy was a friend of Dieudonné's. Clain had rented a place in Molenbeek, the Muslim quarter of Brussels, and was traveling back and forth. In Toulouse, he was in touch with one Larbi Moulaï, a GIA operative who had been the head of the Salafi movement for the southwest region of France since the early nineties, and it was through him that he met a strange but pivotal figure in that story: a tall, white-haired, white-bearded man named Olivier Corel, whom the French press, misled by his name, assumed to be a French convert and nicknamed "the White Sheik." Corel was, in fact, born in 1946 in Homs, Syria, as Abdel llat al-Dandachi. He had come to France in 1973 as an official representative of the Muslim Brotherhood and had changed his name in the early eighties, as a precaution against the Syrian secret police, after Hafez al-Assad, Bashar's father, then in power, started his repressive crackdown against the Muslim Brotherhood. He had then settled on a farm in the Artigat region and it was to this farm that Fabien Clain moved in the early 2000s to start what could be described as "an Islamist commune."

A sort of rhythm began to take place. While Corel, thanks to his contacts with the Muslim Brotherhood, kept proselytizing in the Bellefontaine mosque, where he sometimes served as imam, Fabien Clain toured the Haute-Garonne region to sell his Salafi books, and the two men began to organize weekly religious seminars at the Artigat farm. As it was for Farid Benyettou in Belleville during the same period, recruitment was easy, given the Iraq War. Among the first recruits were Souad and Abdelkader Merah, the latter with the goal of becoming an emir—a religious scientist and propagandist. Mohammed followed sometime in 2006.

During Abdelkader's trial, Anne Chenevat's son Theodore—a young man aged twenty, wedged into a tight-fitting suit—testified that when he was ten, Corel had come to him one day as he was waiting for his parents in a parking lot and announced that "it's okay to hate your parents for not being good Muslims." During that same period, Abdelkader would also take Theodore to religious family gatherings. He'd come home with nightmares, convinced that his mother would soon be killed, for the day was coming when "the Muslims would launch total war against the miscreants."

Proponents of the lone wolf theory seize on Mohammed Merah's own statements to the RAID negotiator after the siege of his apartment, according to which he found religion by himself in jail, then left for the Middle East alone, posing as a tourist as he searched for jihadist training. In the world of terror, where normal rules do not apply, reality lies with the less plausible. While the first part of this assertion is an obvious lie—since Mohammed learned Islam with Corel and Clain and the religious documentation provided by the Belgian Islamic Center—there are all indications that the second one is true. In fact, weary of Mohammed's spontaneous outbursts, Corel and Clain, it appears, were more than reluctant to pass him contacts and information for jihad. Corel, for one, seems to have found him too young, too jumpy, and untrustworthy. So after an initial and unfruitful trip across the Middle East in July 2010, it was during a second trip in November that Mohammed managed to reach Waziristan.

He was received and trained there by Moez Garsallaoui, an Al Qaeda operative of Tunisian background who had set up in the Federally Administered Tribal Areas of Pakistan with the goal of coordinating jihadist networks in Europe. After the Ozar Hatorah slaughter, the terror group Jund al-Khilafah (Soldiers of the Caliphate), of which Garsallaoui was a key member, sent credible statements claiming close ties with Yusuf al-Faransi, another of Mohammed Merah's noms de guerre, and praised his deed.

It is important to note also that in 2003, Garsallaoui had married, in Brussels, Malika El Aroud, the daughter of Moroccan immigrants in Belgium and the widow of one of the killers of Shah Ahmad Massoud, "the Lion of Panjhir," whose killing in Afghanistan, two days before September 11, had been engineered from Molenbeek by Belgians of Moroccan background, at the behest of Osama bin Laden and as a prerequisite for the attacks on the United States. Massoud was the only personality whose aura and authority could have countered bin Laden. There is no way that such a high-ranking operative as Garsallaoui would receive and train a kid as inexperienced as Merah without some sort of an introduction. Given Fabien Clain's connections with Molenbeek, there is every reason to believe that this introduction to Garsallaoui came from Clain. Which would mean the lone wolf was connected to the very heart of jihadism after all.

DCRI Toulouse knew plenty about what was going on. After his return from Waziristan, Mohammed Merah was followed, and his phone conversations studied. DCRI Central sent instructions for a debriefing and two specialists to perform it. Their conclusion: "The dangerousness of Mohammed Merah has not been established."

On March 15, 2012, the link between the murder of the three soldiers in Montauban and the killing of Imad Ibn Ziaten, four days prior, was immediately established. DCRI Toulouse pointed out the Salafi trail at once. But Paris, in response, judged it "not clear" and, because the victims were of Maghrebian origin, as I explained earlier, ordered them to investigate neofascists instead.

France was in the midst of a presidential race, in which incumbent president Nicolas Sarkozy freely borrowed slogans and ideas from the National Front. The question is worth asking whether, paradoxically, he did not need something to distance himself from the NF, as he was also trying to reach Muslim voters.

The next day, in any case, was a Friday, and DCRI Toulouse sent a note profiling fifteen possible suspects. Half were extreme-right activists, as DCRI Paris required, and half were Salafis. Mohammed Merah's name was on the list. The weekend passed. Nothing was done. Monday morning came and Mohammed showed up at the Ozar Hatorah school.

On March 21, two days after the killings, the siege at Merah's apartment was a circus, with the minister of the interior giving instructions to the RAID squad while appearing on news channels to give free PR for President Sarkozy all night long. Meanwhile, Merah was free to leave his apartment to send the videos of his killings to Al Jazeera and then return home, unseen by anyone.

The final assault on Merah's apartment took place on March 22 at 10:30 a.m. The RAID team had begun to drill through the bathroom wall of the place where Merah had sought refuge when suddenly, wearing a bulletproof jacket and a *jellaba,* he sprang up and began to shoot. Three hundred gunshots were exchanged, thirty of them fired by Merah. He was killed by a sniper as he tried to escape through the balcony.

Two days later, the head of DCRI Central, Sarkozy man Bernard Squarcini, gave his full-page interview to *Le Monde,* saying, "Mohammed Merah radicalized himself alone, in jail, by reading the Koran. There is no belonging to any network."[7]

From Algiers, Mohammed Sr. threatened to sue the French state for "the murder" of his son. His French lawyer, not surprisingly, was none other than Isabelle Coutant-Peyre, Carlos's wife and Youssouf Fofana's former lawyer. The case never amounted to anything.

"THE GREATEST GUY FRANCE EVER PRODUCED"

The importance of Mohammed Merah's murder spree, particularly the Ozar Hatorah massacre, for what happened in France afterwards cannot be overstated. What I remember best about those days is the dreamlike quality of the shame that France was now the one country in Europe since World War II where Jewish kids could be killed in the street in broad daylight for the sole reason of being Jews. The most unbearable of all, I think, was the feeling of recognition, of nightmarish fantasy come true in light of the event, as if everybody had thought about it beforehand. *Oh, so it really happened again, this time.* It was a terrible shock, but somehow it wasn't a surprise, and this lack of surprise made the shock even worse.

Whether it was legitimate or not is a different matter, but the collective guilt, in other words, was palpable, especially in the media and political world, and this guilt probably accounts, paradoxically, for the Salim Bachi piece *Le Monde* published and the fascination, already mentioned above, for who the killer "really" was and what had "really" motivated his actions, as well as for a certain level of aggressiveness toward Jews perceptible everywhere. To find reasons for such a deed was the only way to come to terms with the deed — and by acknowledging the killer's motivations as somewhat understandable, the country could keep that guilt at bay.

But isn't there, at core, a profound connection between guilt and narcissism? The murder of Jews in a European country has a special weight, harks back to a special curse. As irrational as it may have been, the hope of exorcising that curse may well have been the real, if unconscious, reason the rhetoric we began to hear was so successful, namely, that the killer was "a product of French society" and nothing else. Boosted by Bachi's piece and Tariq Ramadan's tweets, the notion that "neocolonial racism," "discrimination," and "social conditions" were the "true" and only causes of the killings was everywhere in the weeks and months that followed. It sounded as if, even with anti-Semitism and hate, the unique active forces in history were Europe and the West.

Investigation, meanwhile, showed that Merah's initial target that fateful Monday was, in fact, another French soldier, an officer whose house was located a few hundred yards from the school, but when Merah, for some reason, was unable to reach it, he fell back on the school instead. Yet, as he admitted, Ozar Hatorah and Jews in general were on his list from the start.

In his four-hour-long conversation with a RAID negotiator on the night of the siege, he had made it even clearer in explaining his choice of targets:

In the beginning, the brothers [his Waziristan trainers], they told me to kill. They said I should kill everything—everything that is civilian and miscreant, everything. The gays, the homosexuals, the ones that kiss each other in public. They said, "Shoot them down," see? But me, I had a message to carry. And, er . . . I targeted Jews and French soldiers because I thought the French would understand better. 'Cause if I were to kill just civilians, the French population, they'd say, "Oh, he's just another crazy terrorist." Even if I had the right. But now the message is different. Now I just kill soldiers and Jews, see?

Although the passage was lost in the entirety of the conversation later leaked online by the daily *Libération*,[8] it was a clear confirmation of the most terrible fear in the country—and of the centrality of the Jews in the process of activating hate.

It seems that this element escaped neither President Sarkozy nor François Hollande, who replaced him at the Élysée Palace in May of that year—nor Hollande's minister of the interior (and future prime minister), Manuel Valls. All provided public support to the victims' families, governmental officials made a point of traveling to Jerusalem for the funerals of the children, and, for the first time since the beginning of the anti-Jewish violence, all emphasized, in their speeches, France's solidarity with its Jewish fellow citizens.

And yet, the necessity to cover up the blunders of the investigation—blunders whose roots were to be found in the denial of Islamist networks in the first place—this necessity prevailed and, with it, the lone wolf theory and its corollary: that there was no issue with anti-Semitism in the country.

The curious mindset resulting from all of this was a "firm moral condemnation" of "any" anti-Semitism going hand in hand with its denial, and this was not without consequences. As no further investigation was undertaken on the Artigat network, Fabien Clain, who had been arrested in 2009 for sending people to Iraq, was released from jail. Nobody paid attention to him—nor to the fact that his name figured in a police file in connection with yet another attack that had occurred the very year of his arrest, in Cairo—where he and his family had moved between 2006 and 2008 to study at the Al-Azhar University, the very one where Abdelkader Merah would spend time in 2011. In February 2009, a bomb at the souk had targeted a group of French high school students, wounding twenty-four and killing one. One of the suspects at the time, Farouk Ben Abbes, interrogated by French intelligence, had mentioned Fabien Clain in this context, and in the context of a plan for a future attack in France, whose target was the Bataclan theater, in Paris, then owned by two Jewish brothers, Joel and Pascal Laloux, and seen for that reason as a "Zionist" establishment. But as Mohammed Merah was "a lone wolf," Clain was released from jail the year of the Toulouse and Montauban killings and was not interrogated further.

As Farid Benyettou witnessed firsthand in Belleville at the time, the youths in some mosques had begun to openly ask whether killing children was a Muslim duty. (Killing Jews, it seems, was a given.) Meanwhile, in several places in France, walls began to be tagged with graffiti in Merah's memory, and in Toulouse, people contributed money to the Merah family.

Until the killings at the school, Salafi and Dieudonné political propaganda and spontaneous anti-Jewish acts had existed throughout the country side by side, albeit in parallel universes, as it were. One could not make any connection, for instance, between Benyettou's teachings at the Belleville mosque and the crazy murder of Sébastien Selam by Adel Amastaïbou, some hundred yards away. But after March 2012, this changed. To some, because of the double transgression represented by consciously, willingly killing children and Jews — as opposed to killing them impulsively — Merah's murderous spree acted as a kind of revelation. An idea had taken form. A hate finally had been shaped.

Jailed in Toulon for burglary, Mehdi Nemmouche, thirty, a petty criminal from Roubaix, born into a family of Harkis — the Algerians who worked with the French army during the War of Independence — watched, transfixed, the night of Merah's siege on TV. "Mohammed Merah's the greatest guy France ever produced," he is reported to have said in the days following. "I feel great this morning, I could well picture myself shooting up a little Jew girl today." (Recorded by a warden, the sentences are now part of his accusatory file.) Raised partly in foster homes and partly by his grandmother during the nineties, Nemmouche, as a teenager, had been exposed to the FIS propaganda, which was locally very strong at the time, and had watched the exploits of Caze and Dumont's Roubaix gang, recounted above.

Two years after the Toulouse killings, on May 24, 2014, four months after the Day of Wrath demonstration in Paris, where anti-

Semitic slogans had been heard, seventeen days after the anti-Semitic demonstration set up in Brussels by the comedian Dieudonné and Alain Soral and dispersed with water cannons, and with the number of spontaneous anti-Jewish acts in France hitting the roof, a man appeared at the doorstep of the Jewish Museum in Brussels. A cap on his head, sunglasses over his eyes, and—just like Merah—a GoPro camera attached to his chest, he pulled a Magnum .357 out of his bag and fired. The first to be hit were Emanuel and Miriam Riva, Israeli tourists in their mid-fifties who had just entered. Each was struck in the back of the skull and died on the spot.

Dropping the Magnum, the shooter then took from his bag a Kalashnikov, aimed it at a sixty-five-year-old woman by the name of Dominique Sabrier, and shot her, also in the head. A retired art publisher of Polish descent, Sabrier had left France only two months before. In Brussels, she had registered for law classes at the Free University and was volunteering as a tour guide at the museum. According to friends, her reason for moving was the anti-Semitic atmosphere permeating France: The Toulouse killings had scared her, as had the hate demonstration in Paris four months earlier.

Alexandre Strens, twenty-five, found the time to seek refuge under his reception desk before the killer found him and shot him, once again in the head. Strens, hired by the museum's communications department the previous year, was the only victim still alive after the shooting. Sent to the Saint-Pierre hospital of Brussels, he was declared brain dead the next day. He died on June 6. Although Strens's mother is Jewish, his father is a Muslim Berber from Morocco. In accordance with the wishes of both families, he was buried in the Muslim cemetery of Taza.

With Strens, and with no more reason than it had started, the massacre ended. The surveillance video showed the shooter running away, bag in hand. He disappeared.

The mayor and various members of the Belgian government soon showed up at the scene. King Philippe declared himself "outraged," while the UN Security Council condemned "the terrorist attack and its probable anti-Semitic motivations." The president of the European Commission, José Manuel Barroso, and the EU foreign secretary, Catherine Ashton, both denounced the "intolerable attack against the values of Europe," while European Parliament president Martin Schulz, Italian prime minister Matteo Renzi, and French president François Hollande all made the trip to the museum three days after the killings to pay homage to the victims. On the other end of the spectrum, the esteemed intellectual Tariq Ramadan tweeted on May 27, "According to [Belgian daily] *Le Soir,* the two Israeli tourists targeted in Brussels worked for the Israeli services: Antisemitism or diversion?" *Le Soir* had said no such thing, and the Rivas were, in fact, public accountants. But the hoax and the use of the word "targeted" implied that the murders were part of some larger "Zionist" conspiracy: a diversion to hide the true motives and the real perpetrators, as Ramadan helpfully added.[9]

That same day, back from Syria, where he had worked as jailer and torturer for the Islamic State, Mehdi Nemmouche was arrested in Marseille during the routine inspection of a Eurobus from Amsterdam, known to be commonly used by petty drug traffickers on their way to Algeria. Asking for Nemmouche's ID, the cops noticed a gun at his side. They searched his bag, found not only a cap similar to the one seen in the surveillance video, but also a Kalashnikov, bullets by the dozen, and a miniature GoPro camera with a video on it showing those weapons, with Nemmouche's voice over the images claiming responsibility for the attack. (The camera, apparently, had not been working well during the killings.) Also in the bag, they found a simple white sheet. On it were Arabic letters painstakingly drawn with a felt-tip pen that, once deciphered, read ISIS.

In July 2014—as riots erupted in France, protesting the war in Gaza, and two synagogues in Sarcelles and Paris were attacked to cries of "Death to the Jews"—Nemmouche was sent to Brussels to be judged there, and was charged with the terror attack at the Jewish Museum and with the guarding and torturing of four journalists held hostage in Syria between July and December 2013. One of the former hostages, Nicolas Hénin, testified in *Le Parisien* to the sadistic pleasure Nemmouche took in the torture sessions: "He would look at his hands, crack his knuckles, and take a boxer pose and say: 'Do you see these gloves? I bought them to hit you. Just for you. Do you like them?" Nemmouche used to sing Charles Trenet songs, especially "Douce France," and Hénin said that "when he did not sing, he would torture. He was part of a group of French whose mere appearance terrorized the Syrian prisoners who were there ... What he wanted [if he came back to France] was to make it front page like Mohammed Merah, whom he quoted often."[10]

As of this writing, Nemmouche's trial is still pending. His lawyer in Belgium is Henri Laquay, who was awarded a Golden Quenelle by Dieudonné.

SEVEN

The Terror Wave of 2015–2016: Beyond the Real and the Fake

THE *CHARLIE HEBDO* / HYPER CACHER KILLINGS

Seven months after the Jewish Museum killings, on January 7, 2015, at approximately 11:15, Chérif and Saïd Kouachi, in black attire, balaclavas on their faces and Kalashnikovs in their hands, mistakenly entered the office of SAGAM, a company selling childcare products, situated in the building next door to *Charlie Hebdo*, on Rue Nicolas Appert near the Bastille. Among the cradles and baby carriages, they pointed their guns at a fifty-year-old woman who was being interviewed there that day for a job and, realizing their mistake, ran back outside, entered building number 10—the right one this time—and in the entrance hall killed their first victim, a maintenance employee named Frédéric Boisseau, forty-two and a father of two. Looking for the right door, they lost themselves in the stairwell until running, by chance, into Corinne "Coco" Rey, one of the cartoonists at the journal, who was coming out of an editorial meeting for a cigarette, and whom they forced at gunpoint to climb back up, guide them, and type the digital code to the reinforced door that had been installed as a security measure, which, ironically, prevented the journalists inside from hearing what was going on in the stairway. The Kouachi brothers entered the magazine's offices and at the tedious cry of *"Allahu akbar!"* started shooting, hitting first the webmaster, Simon Fieschi, whose desk was the closest to the door (he survived), then, in the editorial room, Stéphane Charbonnier, forty-eight, the chief editor, and his bodyguard, Franck Brinsolaro, forty-nine, who never had a chance to reach for his gun. (Given the high level of threat, Charbonnier was under constant police protection.) In his chilling account of the event, the journalist Philippe Lançon, who was gravely wounded but survived, testified to the slowness of the action as they shot one bullet after another, punctuating each shot with an *"Allahu akbar"* that Lançon said they chanted almost softly.[1] Chérif Kouachi found Sigolène Vinson, a columnist for the magazine, hiding behind a wall with the proofreader Mustapha Ourrad, sixty. After killing Ourrad, he turned toward Vinson to say they didn't kill women and that because she was to be spared, she should spend her remaining life improving herself by reading the Koran. Going back to the main room, where the massacre was unfolding, Chérif apparently repeated it three times—"We do not kill women! We do not kill women! We do not kill women!"—and women were indeed spared except for the psychoanalyst Elsa Cayat, who happened to be Jewish (whether the killers knew this or not is unknown) and was one of the first victims. Eleven people were lying dead in the room when they left, and eleven others were wounded.

There was a small press agency, Premières Lignes, neighboring the magazine, and journalists there, hearing the noises from the stairs and seeing the killers enter through the spyhole of their own door, had taken refuge on the roof, where they called the cops. Fifteen minutes after the killers had come out of SAGAM's office, the police had received eleven calls—almost one per minute. Other calls were made from the building facing number 10, and soon police lines were jammed.

Doubts about what was "really" happening were expressed almost immediately, thanks, paradoxically, to the videos of the event taken that day by the Premières Lignes journalists and by a neighbor. Today these films are known worldwide—which means that they're half-forgotten, buried deep in the global memory under newer images, fresher killings. One shows the Kouachi brothers coming out to the street and walking to their car, shouting, "We avenged the Prophet Muhammad, we killed *Charlie Hebdo*." Another shows the car stopped, a few minutes later, in the middle of the Boulevard Richard-Lenoir, and Chérif and Saïd Kouachi hidden behind one of the doors, firing at a patrolman whose name will be known only later—Ahmed Merabet, forty, a Muslim, who has heroically drawn his gun. We soon see Merabet lying down, hurt, on the asphalt, as one of the killers approaches him at a run, then Merabet raises a hand from the ground, saying, *"Non, c'est bon, chef"*—"No, it's okay, boss"—and the killer shoots him nonetheless at point-blank range and comes back to the car, slowly, and distractedly picks up a sneaker that has fallen from the passenger's seat, before he closes the door and the car disappears from the video frame toward the Bastille traffic.

"I needed to speak to someone, I panicked," said Jordi Mir, the fifty-year-old engineer who videotaped the scene from his window and immediately posted it on his Facebook page. "When I realized what I'd done, I went back on Facebook and deleted it, but it was too late." The images were picked up by news channels and soon were being broadcast on a loop. On the TV screen of the restaurant where she was having lunch, Morgane Merabet, the patrolman's wife, saw them repeatedly during her whole meal, but, due to the poor quality of the filming and her distance from the screen, she could never guess that the man repeatedly being killed in front of her during lunch was her own husband. As she testified a few days later, in a poignant press conference, it took a phone call from Merabet's sister after she got back to work, at approximately 2 p.m., for her to put a name and a face to the silhouette.

In the meantime, Jordi Mir's film had gone viral on the Web, almost immediately raising the issue of what, in the event, was true and what was fake. Disregarding the most obvious fact, which was the slaughter itself—a slaughter that had attracted them in the first place—thousands of Internet users had started to scrutinize each frame, focusing on details like the side-view mirror on the killers' car allegedly changing colors, or the lack of visible blood on Merabet's body and the fact that his face could not easily be distinguished.

Terror is not about killing alone. It's the waiting that undoes everyone, the aftershock that's also a pre-shock. The waiting as narrative: it was unpredictable, it was unthinkable, it couldn't ever happen—but it did, *and yet, it remains impossible.* And while it is true that the probability for each one of us of being hit in a terror attack remains close to nil, the possibility of this impossibility has now risen. And so everyone was commenting on the event as best they could, because that's what you do while you're waiting: you speak. You speak as if you could restore, through words, some semblance of a line between the you that is safe and the you that's a potential victim—a random variation on the statistic scale of terror. And conspiracy theories and speculative paranoid narratives spread online that day like part of the event itself, while it was still happening and the killers were still in the streets.

Their car was spotted in the northeast part of town, on Place du Colonel Fabien, where it had accidentally smashed into a Volkswagen. It was left empty a few streets further on, on the Rue de Meaux. A few hours later, police found in the car an empty cartridge clip for a Kalashnikov and an identity card with the name Saïd Kouachi. That piece of ID, once it was made public, triggered new conspiracy theories—for what "reasonable killer" would be dumb enough to leave a thing like that behind? Obviously, the ID had been planted in the car by French secret services and the shadowy deep state that controlled them, to better discriminate against Muslims at large. As for *who* controlled that deep state, it was the same cabal that controlled *Charlie Hebdo* in the first place. As the "professor of Islamic studies" Tariq Ramadan would have it the next day in a TV debate with Art Spiegelman on *Democracy Now,* *Charlie Hebdo*'s team firing a cartoonist some years prior for having dared to mock the Jews was a significant clue to what was *"really"* going on and who *"really"* pulled the strings.[2]

Meanwhile, the Kouachi brothers had traded their smashed car for a Renault Clio they hijacked and they were driving north through the Porte de Pantin district on the Périphérique, the beltway surrounding the city. Due to an insistent rumor that they were on their way back to town, that they were actually charging *into* Paris, the police, acting as if such a wild idea were even remotely possible, closed the northern points of entry on the Périphérique, and more than one cop standing guard at the checkpoints that day texted his wife and kids to stay home just in case the two men suddenly showed up on some random street of the capital and started shooting. Such was the helpless and confused state of the police force on the first afternoon of those three days of tension and murder.

In fact, the Kouachi brothers were on the run. And as they switched cars time and again after that afternoon, they always appeared polite, almost friendly, to the various drivers they stole the cars from. It wasn't their fault, they explained — they had do what they had done because of the Jews — because of Israel and the Zionists.

"Are you a Jew?" was one of the first things they asked Michel Catalano, the owner of the printing factory where they finally took refuge the next day at dawn, in the small village of Dammartin-en-Goële, twenty miles northeast of the city. Catalano, the son of Italian immigrants, was not Jewish and said as much; they took him hostage, and he managed to keep his composure during the two days they held him, making coffee for the brothers and even treating Saïd's wound, while one of his employees remained hidden for eight hours before he managed to escape. Later, Catalano testified that when he was asked this question—"Are you a Jew?"—it was the only moment when he felt his life was in immediate danger. This aspect of the attack was barely noted by the press.[3]

That same morning, while the Kouachi brothers were entering Catalano's printing factory, a man dressed all in black showed up at the market of Montrouge, a suburb south of Paris, and shot and killed a patrolwoman there, Clarissa Jean-Philippe, twenty-six, from Martinique, with a burst from a Kalashnikov in the back, also wounding Eric Urban, a maintenance employee who had tried to stop him. The unknown man then disappeared into the subway without being identified. French commentators making the connection with the *Charlie Hebdo* attack were at a loss to explain what had just happened and why. None reported that a Jewish school, Yaguel Yaacov, was situated a few dozen yards from the attack. I myself had to turn on CNN, a foreign channel, to learn it. As investigations would reveal, the shooter, Amédy Coulibaly, thirty, the son of immigrants from Mali, along with his wife, had spent time the previous summer identifying several Jewish establishments as potential targets.

The next morning, January 9, a Friday, at around 1 p.m., Coulibaly, still unidentified, entered the Hyper Cacher market, in the suburb of Vincennes, on the southeast edge of Paris, with a Kalashnikov, two Scorpio submachine guns, two Tokarev pistols, a bulletproof jacket, and fifteen sticks of explosives. He killed his first victim, Yoav Hattab, twenty, son of the great rabbi of Tunis, on the spot. "You got it?" he is reported to have asked right afterwards. "What origin are you? Jewish? There you go! So now you know why I'm here." Yohan Cohen, twenty-three, an employee at the store, died trying to fight Coulibaly and to steal one of his guns. Philippe Braham, forty-five, was also killed; coincidentally, Braham had his children enlisted in another Jewish school in Montrouge, neighboring the market where Clarissa Jean-Philippe had been murdered the previous day. The last victim, François-Michel Saada, sixty-three, lived in Israel.

While these killings were unfolding and Coulibaly improvised speeches for the rest of his hostages, Lassana Bathily, a Muslim, also from Mali, who was an undocumented immigrant employed at the market, helped several customers hide in the basement before escaping and, once outside, helped the police take up positions outside the store for what turned out to be a six-hour siege.

According to the best available police reconstructions, both attacks, in Montrouge and Vincennes, were half autonomous actions and half backup strategy for the Kouachi brothers' getaway: one of the reasons the police waited six hours to move against Coulibaly that day was the fear that the Kouachi brothers would retaliate. The police and the military surrounding the Kouachi brothers in Dammartin-en-Goële were as paralyzed by Coulibaly's potential action as their colleagues were in Vincennes, fearing the Kouachis' response if they moved. It was only when the Kouachis finally charged the police in a suicidal action that the authorities in Vincennes gave the order to move in. The Kouachi brothers had controlled the timing all along.

Coulibaly had registered the various videos claiming responsibility for the attacks in the name of the Islamic State, while the Kouachi brothers, for their part, had mentioned Al Qaeda Yemen, where Saïd had briefly trained. Chérif Kouachi had met Coulibaly in jail in the aftermath of the dismantling of the Buttes-Chaumont gang, and both had entered the ideological tutelage of another detainee, Djamel Beghal, a forty-three-year-old Algerian immigrant Al Qaeda operative and a former member of the Algerian GIA. Freed in 2009, Beghal and Coulibaly had later been arrested again, on suspicion of abetting the escape of GIA operative Smaïn Belkacem, jailed as one of the main perpetrators of the 1995 terror wave engineered by Khaled Kelkal. So the nineties were finally yielding results.

Then, a month later, on February 14, the Krudttønden cultural center, in Copenhagen, was attacked during a debate on "Art, Blasphemy, and Freedom of Speech," which starred the artist Lars Vilks and the Russian feminist militant Inna Shevchenko. Armed with a Kalashnikov, one Omar Abdel Hamid El-Hussein entered and shot a burst of some two hundred bullets in the room where the discussion was taking place, killing the documentary filmmaker Finn Nørgaard, fifty-six, and wounding three policemen before running away. That same night, at around 1 a.m., El-Hussein, who had escaped and could have tried to hide, chose instead to show up in front of the Great Synagogue of the city, which was full. Barred from entering by a security guard, he shot at the building from the street, killing the man, and then ran. El-Hussein was subsequently killed that morning at dawn, in a shootout with the Copenhagen police. In the days that followed, unknown hands deposited flowers at the place where he died.

THE REALITY OF AUTHENTICITY

In 2015, in the wake of the *Charlie Hebdo*/Hyper Cacher killings, the lone wolf theory born in the aftermath of Merahs' murder spree began to lose relevance as the issue of what had *really* motivated the killers and who they *really* were gained special prominence in France.

Not that the anti-Jewish aspect of the violence gained any more attention from it. In the media, the Hyper Cacher attack somewhat paled in comparison with what had happened at *Charlie Hebdo*. Despite the fact that these three days constituted only one attack, the connection between the two phases of it was not really made—in particular, the comparison between the caricatures of the Prophet and the mocking of the Shoah so widespread during the 2007 *Charlie Hebdo* trial was neglected—while the debate soon focused exclusively on the issue of "freedom of speech" and secularism. Instead of trying to track the violence back to its ideological source, then—that is to say, to the accusation against *Charlie Hebdo* of being a Zionist-controlled newspaper set up to humiliate the faithful, which would have established a logical link between the attacks against the journal, the attack against the Hyper Cacher store, and Merah's killings two years earlier—the entirety of French Muslims ended up being recruited, in the media and on social networks, to answer questions on the general issues of freedom of the press and religion. These issues may have seemed, at first, more innocuous and manageable than the virtually infinite question of anti-Semitism, but they helped confuse the matter more.

On January 11, 2015, two days after the end of the attacks, a silent, civil march against terror gathered 1.5 million souls, flooding the streets of Paris. There were four million nationwide. Not since the end of the 1960s had such a crowd marched united in France. Placards and stickers proclaimed JE SUIS CHARLIE ("I am Charlie"), as well as JE SUIS JUIF (Jewish), JE SUIS FLIC (a policeman), and JE SUIS MUSULMAN (Muslim), so as to identify with all the victims of the attacks, regardless of their origins or of who they were. Yet, partly because, at Mr. Hollande's initiative, the first ranks of the march were solemnly filled with state leaders whose presence was seen as debatable at best (Benjamin Netanyahu's appearance was especially criticized; that of Mahmoud Abbas, chief of the Palestinian Authority, wasn't), partly because the crowd spontaneously sang "La Marseillaise" several times and applauded the policemen deployed in the streets for protection—two deadly sins in one for the extreme left—a debate soon erupted as to whether or not Muslims in the suburbs had been somewhat excluded from the march, and whether the event and its slogans were discriminative, perhaps even downright racist. Prominent intellectual figures such as Alain Badiou and the less well-known (internationally) sociologist Olivier Todd argued this case, with the support of Tariq Ramadan, who dutifully declared, "I am not Charlie," and of Dieudonné, who, for his part, stated that he felt like "Charlie Coulibaly."

In fact, while it is true that no Muslim representatives and no Muslim organization had been called to the march, Muslim individuals had indeed been present in its ranks. Veiled women marched, some even wearing strict, heavy black cotton dresses, French flags in their hands, and, in at least two separate incidents I witnessed, tensions rose as they were briefly attacked for being there by small groups of Muslim men hostile to the demonstrators. The debate, however, focused on the Muslims who were *not* there, the disgruntled ones who, once again, seemed to carry the day, who sometimes felt and said that what had happened to *Charlie Hebdo* was somehow justified—the Hyper Cacher store vanishing from the issue altogether in the process—and, even, on understanding the killers themselves. That these voices were in fact a minority did not stop either the left-wingers or the extreme right from emphasizing them as representatives of what "real" Muslims were.

Who, then, were the killers, *really,* and what were their real motivations? In Cartesian France, to add to the confusion, such a question meant implicitly that religion, being only a culture, could not rationally be the true reason for the rage. It had to be social. This was seen—rightly—as a contradiction by Muslims at large, who were asked to publicly condemn the killings *because* they were Muslims, as if not doing so and being Muslims made them accessories to murder. As a result, more and more they refused to answer, which, in turn, reinforced the suspicion.

In any case, the question gained in complexity with the discovery of two series of disturbing pictures on the computer of Amédy Coulibaly. Taken during the same period, between 2012 and the attacks, one series showed Coulibaly and his wife, Hayat Boumeddiene, twenty-six, on the beach—Coulibaly in a bathing suit, muscular, a gold necklace around his neck, standing in the surf while Boumeddiene, in a bikini, nuzzles up against him, smiling—while in the other series, Coulibaly appeared, pistol in hand, aiming at a target off-camera and Boumeddiene, her body fully hidden under the *niqab,* pointing a crossbow at the photographer.

That last picture in particular baffled everyone. Especially disturbing was the fact that both series seemed to have been taken for private use only—not for propaganda purposes—which implied that they were self-portraits. So which was which? Did these pictures prove that they were religious or that they weren't?

None of what has emerged about the couple's lives—that they were religiously married in 2009 after Coulibaly was released from jail for petty delinquency and went to work for Coca-Cola; that he was received that year by President Sarkozy at the Élysée Palace as an example of success in a PR campaign to promote Coca-Cola's involvement in social partnership for rehabilitating former inmates; that he worked on the side as a sports coach, his all-female clientele testifying unanimously that he had always appeared to them competent, charming, and agreeably flirtatious; that, at some point in her life, Hayat Boumeddiene, raised in foster homes after her mother died and her father remarried, had tried to change her name to make it sound more French; that after failing at the *baccalauréat* exam, she found a job as a cashier in a computer chain store, from which she resigned for not being allowed to wear the *niqab* in 2010, which was two years before the bikini pictures were taken; that soon after their wedding, she got into a fight with Coulibaly, who had expressed the wish to take a second wife, as he thought Muslim law allowed him to do; that she was nonetheless the one who dragged the couple toward "radical" circles and that, during the summer of 2014, when they took out a loan to buy a car, which they would resell immediately and use the money to buy the weapons for the attacks, she did all the talking while Coulibaly remained silent and passive, "as Muslim women do," to quote the car salesman who testified after the killings—none of this made sense. The strange, morbid association of the crossbow—an archaic, impracticable weapon—the *niqab,* and the bikini, in particular, combined to fix the couple's image in French opinion—and especially Hayat Boumeddiene's.[4] There was also the fact that the Eastern European weapons were bought in Belgium, from a network connected with right-wing groups.

Then, on April 19, a new attack occurred, as unforeseen as the previous ones. An Algerian Islamist and computer student by the name of Sid Ahmed Ghlam, twenty-four, shot and killed Aurélie Châtelain, twenty-eight, a fitness instructor from whom he was trying to steal a car, wounding himself in the process, in an apparent attempt to use the car to attack two Catholic churches in the Ville-juif *banlieue.*

"We are facing individuals who come from nowhere," asserted the state prosecutor François Molins, in charge of the investigation, somewhat existentially. "They are adepts of the *taqiya* and give out only very weak signals, undetectable by intelligence services." It was a complete rebuttal of the DCRI line at the time of the Merah case. Terror agents, who previously could not be detected because they did not belong to any network, were now undetectable because they belonged to one—an invisible network where they had learned the subtleties of the *taqiya,* the Islamic ruse. So, were they authentic Muslims after all?

That question of the Islamic ruse—of what one seems to be and of what he really is—leads us back to the paradoxes of identity politics as Ismayl Urbain tried and failed to solve them during the French Empire. It is worth noting that it is also at the heart of contemporary Islamic terrorism. As intelligence services all across the globe know, one of the sure signs that a terrorist is about to take action is his getting rid of his beard and of any sign of Islamic identity —the rationale for this in the doctrine being that, since he is assured to go to paradise, the future martyr is allowed to transgress the law. The *taqiya* is also reported to have been one of the major points of contention between the Muslim Brotherhood and Al Qaeda, as well as between Al Qaeda and the stricter Islamic State, and even to have created serious divisions inside ISIS itself—where the issue is even complicated by the fear of being infiltrated. All this suggests the centrality of the issue.

The most interesting definition of the *taqiya* I was able to find is provided by the Lebanese-Jordanian artist Lawrence Abu Hamdan. Hamdan works with Forensic Architecture, a London-based nongovernmental international research group gathering people from several mediums—from artists and architects to journalists, lawyers, and computer designers—with the purpose of denouncing war crimes and violations of human rights around the globe. In this context, Hamdan studied the practice of the *taqiya* in the Druze communities of northern Syria who were coerced into converting to Wahhabism by the pro-Saudi Al-Nusra terror group in December 2013. In *Contra-Diction: Speech Against Itself,* the conference-performance drawn from that study, which he presented at the Georges Pompidou Center, in Paris, and at New York's MoMA in 2016, Hamdan defines the *taqiya* as "the legal permission by which the faithful can deny his faith, or furthermore commit illegal acts when he is exposed to risks of persecution. The *taqiya* is often understood as a divine right to lie. But the *taqiya* is neither lie or not to lie. It is a self-contradictory condition consisting in finding oneself simultaneously in the law and out of it."[5]

The law here, of course, is God's. The *taqiya* is understandable only in a world where the language itself is a divine creation. But what unites the *taqiya* practitioner with the divine is complex, as it involves a third party who is the listener.

"In every act of the *taqiya*," Hamdan continues, "the truth resides in the ear of the observer. The *taqiya* is never the expression of a clear position, but a multitude of positions emanating simultaneously from a single voice. Each of these multiple truths is forged by and for the listener."

Crucial importance is thus given to the *sound* of the word, rather than to its writing.[6] Pronounced words are sacred because, as they are not written, but spoken, they stop being "representations of things," Hamdan says. "They *are* the things. Language is reduced to a series of onomatopoeias." The key to this esoteric conception of language, then, is pronunciation. In Arabic, some letters resemble others—such as *kaf* and *qaf*—but they are nonetheless pronounced slightly differently in words that only seem to be synonymous but aren't. In this almost imperceptible difference lies the line between the sacred and the impure, the absolute and the ambiguous. The mistake the uninitiated listener makes in confusing the two reflects his own impurity.

Originally conceived around the eighth century among Shiite communities facing persecution from the Sunni Abbasid caliphate, the *taqiya* was at first a tolerant doctrine, arising in order to help the faithful survive in times of pressure. When faced with persecution, the true believer was permitted to lie and break Islamic law in order to conceal his faith. He would not be judged as an apostate if he did so—what really mattered was the secret heart of his true piety burning inside him.

The contradiction between such a position and that of the martyr —whose heroic death in the eyes of the world is supposed to prove the true faith, regardless of his behavior—is obvious enough. To solve it, Islamist propagandists rework the *taqiya* perversely in suggesting that the lie is the sign of the truth. The lie, in other words, is all that remains of subjectivity, while neither survival nor interiority matters.

The "true" member of the faithful is thus the one who will so closely resemble the unfaithful that no one outside the community of the faithful can tell the difference. The crucial point, because it gives room for rage, is that this resemblance is forced upon the believer by the hostile surroundings. It's another thing to be angry about, and to destroy. The reasoning goes more or less like this: *Thanks to the* taqiya, *I am allowed to smoke a joint* (which Salafis are forbidden to do, but which is current practice among terrorists), *I am allowed to go out with loose girls, and I do it, but not because I want to, for wanting would be a sin. I do it because everybody does it, and to adopt this behavior allows me to hide from my many enemies the true extent of my virtuous nature.* They *bear the responsibility of my sins,* they *are the guilty party forcing me to lie and to submit to these pleasures that* they *practice genuinely. The sweeter these pleasures are, the more secretly I suffer, and the more I am humiliated. Indeed, the humiliation of my sins is the sign of my virtue, and in the name of that virtue, I can kill.*

The profit a sociopath can derive from such a concept does not need to be emphasized. Needless to say, state prosecutor Molins did not go as far as to explain all this. That kids from the French suburb could have been initiated to a notion dating from the eighth century was bizarre enough. But was it the case?

The investigation showed that at least some version of the *taqiya* was taught to Coulibaly by Djamel Beghal, the GIA operative he met in jail, who later received him, along with his wife, Boumeddiene, and the Kouachi brothers, in the small village of Murat, where he had been put under surveillance by French authorities but where he was left free to give his pupils weapons training and where, in all likelihood, Boumeddiene's crossbow pictures were taken, probably by Beghal himself. Beghal, who had connections with Al Qaeda, is said to consider the use of the *taqiya* as legit.

One of the problems with such a conclusion, however, remains the status of the *niqab*-crossbow pictures found in Coulibaly's computer, taken *for private use,* just as the bikini pictures were. No one was being lied to here. Both images appeared to be equally true, and both equally false. So something other than the *taqiya* is at stake.

What Coulibaly and Boumeddiene present us with are two antagonistic ways of life, mutually exclusive. But they're far from isolated in this, and such split behavior has been noted ever since the defining act of this century, the attacks on New York and D.C. on 9/11, whose perpetrators lived in the United States for years, regularly drank alcohol, and spent their last night in a strip club while getting ready to punish Americans for doing exactly the same things.

In France, similarly, Mohammed Merah kept going to nightclubs in Toulouse almost till the end of his life, and the sole surviving attacker from the synchronized assaults on Paris on November 13, 2015, Salah Abdeslam, is reported to have been a regular patron of gay nightclubs in Brussels. One of the Kouachi brothers, Chérif, is reported to have had at least one homosexual affair, and pedophile pictures were found by police in both his and Coulibaly's computers. While an explanation for this was that terror groups use porn websites to send encrypted messages, the very choice of such websites adds to the general ambiguity. Before they left for Syria, many jihadists also ordered brand-name sneakers online from websites set up in Tunisia that specialized in providing trendy outfits to jihadists, which does not fit with any definition of the *taqiya*.

The most spectacular example of such split behavior would be provided in 2016 by Mohamed Bouhlel, a Tunisian national living in Nice, who on July 14 of that year, for Bastille Day, drove a massive truck into a crowd watching the fireworks, killing eighty-six and wounding 450. Bouhlel was known to drink alcohol, eat pork, and insult God with the sole purpose of hurting his pious wife, whom he beat up on a regular basis; he also had a habit of defecating in the bedroom when angry, and engaged in several sexual relationships with women and with men. His "intimate friend" was a seventy-three-year-old homosexual who testified after the attack that Bouhlel was "a sweet man." Bouhlel also professed not to like Arabs and to love France and the French better. The Tunisian psychiatrist who followed him during his childhood, and with whom I spoke, confirmed to me that he had diagnosed Bouhlel with a psychotic disorder years earlier. However, Bouhlel's father is said to have been a dignitary of the Tunisian Islamist party Ennahda, and Bouhlel himself is proved by the investigation to have had connections with Islamist sympathizers. (During the year preceding his crime, Bouhlel exchanged more than twelve hundred text messages with a Mohamed Oualid G., who had sent a text praising the *Charlie Hebdo* massacre on January 10, 2015, three days after it occurred. Police investigators who at first saw Bouhlel as just another psychotic now think he may have been an adept of the *taqiya*.)

That jihadists never lie — that, thanks to the *taqiya*, they are always "true" even when they lie — is, paradoxically, what makes it so difficult to answer the question. They commit acts as Muslims when, for instance, in the name of what they and several high religious authorities and states recognize as Islam, they kill homosexuals — a common practice of the GIA in Algeria in the nineties and of ISIS in Syria in 2015 that mirrors the Saudi legal system, based on Islamic clerics' opinions. And yet, a "true" believer would never have indulged in homosexual relationships himself, or visited pedophile sites online, nor would he display an expansive Rolex on his arm, like Abu Bakr al-Baghdadi, the self-proclaimed caliph of ISIS, or engage in photo and film sessions, as *all* terrorists do, from Coulibaly and Boumeddiene and Mohammed Merah to Bouhlel, in Nice, and Abdulgadir Masharipov, the perpetrator of the Istanbul bombing, who filmed himself all along the way to the nightclub in which he killed thirty-nine people for Allah on January 16, 2017. The difficulty in trying to establish the degree of "truth" in the faith proclaimed by the terrorist is that his narcissism is the measure of his "authenticity."

In fact, as we've seen with the Merah case, the more we learn about the profiles of the killers, the less we seem to be able to decide between their religion and their psychology. Was the schizophrenic Adel Amastaïbou — Sébastien Selam's killer — an Islamist, or are the ones we call Islamists psychopaths who "have nothing to do" with Islam or with the Islamist propaganda they are submitted to?

To move on from this dead end, let us first call Norman Mailer to the rescue:

"The psychopath may indeed be the perverted and dangerous

front-runner of a new kind of personality, which could become the central expression of human nature before the twentieth century is over. For the psychopath is better adapted to dominate those mutually contradictory inhibitions upon violence and love which civilization has exacted of us."

Mailer wrote this at the dawn of the Cold War, in an essay called *The White Negro,*[7] and it is hard, now that the twentieth century is indeed over, not to see these lines as prophetic. At the time he published the essay, in 1957, the world was becoming aware of the new technological age it had entered after the end of World War II. In Mailer's opinion, two things overshadowed the new face of the modern condition: the atomic bomb and the still fresh discovery of the Nazi death camps. In a word, terror. Mailer went on:

> For the first time in civilized history, we have been forced to live with the suppressed knowledge that the smallest facets of our personality, or the most minor projection of our ideas, or indeed the absence of ideas and the absence of personality, could mean equally well that we might still be doomed to die as a cipher in some vast statistical operation . . . unknown, unhonored, and unremarked, a death which could not follow with dignity as a possible consequence to serious actions we had chosen but rather a death by deus ex machina in a gas chamber or a radioactive city. And so, in the midst of civilization . . . in the middle of an economic civilization founded upon the confidence that time could indeed be subjected to our will, our psyche was subjected itself to the intolerable anxiety that death being causeless, life was causeless as well, and time deprived of cause and effect had come to a stop.

He was not alone in his concern. At roughly the same time, the French writer André Malraux wrote,[8] "We now know that democracy carries inside of itself capitalism and totalitarian polices, that science and progress allow atomic bombs, and that reason is not enough to account for human nature ... We are entering the era of the end of the individual, who is being wiped out by the atom bomb." In a sense, it was the anti-modern critic renewed by the balance of terror.

"In front of the biggest threat imposed on humanity," Malraux famously offered as a solution, "the task of the twenty-first century will be to bring the Gods back into the Man." Mailer thought, for his part, that in order to escape the new deadly conformism brought about by the technological society of the atomic age, one should, regardless of the risks, *awaken the psychopath in oneself.* It is very tempting to think that the jihadists do precisely both.

The hedonist culture of the second half of the twentieth century that they so hate—namely, rock 'n' roll culture, the sexual revolution, and consumerism—was, as a solution, both an expression of and a rebellion against the paradoxes of the new age. This benign nihilism, so to speak, lasted as long as the Cold War did, and now that it is over, it is a bit difficult to escape the feeling that we're back, existentially speaking, if such a word can still be used, where Malraux and Mailer found us.

In such a context, the question of whether or not Islamist terrorists are "really" Muslims may well be turned on its head: in the technological age, how "real" can a religion be—or, for that matter, any form of "authenticity" and "identity"? The role of narcissism in the shaping of the terrorist mindset has already been studied at length, most notably by the psychiatrist Robert Jay Lifton in his groundbreaking book *Destroying the World to Save It,*[9] dedicated to the Japanese apocalyptic sect Aum Shinrikyo, which fabricated sarin gas and, in 1995, launched an attack in the Tokyo subway, killing twelve people and injuring more than five thousand. But in Aum, as in the Manson family, this narcissism was still centered on the person of the guru—in the case of Aum, a paranoid Shoko Asahara who claimed to be Buddha and Christ resurrected and preached the apocalypse while having sex with the female members of the sect. In today's terror organization, by contrast, *every* member may have his or her momentum, every killer walks with God, depending on the way he or she deals with his or her alternate authenticities. It is tempting to assume that this pathological honesty, with its infantilism and its postmodern aura, is precisely what makes the jihadists so relevant for our times. But should we conclude from this that religion has "nothing to do" with what they do?

It is one of the most striking paradoxes of our age that the reactionary personalities most dedicated to the resurrection of "authentic values"—whether national, like Maurras's pupils such as Steve Bannon, or religious, like the Wahhabi leaders—are all narcissistic transgressors. Take Putin and Alexander Dugin, take Marion Maréchal–Le Pen and de Benoist, and, of course, Donald Trump . . . If the choice in the twentieth century was between being normal and being exceptional, it seems that in our century the choice will increasingly be between ordinariness and psychopathy in the sense Mailer gave to this word. Jihadists, in this context, appear merely like an extreme case. But it doesn't make their religion less true. It could well be the other way around: to survive in the scientific-technological world, any system that pretends to authenticity may need to give way to psychopathy and violence, if only because it is the best way to communicate. Just think of what Islam would be in the world today *without* Wahhabis and political Islam, without the murder of women, homosexuals, and Jews. Would anyone speak about it, or, rather, would it be in the same state as the Catholic Church in France, its churches empty and the most dynamic of the Christians reduced to a fringe of believers fighting for the Mass in Latin?

But this leads to another, related issue: the role of communication and new technologies in the spreading of the violence.

THE AUTHENTICITY OF REALITY

Here is, for instance, an extract of an interview conducted by French police detectives with one of the smartest members of a cyber network of teenage girls from mixed backgrounds—some were from Muslim families, some weren't—which was dismantled in the spring of 2014 after one of them spoke openly on her Facebook page of stealing her father's gun in order to attack a synagogue.

POLICE: Do you think it normal to decapitate people?

GIRL: I say to myself: the ones being killed that way, they probably deserved it. For instance if they didn't respect religion as they were nicely asked to.

POLICE: Have you ever watched decapitation scenes?

GIRL: This is not necessarily my cup of tea. But I am not overwhelmed by these videos. I've seen the one of the American journalist having his throat slit. I thought it looked like a cartoon.

POLICE: Are you aware that this is real footage, that it does not stem from video games or films?

GIRL: Yes. I am well aware of that.

When, in the late nineties, the idea of "virtual reality" became common, it was assumed that people would simply create avatars of themselves that they knew were fake. Because they were fake, those avatars would be able to express and act out things that their creators would never do in real life. This police interview, where images that look like cartoons are nonetheless considered real, suggests a more primal and frightening mental process in which things can be apprehended as real without being seen as true. This may explain why so many jihadists who left France inspired by films of beheadings posted by the Islamic State on the Internet could argue at the same time that the images they watched were a hoax—a fabrication emanating from Western secret services. Yet these same "fake" images triggered their vocation, inspired them to join ISIS in Syria.

This process has been especially powerful among converts, a group that in France represents 30 to 35 percent of jihadists and among whom the part played by social media and new technologies appears to have been central. Along with the social differences —for most converts come from a petit bourgeois environment— the most obvious difference between jihadists from Muslim backgrounds and converts lies in the way the members of each group engineer Islam in their dealings with their own parents. All the converts I have encountered present the same pattern, confirmed by their psychiatrists, of an "enmeshed relationship" with at least one of their parents in the years preceding their discovery of Islam. (Enmeshment refers to attachments within a family that are so strong, a child can't establish his or her own identity.) Where Muslim-born jihadists see religion as a way to both overcome and reconcile with a family history often marked by chaos, domestic violence, and humiliation and to reconnect with what they see as their "origins" through a collective process in which the mosque and the group are essential, converts, by contrast, appear to use Islam as a disruptive element in order to break out of an enmeshed family and as a weapon to isolate themselves from their surroundings and preserve some sort of subjectivity. This isolation may explain the disproportionate role played by Islamist recruiters on social media in winning converts. The process of conversion through the Internet after a series of virtual discussions with recruiters assuming fake identities seems disconcertingly simple—you take a shower to purify yourself and pronounce a vow in front of your computer. The simplicity of this has given birth to the persistent assumption that the future jihadist is an isolated, neurotic outlier who spends too much time online. The process, however, is more complex and works only if this virtual conversion is accompanied by real encounters. Future converts who begin by searching for "real" Muslims online, in the privacy of their bedrooms, always meet people in the flesh at some point.

Consider Liliane, a forty-year-old mother from Grenoble whose daughter Nathalie, seventeen, announced to her one morning at breakfast that she had just married, through text messages the previous evening, a man she had never met physically, whose name she did not know, but that as a married woman she nonetheless had to cover herself with a *niqab* 24/7. When I met Liliane in 2015, she explained that in order to "better understand" Nathalie, she had authorized her to wear the *niqab,* while secretly buying an electronic chip that allowed her to hack into her daughter's phone and follow what was going on. She then submitted herself to the torture of watching, powerless, the erotic text messages her daughter and her virtual husband exchanged for months without meeting. Finally, when Nathalie was eighteen, she simply vanished. She left to live somewhere between Syria and a Grenoble *cité,* and, when we met, Liliane had not been able to locate her. It is safe to assume that, without the prospect of a real, physical encounter nearby, Nathalie's seduction and conversion would not have worked so well.

Or consider Luc, who flew to Syria on his eighteenth birthday to join the Al-Nusra group after a conversion he kept secret from his mother, who had raised him alone. Luc's childhood friend Ali brought him to an Islamist recruiter named Omar Diaby in their hometown of Nice. Diaby was in fact a cyber preacher, one of the first in France to use the Internet extensively to preach and post videos calling to jihad, and French intelligence has him sending more than a hundred recruits to Syria between 2012 and 2014. But Diaby also owned a café in a popular neighborhood of Nice that was used as a headquarters for Islamists, and for years before and during his conversion, Luc spent his afternoons in its basement, watching Diaby's films and playing video games such as *Assassin's Creed*.

Launched six years after 9/11 — the date matters — and conceived by the French company Ubisoft, *Assassin's Creed* served as a hugely successful tool for the training of would-be jihadist converts in those years. Its hero, an Ishmaelite monk, is a member of the quasi-historical sect of the Hashishin, said to have been active in the eleventh and twelfth centuries in the Alamut Valley, in the Alborz Mountains of Iran, where they smoked hashish between killing missions, under the guidance of their leader, the mysterious Hassan-i Sabbah. Based on scattered historical references, the legend is a classic of the Muslim world and has fascinated writers of the twentieth century, William S. Burroughs most of all, who wrote extensively, and sometimes presciently, on them. In books like *Cities of the Red Night* and *The Western Lands,* bafflingly enough, Burroughs imagined modern Hashishin as an all-male gang of young men spiritually trained in some Muslim place and aiming to destroy the West, killing themselves in the process during orgasmic suicides. The "creed" that both Burroughs and the title of the game refer to, which is supposed to have been the true rallying cry of the sect, is "Nothing is true; everything is permitted." Again: the physical presence of the Islamist network appears as the necessary complement to the virtual propaganda.

That said, one may wonder whether something in the operating mode of the new technologies itself—something in the "nature" of the algorithm, if such an expression makes sense—might not play a role in all this.

One definition of knowledge, after all, is one's capacity to tell a story in a rational and understandable way: a narrative based on facts and experiences that can be rebuffed only with a better, more accurate one. Whether scientific or literary, in short, knowledge mirrors truth. An algorithm, on the other hand, does not have to mirror truth or falsity: it just needs to be repeated. Why do members of a Facebook "community," for instance, identify as "friends"? For the sole reason that their pages exchange the same information. This is true, in particular, of militant and Islamist pages. At its core, then, data is tautological. To borrow a phrase from the father of information theory, Claude Shannon, information is entropy. Its power depends not on its veracity but on its simplicity—not on its "truth" but on its being "real"—and what makes it real is its capacity to be duplicated. By that standard, "There is no other God than God" is information in its purest, simplest form. "Jews are hypocrites" and "Arabs are rapists" aren't so far behind. These statements—these *memes,* as the theory calls them—are "real" in the sense that they don't need to be demonstrated in order to be considered true. They just need to be transmitted as many times as possible.

Now may be the time to remember Smaïn Laacher's theory according to which prejudices are linguistic tools through which a language binds a group together into a set of virus-like transmitted beliefs and values. Questions about the knowledge and truth of such values arise only when either the group manages to distance itself from it or some individuals succeed in doing so—when children of immigrants, for instance, can confront these inherited values with the values of the host society. We then call this process of distancing oneself from the founding values "modernity," "cosmopolitanism," or, alternately, a "crisis of faith." But information theory suggests that this process may be obsolete—that narrative that inscribes itself in time, with a beginning, a middle, and an end, may be a thing of the past reserved to a complex and twisted elite, while God, neither dead nor alive, manifests himself now as "real"—as a *meme.* It may be worth wondering, in other words, if the operating mode of the algorithm does not open the door to apocalyptic tendencies inside the established religions. If—to repeat—in order to survive in a technological world, any system that pretends to authenticity must not give way to madness.

MASSACRE IN NOVEMBER

As of this writing, here are the findings of the still pending investigation of the coordinated attacks of November 13, 2015.

Months prior to the attack, fourteen fake IDs were commissioned by ISIS operatives in order to rent cars, send bank orders, and sign leases for the necessary logistics. The forgeries necessitated photo sessions of the jihadists in disguise. They were outsourced to intermediaries in Belgium and collected one by one by the sole survivor of the commandos, the former drug dealer Salah Abdeslam, detained today in France. Each of the IDs cost one thousand euros. In addition, seven safe houses were set up for future hiding of the three commandos, in several Belgian cities and in the Paris suburbs of Bobigny and Alfortville. Some of the future killers traveling from Syria through Greece or Hungary, for their part, received two thousand euros each to pay for the trips. Although the money has been traced back to banks in the UK, where it came from, it is still unknown who paid for the cars, the rent, and the six Kalashnikovs used at the outdoor terraces of the restaurants of the Tenth Arrondissement of Paris and inside the Bataclan theater, to kill 130 victims and wound 356 others. All the commando members at some point had traveled to Syria, Iraq, or the Turkish border.

The long planning, the patient secrecy, the meticulous management of the many networks at play that such an operation requires: none of those qualities were among the natural skills of the killers themselves, who were small-time criminals, braggarts, for the most part, barely able to keep an appointment, and whose knowledge of geopolitical issues defies the most basic intelligence. (At some point during the Bataclan theater siege, one of the killers promised to release the hostages if the policeman he talked to could bring him a "signed paper" from his superior promising that France would leave Syria the next day.) Such a gap leaves entirely open the question of who sponsored the attacks. Another issue is the extent of the involvement of supporting players in the French *cités* and the Belgium Muslim quarters. Dozens and dozens of secondary figures were involved who, although they were never informed of the nature of the targets nor of the magnitude of the operation, were sufficiently "radicalized," or indifferent enough, or clannish enough, or individ-ualistic enough, to help at some point or another, knowing that, at the end of the chain, people would die.

While all this was going on, several attacks were perpetrated on French soil. To list only the most spectacular: In June, in the small town of Saint-Quentin-Fallavier, near Vaulx-en-Velin, a truck driver by the name of Yassin Salhi strangled his employer, Hervé Cornara, fifty-four, decapitated him, rolled the body in an ISIS flag, set the head on the corpse's belly, took a picture of the scene, and sent it to a correspondent in Syria. Then, at the wheel of his truck, he charged the small American chemical plant for which Cornera was a supplier, Air Products, and tried to set fire to its warehouses be-fore being stopped by police. (He would later hang himself in jail.) In August, a Thalys train on the Amsterdam–Paris line was attacked by one Ayoub el-Khazzani, armed with an assault rifle, who was stopped by three U.S. soldiers vacationing in Europe.

These attacks were engineered by a man who had already helped to set up the Brussels Jewish Museum attack of the previous year, and would reveal himself to be the main coordinator of the massacre of November 13 in Paris. He was a twenty-eight-year-old Belgian of Moroccan background named Abdelhamid.

Traveling back and forth between Raqqa, Syria, and Brussels be-tween 2012 and 2014, Abaaoud had sent several videos of his activi-ties in Syria to friends and turned into a local legend of sorts, but it is the partial broadcasting of a propaganda reel by the French news channel BFMTV in February 2014 that made him a real star in the jihadist world. Said to have been found in an abandoned cell phone at the Turkish border by soldiers of the Free Syrian Army and sold to journalists, the film showed Abaaoud at the wheel of a van, say-ing to the camera, with a disarming smile: "Back in the day, we used to attach trailers to our cars so we could visit families for va-cations and bring gifts, but now we attach *kafirs,* miscreants, people who fight us and fight Islam." Then a tracking shot revealed seven or eight bodies, civilians, covered in blood and tied to the van, and cries of *"Allahu akbar"* resonated as the vehicle began to move, with Abaaoud's friends running behind. The rest of the video, not aired on television but easy enough to find online, showed the bodies being dragged toward a nearby site in the desert to be buried in a mass grave, and while Abaaoud's friends started digging and exchanged jokes about the stench of the cadavers, everyone could see Abaaoud laughing, playing soccer with a human head.

His father, Omar, who had settled in Belgium to work in the coal mines twenty years earlier, had found success instead as a clothier, and owned two stores in the Muslim quarter of Molenbeek, Brussels, while his mother owned several cybercafés on both sides of the Mediterranean, so when Abaaoud had reached tenth grade, they had the means to send him to Saint-Pierre College, the best Catholic private school in Brussels. Expelled, however, after a year for a lack of aptitude and discipline, Abaaoud had soon fallen into delinquency. He was incarcerated for larceny first in 2006, and, after some time spent between the streets and the clothing stores, where he helped his father, he had been sent by his family to Egypt for one year to study religion there, with the hope that Islam would tame him and set him on the straight and narrow. And it had worked. The repenting son returned from Egypt a true believer: he was a religious man.

On Friday, November 13, 2015, at 9:25 p.m., Abaaoud was one of the three shooters who sprang out of a black Seat Leon car in front of Le Petit Cambodge and Le Carillon, in the Tenth Arrondissement of Paris, and, in less than twenty minutes, sprayed four hundred rounds from a Kalashnikov on the outdoor terraces, killing thirty-nine people and wounding thirty-two. A few minutes after that shooting, one of the two other men in Abaaoud's unit, the ex-small-time drug dealer Brahim Abdeslam, thirty-one, entered the Café Voltaire brasserie, on the Rue Voltaire, and, after apologizing for the disturbance, blew himself up. (By chance, his bomb, misfiring, claimed no other victims.)

Ten minutes earlier at the Stade de France, where President Hollande was attending a friendly soccer match between France and Germany, two other killers had similarly set off their bomb belts, killing one and wounding ten.

Meanwhile, at 9:40 p.m., a third unit of three men entered the Bataclan theater, which had been on the hit list since 2009 for belonging to two Jewish brothers. The U.S. rock group Eagles of Death Metal was playing a show that night. As the commandos began to shoot the spectators inside one by one with the greatest calm, a witness heard one of them explain that this was "for all the bad things Hollande does to Muslims everywhere in the world"—a rephrasing of the justification given by the GIA operative Aït Belkacem to justify the terror wave twenty years before. The killings went on, resulting in a total of ninety dead and casualties by the dozens before the BRI and RAID elite police units began to circle the theater. Entering it around 10:30, they killed one terrorist and managed to secure the main room, where they found bodies everywhere. The two remaining killers, holding some twenty spectators hostage, retreated to the first floor, where negotiations unfolded for two hours before RAID decided to open fire, killing the remaining terrorists without hurting the hostages.

Meanwhile, Abaaoud and his fellow member Chakib Akrouh—the third shooter in the Seat Leon—having left their car in the suburb of Montreuil, emerged from the subway after midnight in front of the Bataclan, where chaos reigned. There were wounded people lying down, waiting for ambulances, police cars and soldiers everywhere, survivors, neighbors, and families in shock. Abaaoud and Akrouh mixed in with the crowd massed in front of the theater to see President Hollande and Prime Minister Manuel Valls, who, against the advice of their secret service guards, had decided to visit the scene. Abaaoud stood there, only feet away. He had three loaded AK-47s in the Leon, which police would find the next day on the street, abandoned.

Both killers went back into the subway and left. They reached the suburb of Aubervilliers, the warehouse zone, and built a makeshift shelter for themselves, down below Highway A86.

What followed involves Abdelhamid Abaaoud's cousin Hasna Aït Boulahcen, twenty-six, who would die at dawn on November 18, in the suburb of Saint-Denis, during the confused police raid on the decrepit safe house she had improvised for her cousin two days earlier. After her death, the media would publish several pictures picked up from her Facebook page — Hasna, her head covered by a *hijab,* doing the "V" sign; Hasna disappearing under a *niqab;* Hasna wearing a jean jacket and a straw cowboy hat; Hasna slumping on a couch drinking vodka; Hasna in a bathtub, her naked body only half-hidden by the bubble bath. She came to be known as "the kamikaze woman."

Born in the Seine-Saint-Denis district, raised in the suburb of Clichy-sous-Bois by her out-of-work mother, Nina, who was in the habit of burning her with a fork previously heated in the oven, she was put into foster care by the age of ten, and by fifteen she was living alone on the street. She was briefly married to a forty-five-year-old Turkish man, "in order to put a roof over her head," according to a Frenchwoman known only as N., born in Djibouti, who knew her in sixth grade and told this to the police after her death.

She left her husband after some time and traveled east to reconnect with her father, who lived near the German border in a city called Creutzwald, in a studio where Hasna began to intermittently crash. The father was employed there as a worker at the local Peugeot factory, where he made a decent salary, of which he apparently gave nothing to the mother of his children.

In Creutzwald, during the weekends, Hasna used to hang out with a gang of ten, of which she was the only girl and with whom she would sometimes hit the nightclubs on the other side of the border or throw parties in her father's studio when he traveled to Morocco to visit relatives. There was lots of weed, and vodka, and the boys called her "the cowgirl" on account of her hat and boots.

In 2011, her father retired and went back to Morocco for good. Hasna, then twenty-two, with no income and jobless, found herself with nowhere to go but Clichy-sous-Bois, where her mother still lived. She began to show up irregularly, sleeping on a simple mattress laid down in the corridor. Most of the time, however, she preferred to crash on girlfriends' couches, in some squat or other, and a few times she slept out on the streets. This was when people began to spot her at night hanging out with Clichy's known drug dealers, or at dawn, completely ripped, wandering the streets. (The bathtub and cowboy pics on her Facebook wall date from this period.)

Living in the popular neighborhood of Nation, in eastern Paris, and also officially jobless, one Elhadi Belaïd, twenty-six, would later recall for the police the first time he ran into her: "She was with a friend when I met her; they were driving from bar to bar in search of some work. We spoke a bit, I left my number. Later that night she called, we fixed an appointment in some hotel and had sex. In the morning she was gone."

Using the number she'd called him from that night, Belaïd was able to contact her several times after that, but either Hasna did not answer or, when she did pick up, it was only to say she was too busy to meet. But Belaïd was persistent and managed to see her again a few times in the months that followed—"just for sex," Hasna made a point of letting him know. "To me," he commented to the cops, "she was a girl who liked to go out and who lived at night. Some sort of a tomboy."

At that time, however, if we are to believe her sister Djamila, Hasna was also a regular visitor at the mosque. She also had a man, an older man she had met in Morocco during a summer break, and who would go back and forth between France and Morocco.

One year for Ramadan, this man went back home to his country. When he returned, he announced to Hasna that he was about to go back to marry someone there. Hasna, although born in France and French by nationality, answered that she, too, would one day marry someone from her "own country," meaning Morocco. Later on, she confided to her sister that this man was a radical and that she didn't want to have anything to do with that.

It was in the spring of 2015, six months before the killings, that Hasna recontacted N. through Facebook. The two girls met in the *banlieue* of Aulnay-sous-Bois, in a brasserie called Paris Nord. "She was veiled when she appeared," N. would later tell the cops. "She wore a *niqab*. I asked her when she'd started this, and she said two days prior. She'd done so many stupid things in her life. Now was time to repent. She was back living with her mother, but her mother robbed her and as a result she was broke."

N., who owned a small café close to the Roissy Airport, offered Hasna a job there so she could make some money on her own. Hasna said yes. But when N. told her that in order to be a waitress she would have to get rid of her *niqab* during working hours, Hasna at first agreed, then changed her mind. She said she would rather find a Muslim husband instead of working, so she could live a righteous Muslim life.

In the beginning of the summer, Elhadi Belaïd, who by now had lost Hasna's number, tried to recontact her through Facebook. "Who the fuck are you?" was her first answer. Then, after he reminded her of their story, her second note was "well, u date back long time." She was off to Morocco for the summer, and he (although unemployed) was going on vacation to Thailand, so they agreed to meet again in September. Whom she was in touch with in Morocco is unknown, but it was from there that, in August, she posted Hayat Boumeddiene's crossbow picture on her Facebook wall. Various statements praising ISIS followed, along with short messages announcing her impending departure to Syria, with several links to beheading videos. At some point that summer, she also sent Belaïd a Facebook message to let him know that, given her new purpose in life, and given the fact that he, on the other hand, was off to Thailand, which meant the Bangkok bars and their whores, she could not imagine being "interested" in him any longer. They stopped talking.

On September 15, N. received a Facebook message from Hasna (I've translated her broken French to the best of my ability):

> Hi sister ithink really its unfortunat u zap me while u a person that I appreciate enormously u dont recall we lost eachother cuz of ur ex u were always withim and then I went to foster home I hope one day u understand if u really have a Heart or its maybe my religion that made u shun I dunno dont forget life's short death comes fast better do things in the hallal way and the main-thing its to regret yr mistake in short Be karful dontlet the shaitan take u we'll meet on the day of the last judgment Inshallah Salam.

Yet, two months later, on November 12, the eve of the killings, Hasna got in touch through Facebook with two former friends from school, Antony P. and Valerie D., and the three got together that same evening in the town of Villeparisis. According to what Antony later confided to N., Hasna appeared that night wearing a pair of jeans and cowboy boots. When he asked her about religion, her answer could not have been more definite: "Well, all that, it's all over, man."

On Monday, November 16, at 2 a.m., a call awakened Elhadi Belaïd. "She asked me whether I could shelter a brother and offered sex in return," he would recall to the cops. Quickly connecting the dots, given the news and her last messages on Facebook the previous summer, he realized she was talking about Abaaoud, whose picture was now on every channel in the country, and said no and hung up. He didn't call the police. He went back to sleep. The next morning, realizing her proposal had aroused him, he called her back, asked to see her. But she wouldn't have any of it—not until he said yes, that he would shelter the man she insisted on calling "a brother." Finally, pissed off, he insulted her and hung up again, and that was the end of it. He never heard from Hasna afterwards. Except of course on the news.

A few hours later that Monday, Hasna met up with a black guy named Mohamed Soumah, a.k.a. Mouss, twenty-five, a dealer she barely knew, who put her in touch with a local thug by the name of Jawad Bendaoud. Bendaoud was operating as an underground slumlord in the *banlieue* of Saint-Denis, running a decayed building that sheltered undocumented migrant workers, where, for money, a safe house for Abaaoud could probably be arranged, he said. When Abaaoud's picture appeared on TV, people from Hasna's *cité* began to frantically call and text her in search of gossip and news. She took refuge at her friend Gladys's house in Bobigny, turned her phone off to avoid calls, locked herself up in Gladys's bathroom, and cried and drank vodka all night.

Cops had wiretapped her phone in the hope of getting information on an unrelated drug case that Mouss was part of, and it is the police transcript of these tapes that allow us to reconstruct Hasna's last day—a day she spent on the phone while progressively losing any perceptible point of reference in space or time during her wanderings between three adjacent suburban towns located in the Seine-Saint-Denis district, which encompasses some of the toughest *banlieues* in the country: Bobigny, where she stayed; Aubervilliers, where she picked up Abaaoud; and Saint-Denis, where she died. In their mundanity, these conversations give us a taste of the empty, Beckettian hell in which people such as Hasna live—a world where indeed nothing seems real and everything's permitted, and one's subjectivity vainly struggles with overwhelming forces such as religion, family, constant gossip, and the urban apocalypse all around.

The first to call was Mouss. It was 10:30 a.m.

HASNA: Hello . . .

MOUSS: Yeah, hello.

HASNA: Yeah, who's that?

MOUSS: *Salaam alaikum.*

HASNA: *Alaikum salaam,* who's that?

MOUSS: It's Mouss here.

HASNA: Ha, you scared me. You all right or what?

MOUSS: Fine, and you?

HASNA: Who's that? It's Mouss there?

MOUSS: Yeah. What you doin' now?

HASNA: Mouss from Saint-Denis?

MOUSS: Yeah, well, yeah!

HASNA: Whoa, you changed. *Wallah* [I swear], you know what? I . . . *wallah hadine* [I swear to God], I haven't even slept. Been drinking and all. On my mother's life, I —

MOUSS: Why didn't you answer last night?

HASNA: I didn't even answer! I turned my phone off. The whole *cité* was calling! They talked to me. They said, "Hey, Hasna, blah-blah." They saw on TV, they called.

MOUSS: Yeah, I was worried and all. I thought, *Whoa!*

HASNA: No, don't you worry. I didn't even go out. I stayed home. *Wallah hadine,* I didn't even go out. I was in the bathroom all night, I just cried. *Wallah,* I thought about you. I thought, *wallah,* you're black, but you don't drink, you don't smoke, cigarettes only. And me? You seen me in drinking mode, Shaitan [Satan] that I am.

MOUSS: I saw crazy things before. Don't you worry.

HASNA: I'm smoking a joint right now. I gotta sleep, *wallah.* I can't even sleep. I can only cry. I'm not well in my head.

MOUSS: Oh yeah, oh whoa! You've been thinking too much.

HASNA: You bet! Hey, what time did you sleep last night?

MOUSS: Frankly? I slept at 10 p.m. or something. Woke up at seven. I brought my little brother to school and all.

HASNA: Me, I didn't even sleep. Okay, I'm going. Hey, *wallah,* as soon I wake up I call you.

She slept until 3 p.m., when a text message from the slumlord, Bendaoud, woke her up. She called him back, and after some tiresome negotiations they agreed to meet at the Saint-Denis squat with Abaaoud at 10 p.m. "sharp" that evening. Another call followed, from a Samir Bouzid, based in Brussels, operating as Abaaoud's direct connection. He was entering a post office in Brussels to send a money order to Hasna so she could buy a new phone with a new chip for Abaaoud and also a couple of business suits, which were necessary for the next terror attack, planned for the La Défense business district. Because he had to wait in line, they agreed he'd call her back as soon as the money was sent so she could go pick it up at the post office. Hanging up, Hasna called Mouss back to give him the news, through coded words she improvised:

HASNA: Hey . . . um . . . My gynecologist. She's sent me money. A money order. Cash. It's gotta be done quick, 'cause the post office, it closes at 6 p.m. . . . So now I'm gonna get a shower and dress up and . . . Gonna go to the post office, pick up the dough. And, um, once I pick up the dough, can you, like, pick me up, please?

She couldn't stay alone. She needed Mouss to help her get in touch with the undocumented cabdriver who, according to plan, would take her to Aubervilliers, where her cousin and his accomplice had been hiding in the bushes since the day of the massacre, three days earlier, and then drive them all back to Saint-Denis.

HASNA: I lost the taxi number is why. *Wallah!* I lost the paper. . . . It's in the trash bin. I was high yesterday, I was drunk. The cousin of my mother's girlfriend, she threw it away, and the paper was like really dirty after that. So I took it and I wrote down the address. But I forgot to write the taxi's number, on account of I was drunk. *Wallah!*

Mouss texted her the number back and reluctantly agreed to pick her up.

It took no less than two hours for Bouzid to finally call again and announce that the money had been sent and she could go to the post office. Shredded landscape of black towers under the black November sky, filthy stains of yellow-green lawns where rats run for garbage. On the way, she tried several times to reach the cab-driver, in vain. She finally called Mouss back again to chat and, through flirting with him, to make sure he would not leave her alone.

MOUSS: But I'm having lunch now! I was at the mall. My friend, he bought a tablet for his little sister, and now we're eating . . .

HASNA: Why? Why are you eating? You'd've come with me to the post office, we'd've eaten together, you little douchebag! I would've even paid for your meal, man.

MOUSS: Aaah! I ain't no douchebag, Hasna! First of all, if I had eaten with you, it's me who would've paid for you, not you me.

HASNA: Kif-kif, same diff! Lol!

MOUSS: Anyways, don't you worry, I'm coming to pick you up. I feel like seeing you.

HASNA: Yeah, well, you'll see me sober then.

MOUSS: Yeah. It shows you can't manage all that on your own.

HASNA: Oh yeah?

MOUSS: It shows! You lose numbers. You lose things . . .

HASNA: Yeah, yeah, yeah. Anyway, you know what? It's all too crazy, is what it is. All that shit. It's too much! Forget about it! It's abusive, it's impossible!

MOUSS: I know, I know, I know! But don't you worry, now. We're gonna get together tonight.

HASNA: No, but that's what I'm saying . . . I mean tonight . . . It's a fucking drag. 'Cause he told me, "You stay with me," he said. "I don't trust them," he told me.

MOUSS: But I thought we'd stay together tonight.

HASNA: Not tonight, I can't sleep with you, tonight, you crazy? You know damn well what's going on! When it's all over, all that shit, sure. Even tomorrow. Even every day, I don't give a fuck! But don't take it personal, okay?

MOUSS: Okay. Okay. I'll call you back.

HASNA: Oh yeah? Like, what does that mean? Like you're not coming anymore, is that it?

MOUSS: No, no, no! I do. I do! I gave you my word, didn't I?

She arrived at the post office five minutes before closing time and had to stand in line. At 5:57, she realized that Bouzid had forgotten to send her the Western Union code required to collect the money order. She called him, and while the phone rang, she had to argue with the clerk who was closing the office. A three-way conversation ensued, with the clerk filling out the form for her as Bouzid dictated his (fake) name and the code number. Finally, she picked up the money for the attack, but the incident had pissed her off and, once in the street again, she was in a rage. That is when she finally received the call from the unregistered cabdriver she'd been trying to reach, but, blinded by anger and anxiety and unable to identify the number, she flipped out.

CABDRIVER: Yeah, hello.

HASNA: Yeah, hello. You who?

CABDRIVER: Um, you, you who?

HASNA: Um, I don't know who you are. You the one calling, so who're you?

CABDRIVER: You called me three-four times, I believe.

HASNA: Whoa, the dude!

CABDRIVER: Who?

HASNA: There's a dude, he's talking to me!

CABDRIVER: Yeah, he's crazy.

HASNA: Yeah, a nutcase, *wallah*.

CABDRIVER: Who you talking to?

HASNA: Wait, listen. I dunno who it is you are. My phone, it ain't registered, right? I'm pissed right now. I'm gonna fuck it all up, Kalashnikov mode, *wallah hadine,* I shit you not. If you don't know me, don't tell me I know you. 'Cause anyway, my number, nobody gives it to nobody. So who the fuck are you?

CABDRIVER: Hey, listen to me carefully. I don't know who it is you are. You called me three-four times, I just called back. And no, I don't know you.

HASNA: [*realizing*] Aaahh, sorry, ohlala! Ohlala! I'm really sorry, brother. I've been calling you forever . . . I'm really sorry. Um, good evening. Let me introduce myself. Um . . . In fact, I'm calling 'cause I need you.

CABDRIVER: But who's speaking?

HASNA: It's Hasna. My pal, he gave me your number, my pal from Saint-Denis. I need a cab urgently, 'cause my brother, he got thrown out by his old lady and he sleeps outside. He with my cuz. In fact, in short, I'm gonna pay you, see? Dunno how much it is, but you come over to Saint-Denis, we pick up my bro and my cuz and I give you money. Is that okay or what?

CABDRIVER: But wait. Who's that that gave you my number?

HASNA: *Wallah hadine,* it's a guy that gave me your number, it's a pal. His name's Mouss. If you want, well, when I'm in Saint-Denis in the *cité* I call you, you talk to him. You're a . . . That's your trade, right? You're a cabdriver?

CABDRIVER: Yeah, yeah, yeah.

HASNA: So okay, so that's cool. So today you're my cabdriver.

Wallah. Wallah, I'll pay you. I'll pay you good. [*The cabdriver laughs*]

CABDRIVER: What time you want it?

HASNA: Me, when I say something, it really is something. I'm not even lying to you.

CABDRIVER: Ten?

HASNA: Listen! Around ... at 9 p.m. . . . . around 9:30 p.m. . . . . I'm calling you, *inshallah,* and you, you're coming to Saint-Denis, see? You listening? Listen to me well, I'm speaking serious. When you come to Saint-Denis with the car, I get into it and then we go pick them up. There will be my brother and my cuz, so, um . . . In short, we go pick them up, you let me out of the car somewhere, and me, I'm gonna run, I'm gonna call them and tell them to come out. I'll tell them to come out, see? It's right nearby.

CABDRIVER: Right.

HASNA: Look, listen to me well. My brother? He's a brother [*meaning a Muslim*]. I'm not leaving him behind. You're gonna make a lot of dough for yourself.

Their conversation went on for an incredible amount of time, ending up in flirtation, Hasna's default mode when needing help, before they hung up. Then, as Mouss never came, Gladys arrived with her scooter to bring Hasna back to Bobigny. Boulevard Lénine, Avenue Karl Marx, Cité Robespierre—these are the names of the streets in these suburbs that, in a sense, stand in France as the only real ruins of the Cold War. Back at Gladys's, Hasna bought sandwiches for Abaaoud and his accomplice and packed some clothes for the night.

When Mouss called at 7 p.m. to let her know he had finally reached Bobigny and was now waiting for her in front of the Avicenne hospital in the dark, in the rain, she suggested they meet in front of the KFC restaurant instead. But night had fallen, and

Mouss, being unfamiliar with the desolate landscape of Bobigny, didn't know where the KFC was. Although they kept talking on the phone while running in the Bobigny streets through the rain, they actually never met.

Sometime after eight that night, Hasna ended up reaching the shelter where her cousin and his accomplice were hiding. Unable to advance the time of the meeting, however, the unregistered cab-driver canceled the trip. Hasna, with no options left, simply stopped *a guy in the street* to drive the main perpetrator of the worst massacre in France since World War II, whose face was on every TV screen in the country, to Saint-Denis. This, at least, was what she told Mouss in their last phone conversation. *These are guys from the cités,* he soberly commented to Hasna after a first moment of surprise when she broke the news. *They won't talk.* After having dropped the trio in front of the squat, the man in question left his signature in the form of a text message that said: *this is A. the guy who just dropped you.* Whether or not he recognized Abaaoud is unknown.

How much of this confusion contributed to Hasna's death at dawn the next morning? According to the police, as she called a girlfriend from the squat to boast about being hidden with the most wanted man in the country, Hasna also mentioned a Kalashnikov she had been allowed to play with, and this piece of information led to the deploying of a RAID team at 4:16 a.m. the next morning. This conversation, however, does not appear in the transcripts I could read, and no Kalashnikov was found in the squat after the raid.

That day at noon, after they were all dead and Jawad Bendaoud was in custody and only cops, the ballistics teams, and journalists from all over the world remained around the rubble of the building, half-destroyed by the explosions and gunshots, young kids from the neighboring suburbs started setting up a makeshift souk of sorts at the end of the street, lining up cell phones loaded with footage of the assault on the sidewalk and selling them to journalists. By nighttime these images were being broadcast worldwide and also ended up online.

Of this footage, which, except for rooftops and windows in the night, didn't show much, it was the sounds that remained and contributed to Hasna's legend: Hasna's voice yelling, pleading with the cops to let her come out of the building—"Sir, please can I go, please? Sir, let me go, please!"—gunshots, the male voice of a cop shouting, "Where is he, your boyfriend? Where is he, your boyfriend?" Hasna, now in tears, yelling back, "He ain't my boyfriend! He ain't my boyfriend!" which were her last words before a barrage of shots and the sudden blast of a huge explosion.

The French press has since proved that all of these shots—1,500 in all—came in fact from the seventy men of the RAID team themselves and that, in the general mess and fear, as the ballistic report confirmed, the policemen mistook their own shots for enemy fire, wounding one of their fellow members and killing their own dog.

Though the police said that Hasna was the one who had set off the bomb belt that blasted the building, the autopsy report soon provided a different perspective. The bomb had been triggered by Abaaoud's fellow commando Chakib Akrouh, and Hasna died as a result of the blast, asphyxiated under a mix of concrete and wood debris after the floor collapsed beneath her feet, taking her three stories down.

That same Wednesday, at 3:15 p.m., a last call was received on her phone and registered by the cops. It was a girlfriend of Hasna's trying to reach her. She was recorded on the phone's voice mail as she spoke to the friend accompanying her:

ANONYMOUS GIRL: Yeah, it's that bitch. The bitch that blew herself up.

FRIEND: Yeah?

ANONYMOUS GIRL: In fact, she was a friend of mine.

FRIEND: And so?

ANONYMOUS GIRL: Well, two days ago I call her, see?

FRIEND: Yeah?

ANONYMOUS GIRL: And I said, "You okay?" And then she said, "Hey, why you calling and all? Is it 'cause my cousin, he's on TV?" And I said, "No, it's not even 'cause of that." For she had badly showed me the videos on YouTube, see? She badly wanted to go to Syria and all. And us, the people from the *cité*, me and all, I told her, I said "Don't go" and all that and blah-blah, see? And she used to come to my house and all, and we talked, and so after a while she didn't wanna go there that much anymore, she cooled off. And now, I see her on TV! And they said what? On TV? They said the person, the bitch that got killed, she had blood ties with the guy over there with whom it all happened. And I recognized her.

The recording stops there, and with it ends the eulogy of Hasna Aït Boulahcen by the Greek chorus of the *cité*. Amid the rubble where her body lay, the cops found her bag. Inside it was electrical wire, a push button, and a Scotch tape roll: all materials necessary for the fabrication of a bomb.

EIGHT
The War Within

Thehe transcripts on the previous pages offer a naked and rare glimpse at the social but also the narrative misery pervading the world of the *cités,* which serves as compost, as it were, for the hate propaganda in France, which is why I chose to reproduce it at length.

Time never seems to pass in these *cités* of concrete and plastic, so stripped of basic needs and infrastructure that they seem to have been built *as* ruins by some questionable architect to be used by their residents as mirrors or metaphors for the static existence they have been sentenced to forever, in a border zone for no specific country.

They are from the former Yugoslavia, from Russia, from all parts of Africa, from Pakistan, from India, from Syria, from Iran, from Afghanistan, from France, and of course from the Maghreb. They're legal workers and undocumented migrants, political refugees and survivors of clandestine Mediterranean crossings — but, above all, they are strangers among strangers, barely speaking to anyone except on their cell phones on the buses or the tram that takes them to and from work or to and from an employment agency, to and from the hospital or to and from the Bobigny law courts where, every other day in midwinter, the courtrooms' heating system is broken and rain sometimes leaks from the roof. This is not multiculturalism, and it has nothing to do with cosmopolitanism, either—this is global displacement. For family outings on weekends, since they have no money to spend in Paris, only fifteen minutes away by subway but in another universe, they wind up at the McDonald's in the mall or in the KFC that Mouss never found, which is also where they spend most of their free time during the week.

In the memories I keep from my visits to my parents once a month for lunch—from which I would invariably come back with a headache, set off as much by the loud political arguments my parents could not refrain from starting while the TV was on as by the ugliness of the general landscape all around—it always rains here. To come by car means to come by way of the Périphérique, the beltway boulevard surrounding Paris, which in Bobigny was under permanent construction at the time, with detours that were never the same from one visit to the next, so you had to cross an always changing labyrinth of one-way streets, construction sites, and detours, under the towers that resembled vertical tombstones, their dark gray concrete almost black under the rain as the sole fixed element.

My parents lived in a five-story building, on a boulevard named after one of the founders of the French Communist Party. Their kitchen window looked out on an empty lot, where gypsies put up their trailers every spring until it was turned into a parking lot, and behind it stood the Avicenne hospital, a Muslim establishment built in the 1930s for the French Muslim soldiers of Africa and the Maghreb, one of the rare remains of the empire. It was there that my father was taken after his stroke in 2005, and there that, coincidentally, Mouss waited for Hasna that November evening ten years later, in the wake of the massacre. I went back there once afterwards so I could visualize Hasna running through these streets in the rain, trying to give directions to Mouss, the signals of her phone rising up into the clouds, to cross wavelengths with the TV news stations whose stuttering *breaking news* and *special editions* on the screens all around covered the aftermath of the attacks.

The last mass killing in France as of this writing was the truck attack in Nice perpetrated by Mohamed Bouhlel — a bisexual Tunisian diagnosed in his adolescence with psychosis, with close ties to Islamist networks in Tunisia and France I have mentioned — which killed eighty-six and wounded more than 450 on July 14, 2016. Since then, fifty-three attacks or attempted attacks have been perpetrated, five with success, of which none approached in scale the terror wave of 2015–16 — the war against ISIS in Syria now bearing fruit at least for a while. The rest is impossible to foresee, and depends in part on how authorities deal with the returnees, as we call the French nationals coming back from Syria.

To this number, however, one must add the ninety-seven anti-Semitic violent aggressions and the 311 "nonviolent" anti-Jewish acts listed during the same period by the Ministry of the Interior, acts and aggressions that are *disconnected* from the terror attacks and were *not* committed by terrorists — this is a point worth repeating. Proponents of the "psychiatric explanation," who attribute these acts and aggressions to mental derangement only, use this fact to make the case that religion has nothing to do with the violence — one falls back here on the logical dead end of the Sébastien Selam murder case in 2003 — but by doing so, they shoot themselves in the foot. For things are *worse* if you consider the implications of the fact that nonpoliticized individuals give in to serial bursts of anti-Jewish violence.

Here are but a few examples:

In February 2017, in the *banlieue* of Bondy, two young Jewish men wearing their yarmulkes were assaulted by a whole group of men, to shouts of "Dirty Jew assholes, you're gonna die!"—an attack during which one of the two victims had one of his fingers cut off by a handsaw.

One month later, in Paris's Ninth Arrondissement, a man escaped from a woman armed with a hammer who jumped on him out of nowhere, shouting, *"Juif! Juif! Juif!"*

That same spring, a Jewish family in the Noisy-le-Grand suburb began to receive death threats in the form of nine-millimeter and Kalashnikov bullets accompanied by the words *"Allahu akbar"* and "You are all dead" in their mailbox, and tags on the walls that read DEATH TO THE JEWS, LONG LIVE PALESTINE, LONG LIVE DAESH, until the family resolved to move out the following fall.

Meanwhile that same season, in another suburb, Garges-lès-Gonesse, Jewish kids building a sukkah in the courtyard of their synagogue were attacked by a group of Muslim youth.

In Strasbourg that fall, a Jewish man was wounded by a knife-wielding man crying out *"Allahu akbar"* and, because he had pressed charges, was then harassed for months afterwards by a group of Muslims who found his address and stood under his window until he, too, was forced to move out along with his family.

Also that fall, a Jewish family from the Livry-Gargan suburb were attacked in their home, held hostage, and beaten for an entire afternoon by aggressors looking for "Jewish money."

On January 30, 2018, in Sarcelles, an eight-year-old kid was attacked in the street for wearing a yarmulke.

And in March, a fourteen-year-old coming out of the synagogue in Montmagny—a suburb near Paris—was attacked by four kids his age.

Then, of course, there was the beating and defenestration of Sarah Halimi, on the night of April 3, 2017, which occurred on the Rue de Vaucouleurs, two subway stations away from the building where Selam had been killed fourteen years earlier.

An observant Sephardic Jew, Lucie Sarah Halimi was sixty-six when she died. Her killer, Kobili Traoré, age twenty-seven, was a Muslim from Mali and an occasional drug user and dealer who lived down the street with his family. He'd had an argument at home and was in a troubled state when he started knocking on doors before entering number 30, Sarah Halimi's building, and asking one of the residents to shelter him for the night. When the man refused, Traoré threatened him physically, and the resident took shelter in his bedroom with his family, leaving Traoré alone in the living room, where he began to quote prayers and verses from the Koran. Then, for no apparent reason, Traoré climbed the apartment's balcony. He ended up in Sarah Halimi's unit on the third floor.

Halimi had time to cry for help and, in an attempt to defend herself and alert people nearby, to throw plates at her attacker. Meanwhile, several people, including Traoré's family, were calling the cops. According to witnesses, as Halimi began to shout for help and was being beaten, some neighbors appeared in front of the building to come to her aid, but they were stopped at the door by three policemen, who not only blocked access to the building but also stayed put. Unwilling to enter until backup arrived, they remained on the street as everybody watched Sarah Halimi's body fall to the pavement. An autopsy determined that she was still alive when she was thrown, and that she died from the fall rather than from the blows she'd received. She was, the report continued, disfigured by the beating. People had heard Traoré shout *"Allahu akbar"* several times, along with cries against "the Shaitan." After the murder, he returned to the neighbor's living room, where he resumed his prayers and where the police backup finally arrived and found him. He was taken into custody and, from there, put under psychiatric care.

From Israel, where he lives, the victim's son Jonathan testified to the Jewish press that his family and the killer's had been neighbors for more than twenty years and that during most of that time, they had had to put up with recurring anti-Jewish insults and jokes on the part of Traoré and one of his sisters. This was more than enough for the Jews on Twitter and other social networks to get inflamed. Rumors spread that Sarah Halimi had been stabbed, that her Islamic murderer had justified his deed with a Koran in hand, and that at the time he entered his victim's apartment, he was being tracked by RAID as a convicted terrorist. Parliament member Meyer Habib, who represents the French abroad and is devoted to the Jewish cause, wrote on his Facebook page: "Is [the killer] a jihadist? I'm afraid so."

But of course, he wasn't. He was just another Adel Amastaïbou. Yet in a cruel twist of sorts, terrorism was so much on everybody's mind that it might literally have led to Sarah Halimi's death. Convinced that they were dealing with a terror attack, the three cops present at the scene had stopped the neighbors from helping the victim for fear of shootings, and had stayed outside as they waited for backup.

It took seven weeks for the national press to even begin to cover the case and to consider whether or not anti-Semitism was involved. An op-ed piece published by the French journalist Claude Askolovitch in *Slate* pretty much reflected the general mindset, stating that the killer was obviously deranged, that "no element of the investigation" authorized him to conclude it had been an anti-Semitic aggression and that by believing otherwise, the Jewish community was giving in to a "ghetto" mentality. Despite public interventions by Bernard-Henri Lévy and several prominent intellectuals, and despite a petition online, the "anti-Semitic character" of the murder was not acknowledged until March 2018.

On the twenty-third of that month, not far from the same neighborhood, there was a second shocking incident: the murder of Mireille Knoll, eighty-five, a survivor of the Shoah, by her neighbor Yacine Mihoub, who stabbed her eleven times before trying to set her body on fire. He was helped by an accomplice, Alex Carrimbacus, who later testified to having heard Mihoub com-

plaining about the Jews and their financial means and yelling *"Allahu akbar"* during the murder. Mihoub's mother was also indicted,
for trying to clean the knife that had been used.

That Mireille Knoll had survived the Vel' d'Hiv' roundup—the
biggest arrest of Jews by French police, in July 1942—and married
an Auschwitz survivor gave the story a particular symbolic weight.
We soon learned that Knoll, a secular humanist, had regularly received Mihoub in her home when he was a child and his mother
was too busy to take care of him. But the previous year, he had been
accused of sexual assault against Knoll's nurse's daughter, who was
twelve: the aggression was said to have taken place at Knoll's home,
and Mihoub had just been released from jail on the day of the murder. He had spent the day drinking port with the old lady before
killing her. Mireille Knoll also had Parkinson's disease.

The reactions, this time, were noisy and immediate. Mihoub was
charged with murder and "the aggravating circumstance of anti-
Semitism," and over the following month, statements from politicians poured in, condemning the anti-Jewish acts, and a march was
organized in the victim's memory, gathering some ten thousand
people. The debate, however, started again a few weeks later with
a petition signed by three hundred personalities—among which
Lévy, Alain Finkielkraut, Élisabeth Badinter, and the former chief
editor of *Charlie Hebdo,* Philippe Val—denouncing "the new anti-
Semitism" from corners of the Muslim population as a "low-grade
ethnic cleansing" against the Jews. Asking that Muslim authorities
renounce some verses of the Koran, they also claimed—wrongly—
that all the Jews murdered in France in recent years had been killed
by "radical Islamists."

While the petition helped raise consciousness about the issue of
anti-Semitism in the country, at long last, it also immediately back-
fired. A few days later, *Le Monde* published a text signed by three
hundred imams denouncing both anti-Semitism and the fact that
some could even suggest that the recent murders had anything to

do with Islam. Journalists who supported them reminded the three hundred that neither Mihoub nor Traoré—nor Youssouf Fofana at the time he killed Ilan Halimi—were Islamists. They were not Muslims but "simply psychopaths full of hate and greed," as the same Claude Askolovitch had it in a new op-ed piece for *Slate*. Once again we were back at the dead end that has plagued the public debate on the issue since the Selam case.

This time there was a clue available, though none went to the trouble of looking into it. It was buried deep inside the psychiatric report issued in December 2017 by Dr. Daniel Zagury, who had examined Sarah Halimi's murderer, Kobili Traoré, to determine his mental state at the time of the crime.

Traoré, the report said, had indeed entered Halimi's home through her balcony by accident. He had no intention of targeting her and, being in an agitated state, convinced he was being pursued by the devil, probably did not even know at first where he was. It was the mezuzah on the doorframe that reminded him that the woman standing before him, whom he knew as his neighbor, was a Jew. This sudden realization, to quote the report, "clashed with his delirious state of mind, producing the immediate association of Sarah Halimi with the devil, and amplifying the frantic outburst of hate and vengeance."

In other words, Traoré did not enter Halimi's apartment to kill her because she was Jewish—contrary to what Jewish leaders and the three hundred petitioners implied—but, remembering she was a Jew, he killed her to exorcise the devil.

Jews being equated with the devil: this was what came back to the surface once reason disappeared.

The link with the murder of Sébastien Selam by Adel Amastaïbou—whose mother tore off the mezuzahs hanging on the neighbors' doors—could not be more obvious. For the first time, Zagury diagnosed in Traoré not simply a "delirious episode," but the "anti-Semitic delirious episode" that no one had been able to see at the time of Selam's murder. But what might link these kinds of anti-Semitic delirious episodes with more structured propaganda and with terrorism? It is now time to come full circle and to hazard my own explanation.

THE THERMODYNAMICS OF HATE

Let me state, then, that, like letters in a child's copybook, once copied and reproduced an adequate number of times—once turned into memes—anti-Semitic clichés such as the ones analyzed by Laacher are like an alphabet with which the propaganda writes itself in people's minds. The dormant hate contained in these anti-Semitic clichés, once acted out, is shaped by the propaganda into a pseudo-rational narrative that allows it to target anyone, the validation of violence through the murder of the Jews remaining effective *even when Jews have stopped figuring as its exclusive target.* Conversely, during a low-intensity terror period such as the one we've known since July 2016, the maintaining of violent anti-Semitism at a low but constant hum makes possible the preservation of the energy of violence, while waiting for the next outburst.

If this assumption is right—that is to say, if the violence against "the Jews" (or the people identified as such) is indeed the initiation threshold, as it were, beyond which "everything is permitted" —then it means that the indifference of French opinion in the face of the rising anti-Jewish aggressions between 2000 and 2015 bears some responsibility for the larger terror wave that ensued. Mohammed Merah's line quoted above—"I targeted Jews and French soldiers because I thought the French would understand better"— rings in this view as no more than the report on twelve years of incubation of hate.

What it also means is that one will find background support for terror in France as long as this backdrop of virulent anti-Semitism persists. It was this backdrop that allowed Hasna Aït Boulahcen to be so confident in asking an unknown driver to drive her killer cousin to the Saint-Denis safe house. As was already established, the investigation of the synchronized attacks of that November night has shown that the commando unit led by Abaaoud benefited from the help of several dozen people who, although not necessarily radicalized, found themselves at ease in the collective inner world from which the terrorists sprang. At the center of that world stand anti-Semitic clichés.

The advantage—and inconvenience—of such a thermodynamic vision of violence, so to speak, is that it leaves aside entirely the usual ideological, political, or social explanations for it. The distinction between psychopathy and rationalized terror acts also falls away, since the gestures of the former appear as the necessary substratum for the actions of the latter, which, in return, nurtures new eruptions of random brutal acts.

Political violence is usually envisioned as a means to an end. The idea is that humans governed by reason have some knowledge of what they want and don't want. The conclusion I'm offering here is based on the reverse assumption: if each of the historical, social, and political factors presented in this book sheds light on the violence that has been going on in France in the past eighteen years, they nevertheless, when taken together, do not give a complete explanation. The reason for this is that the causes of paroxysmal events do not explain *why* they happen. To use the cardinal example, the dramatic unemployment rate, the famine, the political chaos, and the bitterness of the Germans after the Treaty of Versailles all contributed to the rise of Hitler in Germany in 1933, yet, all combined, they do not "explain" Auschwitz.

Needless to say, the rise of anti-Semitism in France and the terror wave that has followed are not Auschwitz—not by a long shot. In fact, compared with most of the biggest tragedies in the world today —and contrary to what the concentration of events in this book may lead one to believe—they do not weigh much. By and large, for the average French citizen, the odds of dying as a victim of a terror attack or an anti-Semitic act in France today are close to nil. Yet it *can* happen, in a way that seemed impossible thirty years ago, so this new state of things needs to be reflected upon, if only to avoid a further degradation. (We are back here to the paradoxes of terror, which consist in making impossibilities possible.)

History, at the end of the day, may well be the history of the tales humans invent to explain to themselves what they do. What needs to be understood, then, is why some narratives work better than others to rationally legitimize sadism and murder. If the Islamist propaganda can rely on a psychopathic anti-Semitism to spread, it is because this psychopathy itself is but the manifestation of a much bigger current—a narrative that goes beyond the simple existence of a minority of disgruntled Muslims in France. A narrative that, in this book, Smaïn Laacher has analyzed and Ahmed Chekhab in Vaulx-en-Velin has illustrated. Can it be quantified?

According to a survey on France from the Anti-Defamation League published in 2015, 49 percent of the Muslims interrogated agreed with at least six of the eleven anti-Semitic statements that were offered to them (as opposed to 17 percent of the general population). The same year, the French sociologists and political analysts Dominique Schnapper and Chantal Bordes-Benayoun conducted a study for the Fondation du Judaïsme Français, in which 51 percent of Muslims interrogated agreed with five of the eight anti-Semitic clichés offered by the study—versus 38 percent of the general population in the country.

But, of course, one will say, those are two "Jewish" organizations—one can't be judge and jury. Let us examine, then, the results from the WBZ Berlin Social Science Center, which has analyzed studies on the Muslim population in France between 2008 and 2009. It says that 43.4 percent of French people of Moroccan or Turkish background claim to distrust the Jews—versus 7.1 percent of the French at large.

Historian and sociologist Günther Jikeli, of Indiana University and the French National Center for Scientific Research (CNRS), for his part, conducted interviews with 117 young Muslim men in Paris, London, and Berlin between 2005 and 2007. According to his conclusions, "the level of anti-Semitism increases significantly with the level of religiosity and/or with the authoritarian interpretations of Islam. By contrast, no correlation could be found between this anti-Semitism and personal experiences of discrimination."[1]

Even taking into account the margin of error unavoidable in this sort of study, that they could *all* be on the wrong track is improbable at best. One is then led to think that the impulsive anti-Semitic violence serving as a basis for the Islamist propaganda is itself a pathological manifestation of an anti-Semitic narrative at work inside the Muslim world today. To try to shed some light on it, without succumbing to the sins of essentialism, one must return to our old friend Ismayl Urbain, Napoleon III's special adviser, and to the crisis of modernity in France and in Europe.

"TO SAY, WITH SOME DISGUST, THAT FRENCH AND JEWS ARE ONE"

This book has tried to show how two anti-modern heritages may have influenced each other and converged in the construction of a common narrative: how, in France around 1830, during the Restoration era, reactionaries and utopians alike found, in the newly conquered Algeria and its dominant religion, an answer to the French spiritual anxiety, an anxiety born out of the contradictions between the dynamics of Industrial Revolution — the social troubles, the anarchic urbanization, and the growing secularism — that was seen as the devilish result of the French Enlightenment ideal of progress; and how, in the Muslim world, some of the most suicidal and destructive elements of that modernity crisis nourished the conservative tendencies of the Muslim clerics against the Enlightenment and the empire that brought it about. Now, in both cases, hostility to the Jews happened to be central.

As we've seen, the notion that France should choose between its Muslims and its Jews was expressed with the utmost clarity almost as soon as the colonization of Algeria began, by Ismayl Urbain. There was at the time, of course, no Arab policy to preserve, let alone a Zionist doctrine or an Israeli state. And yet, to again quote the passage, Napoleon III's future adviser for oriental affairs and the instigator of the future Muslim personal status, which would be so damaging to the Muslims themselves, could consider that to give up "the honor and dignity of France to these degraded pariahs" (the Jews) would only "distance the Arabs from us and make them say, with some disgust, that French and Jews are one."

Whether Urbain is right or wrong about what he perceives as the mindset of "the Muslims" toward "the Jews" is of no importance here. Rather, what matters is his own narrative—and the political consequences he'll draw from it twenty years later when putting together the basis of the Muslim personal status.

I indicated how these oriental clichés on Islam traveled through Europe to influence Nazi Germany and the writings of the Nazi propagandist Johann von Leers, and how von Leers ended up converting to Islam in Egypt, where Nasser appointed him to address the Jewish situation in 1956, and where he had *The Protocols of the Elders of Zion* translated into Arabic and printed. As late as the mid-sixties, before Jean Genet was turning his attention to the PLO and before Alain de Benoist invented the New Right, it is also under the influence of von Leers that, in 1966, Nasser, the hero of the Arab world, made remarks denying the Holocaust in a German neofascist journal. What I'm trying to argue here is that, between the complex heritage of Urbain, in France, and the pride of Arab nationalism in their countries of origin, the French youth of migrant background in search of their "cultural roots" do not have to search very far in order to stumble on the tropes of an anti-Jewish hate.

FRANCE AS THE HEART OF THE
TRANSNATIONAL FORCES OF NATIONALISM

Is it possible now to begin to find meaning in the coincidence in time between, on the one hand, the rise of spontaneous anti-Semitism in the *cités* and the spreading of Islamist militancy and, on the other, the development of a transnational populist—and, at times, crypto-fascist—current, whose success everywhere on the planet appears to be one of the major political phenomena of the new century?

The list is known; it is long, and keeps growing: Putin's Russia, Hungary, and Poland, to which one must now add Italy and, since Brexit, England; Austria, Germany, Sweden, the Netherlands, and Belgium, where nationalist currents are on the rise; and of course there is Donald Trump's USA. Whether in power or deeply ingrained in public opinion, and despite their multiple differences, most of these currents share with the Muslim reactionaries a similar hate for "the liberal elites" and for "globalism," and the same basic quest for "authenticity" and "identity" first theorized by Charles Maurras at the turn of the twentieth century, at the expense of Captain Dreyfus. Such a claim seems at first absurd, since most Western illiberal regimes and nationalist parties in Europe also support Israel and are hostile to Islam and to migrants from Muslim countries. But let us remember the moral dilemma of the French extreme right in the early 2000s, recounted above, a dilemma from which Dieudonné and Soral sprang. Doesn't this dilemma find its equivalent in geopolitics? Although it supports Israel, Poland, for instance, is as anti-immigrant as it is hostile to the Jewish memory of the Holocaust. Donald Trump, said to be anti-Muslim and pro-Israel, has allowed anti-Semitic threats to grow among his supporters in a way not seen in the United States since the thirties. Although officially fighting Islamists, Vladimir Putin relies on the Muslim Chechen president

Ramzan Kadyrov, who, even if he is against ISIS, supports honor killings of women, "understands" *Charlie Hebdo*'s killers, and has homosexuals in Chechnya deported and killed in the name of Sharia; Putin himself occasionally relies on anti-Semitic rhetoric, for instance when he blames "foreign Jews" for the possible Russian manipulation of the 2016 U.S. elections. Hungary, another supporter of the Netanyahu government in Israel, is both racist and anti-Semitic. Even Netanyahu's son Yair has at times posted anti-Semitic, "anti-globalist," anti–George Soros cartoons on Twitter, with the enthusiastic support of David Duke.

In fact, these contradictions solve themselves once you begin to realize that they all drink from the same source, namely the French Charles Maurras. Maurras was the first to politically theorize the notion that a manly, nationalist "authenticity" should fight the feminine, Judaized, modern globalism of his time. (Like Soral and like the Islamists, Maurras was as much an anti-Semite as he was a misogynist, and of course, as we've seen, he was anti-gay.)

But Maurras himself came from a long line of writers. De Maistre, Balzac, Baudelaire . . . Somewhere between the French existential malaise, born out of a reaction to the Enlightenment's contradictions and the political Restoration of the Ancien Régime, France gave birth to its best writers, and to its worst tendencies. It is, as we've seen, the climate born out of these tendencies that gave Russian agents at the Paris embassy the idea for *The Protocols of the Elders of Zion* in 1903. In time, these tendencies would influence currents in both the Arab Muslim world and the Vichy regime, before being resurrected as the New Right, personified in the pages above by Alain de Benoist and Co.

That France is absent from the list of illiberal regimes above is all the more remarkable. But this exception itself is telling. The suffocating atmosphere in the country before the 2017 French presidential elections, which saw the improbable victory of the unknown Emmanuel Macron over the nationalist Marine Le Pen — not to mention over the right-wing (and pro-Putin) François Fillon, the real favorite of the elections — was not the consequence of the terror attacks alone. Rather, these attacks had forced the country to contemplate a disturbing reality: entire segments of the French populace — and not Muslims only — could be attracted if not to the violence itself, then at least to the notion, shared by the terrorists, that democracy and the liberal society should be replaced by something more "traditional" and authoritarian. This attraction, in return, led to a certain "understanding" of the terrorists' motivations — at the expense of the Jews.

In France, both extreme-right and extreme-left ballots combined result in 30 percent of the voters agreeing that a parliamentary regime is rigged by nature. The number has been constant since the early eighties. These illiberal forces in France have not disappeared at all. Ever since he was elected, President Macron, who of course is not Jewish, has had to suffer anti-Semitic caricatures nonetheless. The first emanated from Soral's website, but it was soon picked up by some on both the extreme right and left. It presented him as a puppet, with the traditional big, hooked nose, working at the service of "the Rothschilds" and other global Jewish bankers. In May 2018, a left-wing anti-Macron demonstration presented a placard denouncing the "Zionist" and "crook" "Mac Aaron."

After twenty-five years of a virtually unchallenged anti-modern, illiberal current of an unprecedented magnitude across the globe, it is too soon, at this point, to tell whether Emmanuel Macron's victory in May 2017 is more than a simple accident in history, representing the beginning of a counterattack or the last bastion of what we call liberalism, whose inner contradiction entertains permanent dissatisfaction. Macron's chances of success, in any case, will largely depend on his capacity to mobilize what remains of the liberal forces in Europe, which are thin. His strength at this point is to stand alone, but of course such a position could easily turn into weakness and isolation. And yet his failure would be dramatic.

But the most obvious point linking Islamism with the self-destructive reactionary tendencies and neofascist narratives in the West is simply that the former delivered the latter. Jean-Marie Le Pen's unforeseen victory in the first round of the French presidential elections in 2002, less than a year after the attacks of 9/11, can rightly serve here as a metaphor for a more global dynamic.

During the previous decade, the slow rise of the "red-brown" alliance among European intellectual circles until then inclined to Communism had paralleled the development of political Islam in Sunni countries that had previously been exposed to the influence of the USSR, such as Algeria, and of course Afghanistan. Meanwhile in France and in countries of the former Eastern Bloc, the end of the Cold War, the swiftness, in particular, of the collapse of the Soviet Union, and the pace of the many unrelated events that accompanied it—the Balkan wars, the Algerian civil war, etc.—all this led to the sense that history was becoming unpredictable again. Uneasiness prevailed, and fear soon followed. The 9/11 attacks by Al Qaeda on New York and D.C. came right on time to give this fear a name, and to bring to it a new kind of narrative.

THE VANISHING OF THE NOTION OF TRUTH AFTER 9/11 AND THE RISE OF A GLOBAL COUNTER-KNOWLEDGE

September 11 signaled the end of the global narrative that CNN had broadcast since the end of the Cold War. It is worth remembering what this narrative, sometimes called "neoliberalism," said: In the wake of the crumbling of the Berlin Wall and the dismantling of apartheid in South Africa, and with social democracy getting ever stronger in Europe, even Russia would soon convert to free markets and free speech. The spread of liberal democracy and economic prosperity to China was only a matter of time. Through the Oslo peace process between the Israelis and the Palestinians, a giant Silicon Valley would rise from Cairo to Amman, ensuring the creation of an Arab middle class that would put an end to the dictatorships in the region. Peace, as a result, would reign, not just in the Middle East but everywhere. And what would help to create these "unavoidable" historical changes? Technology. Information. Cameras. The then exclusively American capacity to film anything on the planet "live" would bring an end to political violence. No tyrant anywhere would ever dare to implement his murderous policies under the divine eye of enlightened international opinion, in the glare of television lights. Information was free now. Censorship was over.

What the following years showed, however, is that censorship may not be simply a tool for dictators. Sometimes censorship may be a means by which the human imagination conceals its worst dreams and impulses. In the aftermath of 9/11, as the images of the World Trade Center falling spread through the Internet, new possibilities began to grow. I do not think that Americans were entirely aware of the strange elation, the frightened joy with which these images were received in many parts of the world, central Paris included (not just the *cités*). It wasn't simply the attack in itself; it was the place, New York. New York, the sanctified center of modernity, the capital city of the Diaspora Jews, the best shop window of capitalist America. Just when everybody assumed that the whole planet would follow the same boring road, something incredible had happened—something *real*.

Anything could follow. The implausible event was probably the first to be massively filmed by cell-phone users—the practice was still relatively new at the time. The spread of numerous eyewitness films showing the towers in flames and falling thus coincided with the progress of the Internet, and was immediately accompanied by commentaries casting doubt on what was being shown: How many people had really died? Why had Jews avoided working in the towers that day? And wasn't it obvious that the planes you saw had nothing to do with the crumbling of the towers—that explosives had done it? In other words, the images were too real to be true.

This disbelief was not just the result of political propaganda; it was an effect of the images themselves. I remember that the day following the attacks, as I was waiting in the hall to be called onto the set of a TV talk show, a technician who was watching, shocked, as the constant rerun of the attack played on a screen in front of us suddenly exclaimed, "And they're gonna make us believe that the Arabs did it!" This was a completely spontaneous reaction. It meant contradictory things: one was that, even for him, Al Qaeda equated to "the Arabs"; two was that both were innocent, and the whole thing was a scam.

Such suspicion had already been in the air since the end of the nineties, when there was paranoia surrounding Y2K and a sense that "the truth was elsewhere," as preached the trilogy of the *Matrix* movies, a worldwide success—excerpts of which would later be used by Islamist propagandists in France along with *Assassin's Creed*. In Japan, the terrorist sect Aum Shinrikyo, whose members thought the global world was manipulated by Freemasons and Jews, launched the sarin gas attacks in the Tokyo subway in 1995, killing twelve and injuring more than five thousand. All this was part of a global atmosphere, as was Timothy McVeigh in the United States, who longed for a nuclear holocaust in which all Jews and nonwhites would be annihilated and, as an appetizer of sorts, blew up the Murrah Federal Building, in Oklahoma City, killing 168 that same year. This was the larger context for the episodes of the nineties related in this book: the Islamists' attempt to drown "the global democracy of homosexuals and Jews" in the blood of the miscreants in Algeria; in Europe, the manly visit the partisans of the Franco-Russian "red-brown" ideology paid to Milošević's death squads in order to rebel against the new world order; and, in Russia, the frenetic writings of Alexander Dugin preaching—as Islamists did—that "all content of Modernity is Satanism and degeneration" and that "its sciences, values, philosophy, art, society, modes, patterns, and truths" should end.

After 9/11, as everyone began to turn their attention once again toward the Middle East, this mindset of apocalyptic anxieties, accumulated since the beginning of the atomic age and repressed during forty years by the balance of terror—this mindset blossomed.

Seen that way, what we call "Islamism" simply appears to be the Muslim variation of the global illiberal wave. What gave it prominence—in addition to the millions that the Saudis, Qatar, and Iran spent to sponsor it—was technology.

The footage of the towers falling served as raw material for the building of a new type of counterculture that gave a new strength to conspiracy theories, a self-generated mass production of counter-knowledge on a worldwide scale.

The credibility of this counter-knowledge, with its mass audience, was strengthened two years after the attacks by the public lies told by the U.S. administration about weapons of mass destruction in Iraq. Such a lie to the face of the world, emanating from the guarantor of the world order, could only validate the general feeling that anything labeled as the "official truth" was phony. The combination of these two factors helped to build an alternate narrative of a global scale according to which *things do not need to be true in order to be real.*

By the beginning of the following decade, a whole generation across the world, born with the fall of the World Trade Center, had at its disposal the products of an industry of spectacular videos, speeches, and so-called analysis that either justified the attack or denied any implication of the Muslim world in it, blaming instead Israel or the CIA, or both.

Kate Starbird, a professor of human-centered design at the University of Washington, has conducted a three-year research program on "alternative narratives," conspiracy theories, and the politics of disinformation on the Web in the United States between 2013 and 2016. Published in March 2017, her conclusions draw from a large galaxy of news sites where news has been overtaken by hundreds of computer-generated fake Twitter accounts and Facebook pages, some of which use real profiles and pictures stolen from real people. Whether on the left or on the right, most of the news that is thus conveyed is "antiglobalist," the meaning of the word varying from denouncing a global conspiracy of the rich and powerful to the defense of Muslims against global U.S. influence, from anti-immigration activism to anti-corporate stances and anti-European professions of faith. To quote Starbird: "Due to the range of different meanings employed, the sentiment of anti-globalism pulled together individuals (and ideologies) from both the right and the left of the U.S. political spectrum. Disturbingly, much of the anti-globalist content in these alternative media domains was also anti-Semitic — echoing long-lived conspiracy theories about powerful Jewish people controlling world events."[2] We are back to Maurras.

But why? What connects these conspiracy theories and the hate of modernity with the hate of the Jews?

I CAN'T GET NO SATISFACTION

In 1990, an emblematic figure of what then looked like the new era, Václav Havel, a playwright and a former leading dissident who had just become president of Czechoslovakia, invited the Rolling Stones to play in Prague.

He also appointed the rock 'n' roll star Frank Zappa as cultural ambassador of Czechoslovakia.

These moves were supposed to symbolize the new age: Eastern Europe was going West — was, in other words, joining rock 'n' roll culture, in all its decadence.

The same year, Havel published *Disturbing the Peace,* a telling and prescient title. Havel was at this time a model of the European artist and intellectual dissident, and his aura was exceptional. His plays, influenced by Kafka, had been praised by a writer as imposing as

Samuel Beckett, who, while Havel was imprisoned by the Communist regime in 1982, had dedicated one of his own plays, *Catastrophe,* to him in solidarity. Five years earlier, Havel had also been one of the initiators of the civil petition called Charter 77, signed by most of the persecuted intellectuals in Eastern Europe, the influence of which had reinforced the democratic fight in the USSR. Havel's essay "The Power of the Powerless" was read undercover even in Moscow dissident circles. At the time of his election, in other words, he embodied the resurrecting light of a timeless cosmopolitan European culture against the vanishing totalitarianism. From now on, men of letters and culture—philosopher-presidents —would lead the affairs of the state, and no one would ever be assigned to an identity anymore. Everybody would be free to be and become whatever he wanted.

Published in the *New York Times* in 2010, the testimony of the Czech writer Eduard Freisler, sixteen at the time of the Rolling Stones concert in Prague, gives an idea of what the event meant:

It was a cool August night in 1990; the Communist regime had officially collapsed eight months earlier . . .

I recall the posters promoting the concert, which lined the streets and the walls of the stadium: "The Rolling Stones roll in, Soviet army rolls out."

Soviet soldiers had been stationed in Czechoslovakia since 1968, when their tanks brutally crushed the so-called Prague Spring. My father was 21 at that time, dreaming of freedom and listening to bootlegged copies of "Let's Spend the Night Together" . . . During those years, you had to tune into foreign stations to hear the Stones. Communists called the band members "rotten junkies," and said no decent Socialist citizen would listen to them.

I only knew one Stones song, "Satisfaction"—but I knew it by heart. I had heard it for the first time on a pirated tape my father had bought on the black market in Hungary and smuggled into the country. It put an immediate spell on me. I was hugely impressed by the rough, loud guitar riff, so unlike the mellow sound of Czechoslovakian music. (The Communists frowned on the bass and the electric guitar, but they severely disapproved of the saxophone because they said it was invented by a Belgian imperialist.)

And I'd never heard anything like Mick Jagger's cracking, sensual voice, singing about personal desire. Czechoslovakians had been urged for four decades to sacrifice their inner dreams to the collective happiness of the masses. People who went their own way—rebels—often ended up in jail.

That night in August, waiting for the Rolling Stones to come on stage, we felt like rebels . . .

Two and a half hours later, when the concert was over, people were crying and hugging one another. My father cried and hugged me.[3]

Disturbing the Peace, however, which was published that very year, threw cold water on all this enthusiasm. Presented as a series of interviews realized in the years preceding Havel's election, it summarized the new zeitgeist of permanent change in dispiriting lines that sometimes seemed to echo Leonard Cohen at his darkest mood, or Havel's compatriot Kafka. To quote a single extract:

I get involved in many things, I'm an expert in none of them . . .

In general, then, though I have a presence in many places, I don't really have a firm, predestined place anywhere, neither in terms of my employment nor my expertise, nor my education and upbringing, nor my qualities and skills . . .

I write merciless, skeptical, even cruel plays—and yet in other matters behave almost like a Don Quixote and an eternal dreamer

... For many people, I'm a constant source of hope, and yet I'm
always succumbing to depressions, uncertainties, and doubts ...
How does it all fit together? ... How can I—this odd mix of the
most curious opposites—get through life, and by all reports successfully?[4]

This was hardly what you expected from a victorious new president
opening a new area.

With time, however, such a line would acquire the value of a
metaphor for what turned out to be a disappointing outcome. After resigning from the presidency in 1992, during the partition of
the country, Havel was reelected the next year at the head of what
was now the Czech Republic. Soon after, more and more virulent
critics accused him of deserting the Czech people for international
gatherings and society life. Finally, in 2003, he supported George
W. Bush's Iraq War before being defeated by a conservative government.

What interests me here, of course, is not Czech politics. It is
the seemingly irreconcilable tension between the hope for change
brought about by sophisticated, cosmopolitan dissidents such as
Havel, who risked their careers and sometimes their lives in their
fight against injustice, and the extraordinarily disappointing result
that ensued. Without that hope, no change would ever have occurred; but what did the change bring in the end? What followed
such culture, such reason and courage?

Liberalism's inner contradiction entertains permanent dissatisfaction, and there's an irony of sorts in the fact that Freisler's enthusiasm
was set off by that song of the Stones'. But what was discovered in
the nineties was the extreme to which this dissatisfaction could lead.
Where intellectuals had promised happiness and the right for anyone
to choose his life, people discovered constant instability—what the
literary critic Alfred Kazin once called "the fury of transformation"

brought about by American influence. One could be gay, one could change sex, one could become a shark of the stock market or dedicate one's life to humanitarian causes or do all that in turn. To be anyone meant to constantly choose what to be, take one's place in the baroque carnival of plastic identities and moral uncertainties where no judgment is enacted but your own. What did freedom bring, then, apart from chaos, the plague of moral relativism, or the unbearable weight of a personal confrontation with oneself?

At least in European and Arab countries marked by Communism, this was how the nineties were felt.

As it happens, Jews were overrepresented among the dissidents of Eastern Europe during the Cold War—and even when they were not Jewish, Communist authorities tended to label them as such, convinced as they were that Jews were both "naturally" intellectuals and troublemakers. (This is the reason why, for decades, Israel was the only country where dissidents were allowed to immigrate—along with delinquents and Russian mafiosi.) Upon a closer look, Jews are often overrepresented when hopes of radical change are at stake, and disappointment follows. We were told that there was justice in this world; we were told Judaism carried with it a sense of moral rectitude, and that the Messiah would come. And it *is* true that you find Jews in excess among the revolutionary movements in Europe in the nineteenth and twentieth centuries, in the musical avant-garde of the early twentieth, in today's French intellectual life, in New York intellectual life, in the civil rights movement of the sixties in the United States and in the hippie movement of the sixties and seventies, in disruptive capitalist banks, and in cutting-edge science and new technologies. Everywhere, in short, modernity manifests itself. The Jewish presence *disturbs the peace,* to quote the title of Havel's book.

The French-American philosopher George Steiner wrote, "Everything that makes the pulp of modern urban life, everything that gives it its bite, one can say that it is, above all, Jewishness and homosexuality that gave birth to it (and all the more so when both got down to it, as with Proust or with Wittgenstein)."[5]

He could have added Spinoza, Cervantes, and Montaigne—these founders of modern skepticism, all children or grandchildren of Marranos. Isn't there a certain logic, then, in the fact that anti-modern movements, either in Europe or in Islam, are both anti-cosmopolitan, anti-Jew, and anti-gay?

Another Jewish writer, the Israeli Amos Oz, wrote:

> Anyone who is misled into supposing that the Jewish sickness is merely the result of dispersal among the nations and lack of territory is mistaken . . . We have never been able to settle down . . . Whichever way we have turned, whatever we have put our hands to, we have always caused a mighty stir: sweat, nervousness, fear, aggression, a constant ferment . . . The crux of the matter is the restlessness, that irritating, fructifying fever: anxious, eager Jews, always trying to teach everybody else how to live, and how to tell right from wrong.[6]

There is an understandable tendency today among the left to see Muslim migrants as "the new Jews" of the twenty-first century. These new Jews, it is said, are confronted with a new anti-Semitism ("Islamophobia") that denies them both their rights and their religious identity. The task of antiracism, therefore, is to fight for that identity as a civil right. That people should have the same rights regardless of their origin is of course beyond discussion. But, in the view of the Steiner and Oz quotes above—and I could quote many, many others of the kind—it seems to me that this tendency to equate Muslims of the present with Jews of the past, however well intended, entirely misses the point of what anti-Semitism is about. Something else is at stake. Something that has to do with this anxiety to teach everyone right and wrong, as Oz points out, but also with the dialectic of hope and disappointment that Havel embodies.

There are, as we know, 613 commandments in the Jewish law, which means that nobody, not even the most Orthodox Jews, can follow them all. In the strictest application of the law, in other words, nobody can completely be a Jew. The definition of what it is to be Jewish, then—a matter that I don't pretend to begin to address here—is comprised in a narrative where words and acts never entirely coincide. Something is always missing. This disappointment is symbolized on Yom Kippur, the Day of Atonement, when, in every synagogue in the world, Jews admit, before God, that they haven't fulfilled the conditions to be loved by him—they haven't been "authentically," completely Jewish—and yet they remain Jews. Here, I believe, in this modern incompleteness, which is also a disappointment, lies the heart of the problem.

The first racist theory of the modern Western world was established in the fifteenth century by the Holy Inquisition. It stated that, even when they converted, Jews remained Jews because they had Jewish blood in their veins: a religious belonging, in other words, had been transformed into a biological trait. But it wasn't because the Jews fought to remain faithful to their faith and their identity that the Inquisition had started to persecute them in Portugal and Spain—*it was because they didn't. It was because they had adapted and changed. It was the change that was the problem.*

Mostly under pressure from the Catholic Church, they had converted en masse to Catholicism, and *nothing could distinguish them any longer from the rest of the population.* Paranoia ensued. Under the new pejorative names Marranos, Xuetes, or "new Christians," Jews, crypto-Jews, were now seen as hybrid Christians/Jews while really being neither one nor the other. As Havel would have said, they were now a people with "a presence in many places," and yet without "a firm, predestined place anywhere."

Another example: Religious anti-Judaism in Europe had existed since the Middle Ages at least. But its rapid spread in the wake of the Industrial Revolution—a spread that paved the way for the massa-

cres of the twentieth century—had less to do with the synagogues
and the shtetls than with the new fact that Jews were now coming
out of the shtetl to integrate into public urban life everywhere and
could not be distinguished any longer from their fellow citizens.
The influence of the passing of the Declaration of the Rights of
Man in France, in 1789, followed by the emancipation of the Jews in
France, two years later, had, as I have emphasized all along, allowed
assimilation and secularism everywhere on the continent. This gave
birth to the reactionary theory, first born in France, that the Revolution had been brought about by Jews and Freemasons to destroy,
in the name of international money, the royal courts and the divine
order that had ruled until then throughout Europe.

In France during the war, the Vichy regime always pretended that
its anti-Jewish laws were passed to better protect the assimilated
French Jews, who were "like us," integrated and invisible, and separate them from the foreign Jews of recent arrival, who, by contrast,
could easily be recognized through their religiosity and accent and
were said to be the sole target of the anti-Jewish legal measures.
Yet, in fact, the major part of the anti-Semitic state policy between
1940 and 1945 focused on teaching the population *how to recognize a
Jew*, that is to say, how to identify someone who looks like you but
isn't, and whose appearance is deceitful. By *that* standard, the Polish Jewish family that barely spoke French and crossed the border
seeking refuge, and my family, born and raised in Paris and totally
assimilated, were equally foreigners. (Jacques Helbronner, president
of the Jewish Consistory at the time and a personal friend of Marshal Pétain's, thought it wise to implement the anti-Jewish measures
in the French synagogues, where he instituted a line of separation
between French "Israelites" and foreign Jews. In 1943, though, he
himself was arrested and deported to Auschwitz, where he was immediately gassed.)

This educational program—how to recognize a Jew—was the
main theme of the highly popular exhibit *France and the Jew*, inaugu-

rated by the regime in September 1941 on the Grands Boulevards, and in which portraits of Jews were shown in order for the "real" French to identify the "fake" ones. The basis for the show was a book of the same title, published in 1940 by an anthropologist called Georges Montandon, a former Communist who had supported the Russian revolution and fought against slavery in the 1920s in Ethiopia before turning to anti-Semitism. (The book, like the exhibit itself, was subsidized by the Nazis.) From the thirties on, Montandon had become the first theoretician of political anti-Semitism in France and even inspired the French writer Céline's famous anti-Jewish pamphlets. (The two men were good friends.)

It is telling that Montandon also rebuffed any notion of a French race: "To speak of the French race," he had written in 1935, "is to ignore what a race is. There is no French race. There is a French ethnic group, in the composition of which enter elements of several races."[7] He was not a racist — at least not in the popular sense of the term. In addition to fighting slavery in Ethiopia, he also denounced the genocide of the Native Americans. Having devoted part of his time to working as an ethnologist on North Africa, he also thought, favorably, that the Maghreb was the place where "a fraction probably even more important tomorrow than today, of the French ethnic group," would develop. In other words, he was an adept of "multiracialism," as he called it. And this was the basis for his raw hate against the only "whore ethnic group" in the world, namely the Jews. (In French, the label *l'ethnie putain* carries an untranslatable obscene violence.) "What characterizes psychologically the Jewish ethnic community and legitimates the scientific label by which we name it," he wrote, "is the fact that this community, instead of serving one country, one homeland, puts itself, like a public girl, at the service of all countries while refusing for two thousand years to mix with the populations."[8]

This is a crucial statement. In actuality, of course, one could find many Jewish patriots in France, such as Captain Dreyfus, to name the most familiar, and Montandon himself probably knew more than one. But those were individual cases. If anything, they justified Montandon's scientific hate. Why? Because his labeling the Jews as a whore group was based on the fact that there were Jewish patriots in other countries as well. And while some of them were entirely secular, like my uncle Jean-Louis Crémieux-Brilhac, and all my family, for that matter, they insisted on remaining Jews nonetheless and had done so, as Montandon wrote, "for two thousand years." What really set off Montandon's hate—and not just his—was not simply the Jewish "identity" or the Jewish "religion," but *the Jewish plasticity, so to speak, the Jewish permanence through several (and at times, it seemed, mutually irreconcilable) shapes.* In Václav Havel's words, a presence that could be found "in many places"—in France and Germany, for instance—"without having a firm, predestined place anywhere."

It will come as no surprise, at this point, that Montandon was a proponent of the creation of a Jewish state in Palestine. There was no contradiction. Like many far-right-wingers then and now, he wanted the Jews in one place and one place only. Once the Israeli state existed, he thought, every non-Israeli Jew in the world would be listed as a foreigner in his or her own country and subsequently cast out, with no other choice but to emigrate.

Another example of such a mindset in France can be found in Darquier de Pellepoix, the founder, in 1936, of the Rassemblement Anti-Juif de France (Anti-Jewish Rally of France), who during the war was appointed head of the Commissariat Général aux Questions Juives (General Commission for Jewish Affairs) and supervised the government's official anti-Semitic policy and the deportations. Much later, after the Six-Day War of 1967, Darquier de Pellepoix became both a firm denier of the Holocaust and an enthusiastic supporter of the Israeli state and of its army. The same mindset can be found today among true anti-Semites in the Muslim world who do not just deny Israel the right to exist but fight it as a territorial emanation of an alleged global Jewish lobby, that is to say an underground cabal of Jews in disguise. Today's far-right pro-Israel militants inside the National Front in France or among the U.S. alt-right may disagree with Islamists on the Middle East, but both share a common ground in their hatred for the ability of the Jewish narrative to escape any final definition—any final identity.

Where does such an obsession originate? It is found already in the Gospels, where hypocrite Hebrews are compared to "whitewashed tombs that look handsome on the outside but inside are full of the bones of the dead." Saint Paul probably gave it its deepest expression when he wrote that Jews exhibiting their circumcision as the sign of their covenant with God and the proof of being the chosen people in fact disregarded the law in their daily lives. Moral rectitude, he argued, had nothing to do with what you showed and everything to do with what you felt inside. True virtue was invisible, appearance of virtue deceitful. The *real* circumcision was not the circumcision of the flesh, but that of the heart. According to David Nirenberg, from whom I borrow these examples,[9] this epistemological issue of the circumcision and the divide between what is and what seems to be—the opposition between an inner, ineffable real and the coarse, vulgar appearance of the fleshly world—in its connection with the notion of being chosen has defined the relationship of the rest of the world to "the Jews" ever since. (Fascinatingly, in January 2017, the imam of the Grand Mosque of Paris, Dalil Boubakeur, a moderate, published on the mosque's website a whole exegesis on Abraham, in order to demonstrate that the Jewish circumcision as a sign of the covenant was, in fact, a pretense and a lie, and that the biblical text had been falsified by the Hebrew commentators. The article, still available in December 2017 when I read it, has apparently been removed since.)

Anti-Semitism, in other words, has less to do with "the hate of the other" or with "identity" than with change. The true sedition lies in the metamorphosis, this Kafkaesque word, which infuriated the Inquisition at the time of the Marranos just as it infuriates all the proponents of "identity politics" anywhere at any time.

Which is why, as this book reaches its close, I can only dedicate these pages to all the reticent soldiers ensnared in this war. To the dead, of course, but also to the living: to Jonathan Chetrit, today twenty-three, who successfully improvised the sheltering and protection of the children in the Ozar Hatorah school during the shooting on March 19, 2012; to Sharon Benitah, today fifteen, who not only witnessed the death of her friend Miriam Monsonego that day but stood testifying at Abdelkader Merah's trial with almost no quavering in her voice. I'm thinking of the lawyer Jacques Gauthier, who, in the name of the school, gave what was probably the most affecting speech of the whole trial before falling into tears. To Muslims such as Latifa Ibn Ziaten, the mother of Mohammed Merah's first victim, who, a scarf around her head, has been traveling across the *cités* of France since her son was killed to try to work with the Muslim youth, among whom she says she sees "many Merahs growing," and who, in the aftermath of the death of her son, had to fight the cops because "the commissioner thought my son was drug dealing and that was the reason why he got killed. He said, 'You're all the same anyway, don't lie to me.' He would not let me see Imad on account that the morgue was closed. The next day, they performed the autopsy before I had a chance to see him." Latifa Ibn Ziaten was by no means the only one. All of the Muslim victims' families—all of them—mentioned the same attitude from the cops who broke the news of the killings by addressing them first as suspects, because of their Arab names and their looks. Because of their "identity." And no left-winger, nor any Muslim leaders, came to help.

This book is for them—and for all the solitary champions of impurity, wherever they are. Modernity is at war with itself—and so are we all.

Acknowledgments

Hate is drawn from a five-part series of reports, of four thousand words each, on anti-Semitic brutalities in France that I wrote during the summer of 2014 for *Tablet* magazine and that in February 2015 received the Chaim Bermant Prize in London. Let me first thank the journalists Alana Newhouse and David Samuels, for having welcomed and sheltered my tentative English in *Tablet*. My gratitude extends also to Tom Reiss, who first suggested *Tablet* and made the introduction. The book would never have been written without you guys.

All my thanks to Andrew Wylie, Jeff Posternak, and the entire team at the Wylie Agency, for their constant availability and advice, and, at Houghton Mifflin Harcourt, to Lauren Wein, for her support and patience as I was struggling with the subject, and to copy editor Will Palmer, for his meticulous reading. Stéphanie Polack, as you know, these thanks also extend to you—I could never have accomplished the job of writing in two different languages without your love and your faith, to say nothing of your patience for four years.

But above all, my gratitude goes to Philip Roth. It is not too much to say that, from the early 2000s on, during the years I began to come to New York on a regular basis to escape the increasingly suffocating atmosphere in France, it was Philip's presence and friendship and his vision of New York and of the United States as a place where a counter-history was possible for the Jews that saved me from going insane and made the city, for me, a place in which I could breathe.

Then, in July 2014, after the second installment in *Tablet,* I received from Philip the following email:

> Marc, I have taken the liberty of asking Andrew Wylie if he would act as agent for a book by you about the menacing new predicament of French Jews that you would base on an expanded book-length version of your 5 *Tablet* pieces. He has indicated to me that if you are willing so is he. I have told him that I think such a book, published in the next 12 to 18 months, would find a large Jewish audience here and get extensive media coverage. I base my judgment on the excellent beginning already published in *Tablet* and on my understanding of what literate Jews (and, to be sure, not exclusively Jews) would be interested in reading about. I have absolute faith in the combination of you and the subject and I have told him as much. I will send Andrew a copy of this email and leave it to the two of you to make contact.

To say no was not an option. HMH and I signed a contract in November of that year. Later on, I signed a corresponding contract with my French publisher, Grasset, for a French version of what, in my mind, was a small book that would be "published in the next 12 to 18 months."

That was the simple timetable that got turned upside down by the coordinated attacks on *Charlie Hebdo* and the Hyper Cacher store, in Vincennes, in January 2015 — launching a terror wave of a magnitude not seen since World War II in France or in any European country, for that matter. For the year and a half that followed, as these attacks were followed by others, I faced a strange paradox.

While the new situation seemed to confirm the intuition at the core of the *Tablet* series, it also changed everything. For what could the connection be between random brutalities emanating from regular Muslim people and targeting Jews only and planned terrorist attacks aimed at everyone? And how could all this relate to the rising populism in France, which culminated, in January 2014, in a right-wing demonstration during which anti-Semitic slogans were heard in the streets of Paris for the first time since the 1930s? And why had anti-Jewish brutalities reached the astonishing peak of eight hundred across the country—more than two per day—during that year that preceded the larger terror wave? How did these facts relate to one another, if indeed they did?

These questions would keep me busy for the next four years. Four years during which I wrestled first with the first draft of the present book in English, then with a draft in French, before I came back to the English and back again to the French, writing, in fact, two different books for two different audiences, each time coming to understand different things about a situation that was—and is—constantly changing.

Today, both *Hate* and its French cousin, *Un Temps pour Haïr,* exist, but the world in which they are being published has little resemblance to the world in which Philip sent me his email five years ago. Philip, for one, is gone, and so is his America—at least for now. Who would have thought, in 2014, that the president of the United States would write, as a mental note in the margins of a speech, a sentence such as TRADE IS BAD, as Bob Woodward revealed in *Fear?* The populist wave that is sweeping across the planet has hit the USA, too, with unpredictable consequences.

Its origins are in good part French. As Steven Bannon reminds us in the present book, they are to be found in Charles Maurras's writings and, before him, in the conflict with modernity first born in France in the aftermath of the Revolution and the Napoleonic Wars. But in the first decades of the twentieth century, Maurras's quest for "the real country" also infused Arab nationalism, giving a secular content to what the Wahhabist current, for its part, was looking for in the "true" Islam. And it is very tempting, now, to identify at last the enemy I wrestled with in this book for five years. Not "Islam," nor "the Muslims," but, more simply, a Muslim version of the worldwide populist wave. Many heads for one beast.

As I said, Philip did not live to read this book, and whether it fulfills the promises he saw in the *Tablet* series is not for me to say. One thing, however, is certain: his memory and his strength inspire us all for the fights to come.

Notes

PREFACE

1. Gilles Antonowicz and Françoise Cotta, "Gang des Barbares," *Le Monde,* July 13, 2009.
2. Gilles Antonowicz, *L'Affaire Halimi, du crime crapuleux au meurtre anti-sémite, histoire d'une dérive* (Paris: Nicolas Ebayin, 2014), 13.
3. Institute for Economics and Peace, *Global Terrorism Index 2017: Measuring and Understanding the Impact of Terrorism* (Sydney: Institute for Economics and Peace, 2017).
4. Emma-Kate Symons, "Steve Bannon Loves France," Politico, March 22, 2017 (updated March 23, 2017), https://www.politico.eu/article/steve-bannons-french-marine-le-pen-front-national-donald-trump-far-right-populism-inspiration/; Ed Kilgore, "Zut Alors: Bannon's Taste for Franco-Fascists," *New York,* March 17, 2017.
5. For a complete analysis of Maurras's ideology, see, in particular, Zeev Sternhell, *The Anti-Enlightenment Tradition,* trans. David Maisel (New Haven, CT: Yale University Press, 2009).
6. Amos Elon, *Herzl* (New York: Schocken Books, 1986), 182.
7. For a detailed history of the Protocols, see Pierre-André Taguieff, *Les Protocoles des sages de Sion: Un faux et ses usages dans le siècle* (Paris: Fayard, 2004). The novelist Danilo Kiš takes a more poetic approach to the story in his masterpiece novella *The Book of Kings and Fools.* See Danilo Kiš, *The Encyclopedia of the Dead* (New York: Faber, 1989), 250–315.

1. THE RETURN OF THE REPRESSED

1. David Nirenberg, *Anti-Judaism: The Western Tradition* (New York: W. W. Norton, 2014), 365.

2. Nirenberg, 366.

3. Nirenberg, 367.

4. Daniel Boyarin has famously analyzed how this regeneration of the Jews helped frame a completely new vision of the Jewish male while influencing the rise of Zionism. See, in particular, Daniel Boyarin, *Unheroic Conduct: The Rise of Heterosexuality and the Invention of the Jewish Man* (Berkeley: University of California Press, 1997).

5. Christopher de Bellaigue, *The Islamic Enlightenment* (London: Bodley Head, 2018), 3.

6. De Bellaigue, 10.

7. Joseph de Maistre, *Oeuvres Complètes,* vol. 2 (Paris: Forgotten Books, 2018), 338. I'm simplifying here a subject that is beyond the reach of the present book. For a whole discussion on the link between the counter-Enlightenments, de Maistre, and the roots of fascism and anti-Semitism in France, see, in particular, Isaiah Berlin, *Freedom and Its Betrayal* (Princeton, NJ: Princeton University Press, 2017), and the more debatable book by Pankaj Mishra, *Age of Anger* (London: Penguin, 2017).

8. De Bellaigue, 12.

9. Simone de Beauvoir, *Les Mandarins* (Paris: Gallimard, 1954), 84 (translation mine).

10. Michel's speech is reproduced in full in Jean-Louis Crémieux-Brilhac, *L'étrange victoire: De la défense de la République à la liberation de la France* (Paris: Gallimard, 2016), 50–65.

11. Herzl went to Mayer's funeral. According to Amos Elon's biography *Herzl* (see note 7), it was this incident, more than the Dreyfus affair, that convinced Herzl to fight for the Jews of Europe. Once back in Berlin, Herzl was so influenced by the mood in France that the first idea he came up with was to challenge every anti-Semite in Germany to a duel. The obvious impracticability of such a plan led him to consider, for a while, supporting mass conversion of the Jews to Catholicism. Eventually, confronted with the persistence of anti-Semitism in Europe, he came up with Zionism.

12. Two of the German spies to whom Dreyfus supposedly passed informa-

tion were thought to be homosexuals. This was one of the reasons the military prosecution wanted to keep the Dreyfus file secret. To admit publicly that a French officer had any connection with homosexuals would be insufferable. For a complete account of this aspect of the case, see Pierre Gervais, Pauline Peretz, and Pierre Stutin, *Le dossier secret de l'affaire Dreyfus* (Paris: Alma, 2012).

13. Ralph Schor, *L'antisémitisme en France dans l'entre-deux-guerres: Prélude à Vichy* (Paris: Éditions Complexe, 2005), 145–69.

14. Of the Jewish members of the Popular Front, Léon Blum was the only one to survive the war, and that was only by luck, as he came back from Buchenwald in 1945. His brother René died in Auschwitz. As for Jean Filliol, an active collaborator with the Vichy regime during the war, he found refuge in 1945 in General Franco's Spain as a high-level executive for the L'Oréal Group. Eugène Schueller, L'Oréal's founder, was a fierce anti-Semite and a pro-Nazi militant all his life, and L'Oréal served as a safe house for former Nazis and collaborators until the nineties.

15. These numbers are provided by the French minister of the interior. The cases that follow in the text, each with its own bizarre details, were gathered by the Service de Protection de la Communauté Juive, or SPCJ, the voluntary security service of the Jewish community, which collects information about all anti-Semitic incidents in France for which a formal complaint has been made and an investigation has been conducted by the police.

16. Alain Peyreffite, *C'était de Gaulle* (Paris: Fayard, 2002), 354.

17. Writer/journalist Kamel Daoud emphasizes this point in his novel *The Meursault Investigation,* which presents itself as the Algerian counterpart to Albert Camus's famous novel *The Stranger,* but with the explicit intention of "giving a face" to the anonymous Algerian killed by Meursault in that book. See Kamel Daoud, *The Meursault Investigation* (New York: Oneworld, 2015).

18. Edmund Burke, *Reflections on the Revolution in France* (Manchester, England: Manchester University Press, 2013).

19. Joseph de Maistre, *Les soirées de Saint-Pétersbourg ou Entretiens sur le gouvernement temporel de la providence: onzième entretien* (Paris: L'Herne, 2016).

20. Alexis de Tocqueville, *Travail sur l'Algérie* (1841) (Paris, ed. ink Book, 2013).

21. Unless otherwise indicated, for all information and quotations related

to the life of Ismayl Urbain, I rely on Michel Levallois's *Ismaÿl Urbain: Une autre conquête de l'Algérie,* the only existing biography of this strange character. But I present a completely different view of Urbain than Levallois does. See Michel Levallois, *Ismaÿl Urbain: Une autre conquête de l'Algérie* (Paris: Maisonneuve & Larose, 2001).

22. Levallois, 250.
23. Levallois, 280.
24. Levallois, 320.
25. Levallois, 340.
26. Levallois, 345.
27. Xavier Yacono, "La Régence d'Alger en 1830 d'après l'enquête des commissions de 1833–1834," *Revue de l'Occident musulman et de la Méditerranée* (1966), 229–44.
28. Raed Bader, "Noirs en Algérie, XIXème-XXème siècle, pour une histoire critique et citoyenne, le cas de l'histoire franco-algérienne," Canal-U video, 24:14, June 20, 2006, Maison Méditerranéenne des Sciences de l'Homme, https://www.canal-u.tv/video/ecole_normale _superieure_de_lyon/18_noirs_en_algerie_xixeme_xxeme_siecles .4352. The slave trade in the Maghreb did not disappear unil the 1920s, with the arrival of urbanization.
29. For this and the quotes and information below, see Victor Klemperer, *I Will Bear Witness: A Diary of the Nazi Years,* 2 vols. (New York: Modern Library, 2001); Jeffrey Herf, *The Jewish Enemy: Nazi Propaganda During World War II and the Holocaust* (Cambridge, MA: Belknap Press at Harvard University Press, 2006); and Jeffrey Herf, *Nazi Propaganda for the Arab World* (New Haven, CT: Yale University Press, 2010).
30. Jean Genet, *Un captif amoureux* (Paris: Gallimard, 1986) (translation mine). An English translation of this book was published in 2003 by New York Review Books (NYRB Classics) under the title *Prisoner of Love,* with a foreword by Ahdaf Souief. I have used the French text as my source.
31. Between 1980 and 1986, Paris delivered $17 billion worth of weapons to Iraq, including Exocet missiles and Mirage F1 fighter planes, plus material to manufacture large quantities of sarin gas. In 1987, this gas was used against the Kurdish civilian population of Hallabja, killing five thousand people, mostly women and children. In the scandal that

ensued, the French minister of defense, Jean-Pierre Chevènement, ex-onerated Saddam Hussein from the charge of gassing Kurdish civilians, claiming "a lack of proof." Grisly photographs published the world over proved him wrong.

32. Olivier Carré, *Le nationalisme arabe* (Paris: Fayard, 1993).

33. Hakim El Karoui, "Un islam française est possible," Institut Montaigne, September 2016, http://www.institutmontaigne.org/ressources /pdfs/publications/rapport-un-islam-francais-est_-possible.pdf.

34. Olivier Galland and Anne Muxel, *La tentation radicale: Enquête auprès des lycéens* (Paris: Presses Universitaires de France, 2018). Twenty percent of the young Muslims interviewed in this study also considered it "acceptable in some cases in our society to fight, arms in hand, for one's religion," while only 9 percent of the non-Muslims agreed.

35. Jean-Pierre Obin, interview with the author, winter 2015.

36. Hélène Roudier de Lara, interview with the author, winter 2015.

37. Roudier de Lara interview, 2015.

38. Roudier de Lara interview, 2015.

2. THE YEAR OF THE QUENELLE

1. Respectively, *La Libre Belgique,* December 29, 2014, and *Le Soir,* February 12, 2014, for the train incident and the doctor incident. Other incidents mentioned here have been provided by the Service de Protection de la Communauté Juive (SPCJ) and checked by police.

2. It was another RT journalist, Eva Bartlett, who, in a press conference at the UN in 2016, defended Bashar al-Assad and denounced the coverage of the Syrian war by the Western press. On this, and on the links between RT and Dieudonné, see Mathieu Dejean, "Comment une vidéo sur la Syrie est devenue la deuxième la plus vue sur Youtube," *Les Inrockuptibles,* December 15, 2016.

3. Alain Soral, *Misère du désir* (Paris: Blanche, 2012).

4. Mathias Destal, "Affaire Binti: Alain Soral condamné pour menaces à l'encontre d'une jeune femme," *Marianne,* November 29, 2016, https:// www.marianne.net/societe/affaire-binti-alain-soral-condamne-pour -menaces-l-encontre-d-une-jeune-femme.

5. Marie-France Etchegoin, "Antisémite, 'national-socialiste': Comment devient-on Alain Soral?" *Le Nouvel Observateur,* January 26, 2014, https://www.nouvelobs.com/l-enquete-de-l-obs/20140124.OBS3766/antisemite-national-socialiste-comment-devient-on-alain-soral.html.

6. Alain de Benoist, *Cartouches: Les éditoriaux d'Éléments, 1973–2010* (Paris: Amis d'Alain de Benoist, 2010).

7. Alexander Dugin, *Foundations of Geopolitics* (Moscow: Arctogéa, 2015), 367. For a complete analysis of the book, see John B. Dunlop, "Alexander Dugin's Foundations of Geopolitics," Europe Center at Stanford University. First published in *Demokratizatsiya* 12, no. 1 (January 31, 2004). https://tec.fsi.stanford.edu/docs/aleksandr-dugins-foundations-geopolitics.

8. Alexander Dugin, *Le prophète de l'eurasisme* (Paris: Avatar Éditions, 2006), 156.

9. Dugin, *Le prophète,* 158.

10. Alexander Dugin, *La Quatrième Théorie Politique: La Russie et les idées politiques du XXIème siècle,* foreword by Alain Soral (Paris: Ars Magna, 2016). For the quote in English, I use the translation from Paul Ratner, "The Most Dangerous Philosopher in the World," Big Think, accessed July 22, 2018, https://bigthink.com/paul-ratner/the-dangerous-philosopher-behind-putins-strategy-to-grow-russian-power-at-americas-expense.

11. Beauvoir, *Les Mandarins.*

12. Philippe Muray, *Après l'Histoire* (Paris: Gallimard, 2000), 650.

13. Benoit Faucon and Margaret Coker, "Willing Banks Find Profits in Legal Trade with Iran," *Wall Street Journal,* April 8, 2012, https://www.wsj.com/articles/SB10001424052702303299604577323601794862004.

3. "THE LITTLE PRINCE OF THE MAGHREB"

1. Farid Benyettou, interview with author, winter 2016.

2. Soren Seelow, "Le Pentagone revendique la mort de Boubaker el Hakim, émir français de l'Etat islamique," *Le Monde,* December 12, 2016, https://www.lemonde.fr/police-justice/article/2016/12/08/boubaker-el-hakim-emir-francais-de-l-etat-islamique-et-veteran-du-djihad-vise-par-une-frappe-de-drone_5045975_1653578.html.

4. THE ALGERIAN FACTOR

1. Hassane Zerrouky, *La nébuleuse islamique en France et en Algérie* (Paris: Éditions 1, 2002), Kindle, chap.1.
2. Zerrouky, chap.1.
3. Zerrouky, chap.2.
4. Zerrouky, chap.2.
5. Sammy Ghozlan, interview with author, winter 2015.
6. Marieme Helie Lucas, interview with author, winter 2015.
7. For efficiency and clarity, I am simplifying what was indeed a labyrinthine situation. While French officials sympathized with an Islamism they perceived as the popular expression of a national culture, French intelligence, more diligently, exchanged information with Algerian security in the hope of dismantling the first Islamist networks in France as early as 1993. But this work remained purely technical and fragmentary, and it was not supported politically—in part because the French government did not entirely trust the relationships its own operatives had with their counterparts in Algeria.
8. See, among several sources for this quote, Marc Ferro, *Le retournement de l'Histoire* (Paris: Robert Laffont, 2010), 215.
9. Zerrouky, 835.
10. In April 2017, Smaïn Aït Ali Belkacem was sentenced for attempting to escape prison in 2013 with the help of Amédy Coulibaly, the gunman in the Vincennes Hyper Cacher Kosher Supermaket attacks in 2015. Among other materials in his cell, police found more than 4,500 propaganda videos on Syria and Iraq, a list of "famous Jews in France," and a list of "Jewish Zionists ideologues and non-Jewish neo-Zionists in French media."

5. WORDS AND BLOOD

1. Juliette Selam, interview with author, winter 2015.
2. Georges Bensoussan, interviewed by Alain Finkielkraut, "Le sens de la République," France Culture, October 10, 2015, https://www.franceculture.fr/emissions/repliques/le-sens-de-la-republique.
3. See, among other sources, Sylvain Chazot, "Document: les insultes an-

tisémites d'un élu PS de Vaulx-en-Velin," Le Lab (Europe 1), July 9, 2014, https://lelab.europe1.fr/document-les-insultes-antisemites-d-un-elu-ps-de-vaulx-en-velin-15414.

4. Ahmed Chekhab, interview with author, winter 2015.

5. Patrick Kahn, interview with author, winter 2015.

6. Hélène Geoffroy, interview with author, winter 2015.

7. Adolphe Crémieux, the representative who wrote the decree of the same name in 1870, is an ancestor of my great-uncle Jean-Louis. The decree itself was an unintended consequence of Ismayl Urbain's personal status of five years earlier. According to the original phrasing of the personal status, every Algerian "indigenous" could ask to be naturalized as French regardless of his or her religion. In effect, this made French nationality and political rights optional, thus protecting the Muslim upper classes and the imams from embracing the French Code Civil, which would have forced them to abandon polygamy and slavery. But as the process of applying to be a naturalized French citizen was especially tedious, Algerian Jews, unconcerned with Muslim customs, launched a petition in order to be recognized as fully French as the 1791 Emancipation Law, passed during the Revolution, gave them the right to be. This resulted, after five years, in the Crémieux decree. In return, this made the personal status a measure that, in effect, touched only Muslims. The first victims of it, of course, were the poorer classes of the Muslim population, who ended up deprived of political rights and with no means to own slaves. With time, the origin of this difference of status between Jews and Muslims in Algeria was forgotten, and the Crémieux decree was seen as simply another sign of the double standard that allegedly benefited the Jews, thus becoming one of the roots for anti-Jewish biases. I saw a contemporary example of such bias a few months after Barack Obama won the 2006 presidential election in the United States. I was reporting on a gang in the south Paris suburb of Vitry. As she was driving me to the café that served as headquarters for the gang, my fixer, Saïda, who was of Algerian descent and whose parents returned to Algeria every year, told me that her father explained a black man's unprecedented admission to the White House thus: Since "everybody knew" that no black person could ever be elected president in America, Obama had to be the puppet of "the Zionists" and the Jews.

8. The existence of these additional drawings was revealed on January 12, 2006, by the Danish tabloid *Ekstra Bladet.*

6. A REVELATION AND A DENIAL: THE TOULOUSE AND MONTAUBAN KILLINGS

1. Anne Werthenschlag, interview with the author, June 2014.
2. Nicole Yardéni, interview with author, June 2014.
3. Selim Bachi, "Moi, Mohamed Merah," *Le Monde,* March 30, 2012.
4. See, among several sources, Ian Hamel, "Les deux visages de Tariq Ramadan," *Le Point,* April 10, 2012.
5. Olivier Roy, "Loner, Loser, Killer," *New York Times,* March 23, 2012.
6. Adam Shatz, "Moral Clarity," *LRB Blog,* January 9, 2015.
7. Laurent Borredon and Jacques Follorou, "Bernard Squarcini: 'Nous ne pouvions pas aller plus vite,'" *Le Monde,* March 23, 2012.
8. "Exclusif: Transcription des conversations entre Mohamed Merah et les négociateurs," *Libération,* July 17, 2012, http://www.conspiracywatch .info/tuerie-de-bruxelles-ils-crient-au-complot_a1243.html.
9. "Tuerie de Bruxelles: Ils crient au complot," *Conspiracy Watch,* June 1, 2014, http://www.conspiracywatch.info/tuerie-de-bruxelles-ils-crient -au-complot_a1243.html.
10. Nicolas Hénin, "Mehdi Nemmouche m'a maltraité," *Le Parisien,* September 6, 2014.

7. THE TERROR WAVE OF 2015–2016: BEYOND THE REAL AND THE FAKE

1. Philippe Lançon, *Le Lambeau* (Paris: Gallimard, 2018).
2. "Comics Legend Art Spiegelman & Scholar Tariq Ramadan on Charlie Hebdo & the Power Dynamic of Satire," interview by Amy Goodman and Nermeen Shaikh, *Democracy Now,* January 8, 2015, https:// www.democracynow.org/2015/1/8/comics_legend_art_spiegelman _scholar_tariq.
3. See, among several sources, David Namias, "Dammartin: Les frères Kouachi ont demandé à l'imprimeur s'il êtait juif," BFMTV, March 3, 2015, https://www.bfmtv.com/societe/dammartin-le-film-repasse-en -boucle-temoigne-l-ex-otage-des-freres-kouachi-867555.html.
4. Surveillance cameras at the Istanbul airport spotted Boumeddiene on

her way to Syria on January 2, four days before the *Charlie Hebdo* attack. She has reportedly been living with ISIS in Syria ever since.

5. Lawrence Abu Hamdan, *Contra Diction: Speech Against Itself,* http://lawrenceabuhamdan.com/contra-diction.

6. In contrast with the Jewish mystical tradition, for instance, in which God has given us the written alphabet.

7. Norman Mailer, *The White Negro* (San Francisco: City Lights, 1957). The text can be found in Norman Mailer, *Mind of an Outlaw: Selected Essays,* ed. Phillip Sipiora (New York: Penguin, 2014).

8. André Malraux, *Œuvres complètes* (Paris: Gallimard, 1996).

9. Robert Jay Lifton, *Destroying the World to Save It: Aum Shinrikyo, Apocalyptic Violence, and the New Global Terrorism* (New York: Picador, 1999).

8. THE WAR WITHIN

1. Günther Jikeli, "L'antisémitisme parmi les musulmans se manifeste au-delà des islamistes radicaux," *Le Monde,* April 24, 2018, https://abonnes.lemonde.fr/idees/article/2018/04/24/gunther-jikeli-l-antisemitisme-parmi-les-musulmans-se-manifeste-au-dela-des-islamistes-radicaux_5289764_3232.html.

2. Kate Starbird, "Information Wars: A Window into the Alternative Media Ecosystem," HCI & Design at UW on Medium, March 15, 2017, https://medium.com/hci-design-at-uw/information-wars-a-window-into-the-alternative-media-ecosystem-a1347f32fd8f.

3. Eduard Freisler, "Satisfaction, at Last," *New York Times,* August 17, 2010.

4. Václav Havel, *Disturbing the Peace: A Conversation with Karel Hvizdala* (New York: Faber, 1990), 18.

5. George Steiner, *George Steiner at the New Yorker* (New York: New Directions, 2009), 145.

6. Amos Oz, "Like a Gangster on the Night of the Long Knives, but Somewhat in a Dream," in *Under This Blazing Light* (Cambridge, England: Cambridge Press University, 1995), 170.

7. Georges Montandon, *L'Ethnie française* (Paris: Payot, 1935), 44.

8. Georges Montandon, *La France au Travail,* July 2, 1940.

9. Nirenberg, *Anti-Judaism,* 95.

Bibliography

Abu Hamdan, Lawrence. *Contra Diction: Speech Against Itself.* April 16, 2016. Two-channel video installation at Haus der Kulturen der Welt, Berlin. http://lawrenceabuhamdan.com/contra-diction.

Antonowicz, Gilles. *L'Affaire Halimi, du crime crapuleux au meurtre antisémite, histoire d'une derive.* Paris: Nicolas Ebayin, 2014.

Antonowicz, Gilles, and Françoise Cotta. "Gang des Barbares." *Le Monde,* July 13, 2009. https://www.lemonde.fr/idees/article/2009/07/13/gang-des -barbares-par-gilles-antonowicz-et-francoise-cotta_1218282_3232.html.

Bachi, Selim. "Moi, Mohamed Merah." *Le Monde,* March 30, 2012.

Bader, Raed. "Noirs en Algérie, XIXème-XXème siècle, pour une histoire critique et citoyenne, le cas de l'histoire franco-algérienne." Canal-U video, 24:14, June 20, 2006. Maison Méditerranéenne des Sciences de l'Homme. https://www.canal-u.tv/video/ecole_normale_superieure_de_lyon/18_ noirs_en_algerie_xixeme_xxeme_siecles.4352.

Beauvoir, Simone de. *Les Mandarins.* Paris: Gallimard, 1954.

Benoist, Alain de. *Cartouches: Les éditoriaux d'Éléments, 1973–2010.* Paris: Amis d'Alain de Benoist, 2010.

Borredon, Laurent, and Jacques Follorou. "Bernard Squarcini: 'Nous ne pouvions pas aller plus vite.'" *Le Monde,* March 23, 2012. https://www.lemonde .fr/societe/article/2012/03/23/toulouse-les-revelations-du-patron-du -renseignement_1674664_3224.html.

Boyarin, Daniel. *Unheroic Conduct: The Rise of Heterosexuality and the Invention of the Jewish Man.* Berkeley: University of California Press, 1997.

Burke, Edmund. *Reflections on the Revolution in France.* Manchester, England: Manchester University Press, 2013.

Burroughs, William S. *The Western Lands.* New York: Penguin, 1989.

Carré, Olivier. *Le nationalisme arabe.* Paris: Fayard, 1993.

Chazot, Sylvain. "Document: Les insultes antisémites d'un élu PS de Vaulx-en-Velin." Le Lab (Europe 1). July 9, 2014. https://lelab.europe1.fr/document -les-insultes-antisemites-d-un-elu-ps-de-vaulx-en-velin-15414.

"Comics Legend Art Spiegelman & Scholar Tariq Ramadan on Charlie Hebdo & the Power Dynamic of Satire." Interview by Amy Goodman and Nermeen Shaikh. *Democracy Now,* January 8, 2015. https://www.democracynow .org/2015/1/8/comics_legend_art_spiegelman_scholar_tariq.

Crémieux-Brilhac, Jean-Louis. *L'étrange victoire: De la défense de la République à la libération de la France.* Paris: Gallimard, 2016.

Daoud, Kamel. *The Meursault Investigation.* New York: Oneworld, 2015.

de Bellaigue, Christopher. *The Islamic Enlightenment.* London: Bodley Head, 2018.

Dejean, Mathieu. "Comment une vidéo sur la Syrie est devenue la deuxième la plus vue sur Youtube." *Les Inrockuptibles,* December 15, 2016. https:// mobile.lesinrocks.com/2016/12/15/actualite/video-conspirationniste -syrie-devenue-deuxieme-plus-vue-youtube-11889000.

de Maistre, Joseph. *Les soirées de Saint-Pétersbourg ou Entretiens sur le gouvernement temporel de la providence: onzième entretien.* Paris: L'Herne, 2016.

Destal, Mathias. "Affaire Binti: Alain Soral condamné pour menaces à l'encontre d'une jeune femme." *Marianne,* November 29, 2016. https:// www.marianne.net/societe/affaire-binti-alain-soral-condamne-pour -menaces-l-encontre-d-une-jeune-femme.

Dugin, Alexander. *Foundations of Geopolitics.* Moscow: Book on Demand, 2015.

———. *Le prophète de l'eurasisme.* Paris: Avatar Éditions, 2006.

———. *La Quatrième théorie politique: La Russie et les idées politiques au XXIème siècle.* With a foreword by Alain Soral. Paris: Ars Magna, 2016.

Dunlop, John B. "Aleksandr Dugin's Foundations of Geopolitics." Europe Center at Stanford University. First published in *Demokratizatsiya* 12, no. 1 (January 31, 2004). https://tec.fsi.stanford.edu/docs/aleksandr-dugins -foundations-geopolitics.

Elon, Amos. *Herzl*. New York: Schocken Books, 1986.

Etchegoin, Marie-France. "Antisémite, 'national-socialiste': Comment devient-on Alain Soral?" *Le Nouvel Observateur,* January 26, 2014. https://www.nouvelobs.com/l-enquete-de-l-obs/20140124.OBS3766/antisemite-national-socialiste-comment-devient-on-alain-soral.html.

"Exclusif: Transcription des conversations entre Mohamed Merah et les négociateurs." *Libération,* July 17, 2012. http://www.liberation.fr/societe/2012/07/17/transcription-des-conversations-entre-mohamed-merah-et-les-negociateurs_833784.

Faucon, Benoit, and Margaret Coker. "Willing Banks Find Profits in Legal Trade with Iran." *Wall Street Journal,* April 8, 2012.

Ferro, Marc. *Le retournement de l'Histoire*. Paris: Robert Laffont, 2010.

Freisler, Eduard. "Satisfaction, at Last." *New York Times,* August 17, 2010. https://www.nytimes.com/2010/08/18/opinion/18freisler.html.

Galland, Olivier, and Anne Muxel. *La tentation radicale: Enquête auprès des lycéens*. Paris: Presses Universitaires de France, 2018.

Ganier-Raymond, Philippe. "À Auschwitz, on n'a gazé que les poux." *L'Express,* October 28, 1978.

Genet, Jean. *Un captif amoureux*. Paris: Gallimard, 1986.

Gervais, Pierre, Pauline Peretz, and Pierre Stutin. *Le dossier secret de l'affaire Dreyfus*. Paris: Alma, 2012.

Hamel, Ian. "Les deux visages de Tariq Ramadan." *Le Point,* April 10, 2012. http://www.lepoint.fr/societe/les-deux-visages-de-tariq-ramadan-09-04-2012-1449828_23.php.

Havel, Václav. *Disturbing the Peace: A Conversation with Karel Hvizdala*. New York: Faber, 1990.

Hénin, Nicolas. "Mehdi Nemmouche m'a maltraité." *Le Parisien,* September 6, 2014.

Herf, Jeffrey. *The Jewish Enemy: Nazi Propaganda During World War II and the Holocaust*. Cambridge, MA: The Belknap Press at Harvard University Press.

———. *Nazi Propaganda for the Arab World*. New Haven, CT: Yale University Press, 2010.

Institute for Economics and Peace. *Global Terrorism Index 2017: Measuring and Understanding the Impact of Terrorism*. Sydney: Institute for Economics and Peace, 2017. http://visionofhumanity.org/app/uploads/2017/11/Global-Terrorism-Index-2017.pdf.

Jikeli, Günther, "L'antisémitisme parmi les musulmans se manifeste au-delà des islamistes radicaux." *Le Monde,* April 24, 2018. https://abonnes.lemonde .fr/idees/article/2018/04/24/gunther-jikeli-l-antisemitisme-parmi-les -musulmans-se-manifeste-au-dela-des-islamistes-radicaux_5289764_3232 .html.

Karoui, Hakim El. "Un islam français est possible." *Institut Montaigne,* September 2016. http://www.institutmontaigne.org/ressources/pdfs/publications /rapport-un-islam-francais-est_-possible.pdf.

Kilgore, Ed. "Zut Alors: Bannon's Taste for Franco-Fascists." *New York,* March 17, 2017.

Kiš, Danilo. *The Encyclopedia of the Dead.* London: Faber, 1989.

Klemperer, Victor. *I Will Bear Witness: A Diary of the Nazi Years.* 2 vols. New York: Modern Library, 2001.

Lançon, Philippe. *Le Lambeau.* Paris: Gallimard, 2018.

Levallois, Michel. *Ismaÿl Urbain: Une autre conquête de l'Algérie.* Paris: Maisonneuve & Larose, 2001.

Lifton, Robert Jay. *Destroying the World to Save It: Aum Shinrikyo, Apocalyptic Violence, and the New Global Terrorism.* New York: Picador, 1999.

Mailer, Norman. *The White Negro.* San Francisco: City Lights, 1957. Reprinted in *Mind of an Outlaw: Selected Essays* by Norman Mailer. Edited by Phillip Sipiora. Introduction by Jonathan Lethem. New York: Penguin, 2014.

Malraux, André. Œuvres complètes. Paris: Gallimard, 1996.

Montandon, George. *L'Ethnie française.* Paris: Payot, 1935.

Muray, Philippe. *Après l'Histoire.* Paris: Gallimard, 2000.

Namias, David. "Dammartin: Les frères Kouachi ont demandé à l'imprimeur s'il était juif." BFMTV, March 3, 2015. https://www.bfmtv.com/societe /dammartin-le-film-repasse-en-boucle-temoigne-l-ex-otage-des-freres -kouachi-867555.html.

Nirenberg, David. *Anti-Judaism: The Western Tradition.* New York: W. W. Norton, 2014.

Oz, Amos. "Like a Gangster on the Night of the Long Knives, but Somewhat in a Dream." In *Under This Blazing Light.* Cambridge, England: Cambridge University Press, 1995.

Peyreffitte, Alain. *C'était de Gaulle.* Paris: Fayard, 2002.

Ratner, Paul. "The Most Dangerous Philosopher in the World." Big Think. Accessed July 22, 2018. https://bigthink.com/paul-ratner/the-dangerous -philosopher-behind-putins-strategy-to-grow-russian-power-at-americas -expense.

Roy, Olivier. "Loner, Loser, Killer." *New York Times,* March 23, 2012. https:// www.nytimes.com/2012/03/24/opinion/loner-loser-killer.html.

Samraoui, Mohamed. *Chronique des années de sang.* Paris: Denoël, 2003.

Schor, Ralph. *L'antisémitisme en France dans l'entre-deux-guerres: Prélude à Vichy.* Paris: Éditions Complexe, 2005.

Seelow, Soren. "Le Pentagone revendique la mort de Boubaker El Hakim, émir français de l'Etat islamique." *Le Monde,* December 12, 2016. https:// www.lemonde.fr/police-justice/article/2016/12/08/boubaker-el-hakim -emir-francais-de-l-etat-islamique-et-veteran-du-djihad-vise-par-une -frappe-de-drone_5045975_1653578.html.

Shatz, Adam. "Moral Clarity." *LRB Blog,* January 9, 2015.

Sifaoui, Mohamed. *Histoire secrète de l'Algérie indépendante.* Paris: Nouveau Monde Éditions, 2014.

Soral, Alain. *Misère du désir.* Paris: Blanche, 2012.

Starbird, Kate. "Information Wars: A Window into the Alternative Media Eco-system." HCI & Design at UW on Medium, March 15, 2017. https:// medium.com/hci-design-at-uw/information-wars-a-window-into-the -alternative-media-ecosystem-a1347f32fd8f.

Steiner, George. *George Steiner at the New Yorker.* New York: New Directions, 2009.

Sternhell, Zeev. *The Anti-Enlightenment Tradition.* Translated by David Maisel. New Haven, CT: Yale University Press, 2009.

Symons, Emma-Kate. *Steve Bannon Loves France.* Politico. March 22, 2017 (up-dated March 23, 2017). https://www.politico.eu/article/steve-bannons -french-marine-le-pen-front-national-donald-trump-far-right-populism -inspiration.

Taguieff, Pierre-André. *Les Protocoles des sages de Sion: Un faux et ses usages dans le siècle.* Paris: Fayard, 2004.

Tocqueville, Alexis de. *Travail sur l'Algérie.* Paris: ed. ink Book, 2013. First pub-lished 1841.

"Tuerie de Bruxelles: Ils crient au complot." Conspiracy Watch, June 1,

2014. http://www.conspiracywatch.info/tuerie-de-bruxelles-ils-crient-au
-complot_a1243.html.

Yacono, Xavier. "La Régence d'Alger en 1830 d'après l'enquête des commissions
de 1833–1834." *Revue de l'Occident musulman et de la Méditerranée* no. 1 (1966).
https://www.persee.fr/doc/remmm_0035-1474_1966_num_1_1_921.

Zerrouky, Hassane. *La nébuleuse islamique en France et en Algérie.* Paris: Éditions
1, 2002.